Cheated not poisoned?

Cheated not poisoned?

Food regulation in the United Kingdom, 1875–1938

Michael French and Jim Phillips

Manchester University Press
Manchester and New York

Copyright © Michael French and Jim Phillips 2000, 2009

The right of Michael French and Jim Phillips to be identified as the authors of this work has been asserted by them in accordance with the Copyright, Designs and Patents Act 1988.

Published by Manchester University Press
Oxford Road, Manchester M13 9NR, UK
and Room 400, 175 Fifth Avenue, New York, NY 10010, USA
www.manchesteruniversitypress.co.uk

Distributed exclusively in the USA by
Palgrave, 175 Fifth Avenue, New York NY 10010, USA

Distributed exclusively in Canada by
UBC Press, University of British Columbia, 2029 West Mall,
Vancouver, BC, Canada V6T 1Z2

British Library Cataloguing-in-Publication Data
A catalogue record for this book is available from the British Library

Library of Congress Cataloging-in-Publication Data
A catalog record for this book is available from the Library of Congress

ISBN 13: 978 0 7190 8128 6

First published in hardback 2000 by Manchester University Press
This paperback edition first published 2009

Printed by Lightning Source

Contents

Tables		*page* vi
Acknowledgements		vii
1	Food and state regulation	1
2	The food business and interest groups, 1875–1938	11
3	The evolution and operation of the Sale of Food and Drugs Acts, 1875–1907	33
4	Food scares and the Local Government Board	66
5	Assessing food additives: regulating chemical preservatives, 1888–1938	96
6	Standards and central government, 1899–1938	124
7	Conflicts of interest: milk regulation, 1875–1938	158
8	Conclusion	185
	Bibliography	194
	Index	204

Tables

2.1	Food employment by sector, 1891–1931	*page* 15
2.2	Distribution of employment and output by size of firm, 1930	19
3.1	Level of adulteration of formally purchased food samples in England and Wales and Scotland (%), 1899–1938	53
3.2	Adulteration (%) of formal and informal samples in Scotland, 1904–13	53
7.1	Rural and urban coverage of the 1885 Dairies, Cowsheds and Milkshops Orders in England and Wales (outside London), 1907	162
7.2	Grading definitions under the 1923 Milk (Special Designations) Orders	172

Acknowledgements

This study was made possible by financial support from the Leverhulme Trust (Grant F/179/AI) for which we are most grateful. Additional support, both financial and in many other ways, was provided by the Department of Economic and Social History and the Centre for Business History in Scotland at the University of Glasgow. Staff in the University Library and the University Archives, especially the Business Records Centre and the Scottish Brewing Archives, supplied valuable guidance to relevant sources and collections. Similarly helpful assistance was given by staff at the Public Record Office, the National Archives of Scotland, the National Library of Scotland, the British Library, the Royal Society Library, Edinburgh University Library, the Wellcome Institute for the History of Medicine, the National Museum of Labour History, the Mitchell Library, Dundee City Archives, and the Borthwick Institute, York. We owe a particular debt to Margaret Morrison for guidance to the materials in the Food and Drink Federation Library and Archives. At various stages the project benefited from the opportunity to present papers based on the 'work in progress'. We are grateful for the comments of participants in the International Business History conferences in Glasgow in 1997 and 1999, the conference of the Society for the Social History of Medicine in Aberdeen in 1999, and at seminars at the Department of Economic History, Goteborg, the University of Edinburgh's Modern History Research Seminar, the Department of Economics and Related Studies at the University of York, and the Historians and Nutritionists seminar at Kings College, London. In exploring the food industry's diverse highways and by-ways, we have gained a great deal from the work and encouragement of colleagues. David Smith and Margaret Barnett, Sally Horrocks and Derek Oddy were generous in sharing materials from their own researches on nutrition and science in the food industries. We thank Andrew Philip for lending items on agriculture and meat inspection from his private collection. We thank the editors of *Rural History*, for allowing us to recast in chapter 4 parts of an article which appeared in Vol. 9, No. 2, 1998, and the editors of *Social History of Medicine* for allowing us to reproduce in chapter 7 parts of an article published in Vol. 12, No. 3, 1999. Sections of the manuscript were read by Anne Crowther, Marguerite Dupree, Roger Davidson, Neil Rollings and Tony Slaven; their comments and advice were much appreciated. The responsibility for any remaining errors lies with the authors. Mike's greatest debt is to Roma, Nicky and Kieran for their patience, encouragement and much else. Jim owes thanks and gratitude to Anna.

1

Food and state regulation

In 1874 the President of the Local Government Board for England and Wales, George Sclater-Booth, asked the House of Commons to establish a Select Committee to investigate the continuing problem of food adulteration. This had persisted despite the introduction of three separate pieces of anti-adulteration legislation between 1860 and 1872. The Select Committee duly gathered evidence from food manufacturers and retailers, chemical analysts and local public health officials, who collectively provided a review of adulteration's recent history. Identified as a significant health and commercial problem in the 1850s by analysts and medical doctors, adulteration had been given considerable publicity in the emerging national press. The published evidence of dangerous or fraudulent ingredients was accompanied by demands for corrective government action. This was provided in the shape of the three Adulteration Acts, but the Select Committee of 1874 reported that these measures were largely ineffective because they were permissive rather statutory. Local Authorities were allowed but not compelled to appoint food inspectors and analyse foods sold in their area. This defect was remedied in the 1875 Sale of Food and Drugs Act (SFDA), drafted by the Select Committee, that was to form the basis of food law in the United Kingdom until 1955.

In emerging from a sequence of highly publicised scandals followed by permissive and then statutory legislation, the SFDA conforms to Oliver MacDonagh's interpretation of Victorian social reform.[1] Initial permissive legislation was often superseded by statutory legislation and local administration was subject to greater central direction and oversight. These themes form the basis of a collection of essays on the role of professional experts in Victorian state intervention, edited by Roy Macleod, which charts the varying degrees of influence on public policy of inspectorates and scientific advisers and other officials.[2] These studies highlight the piecemeal development of state regulation during the late nineteenth century. In addition to the legislative cycles driven by specific crises, George Kitson Clark too

---

[1] Oliver MacDonagh, *Early Victorian Government, 1830–1870* (London, 1977).
[2] Roy Macleod (ed.), *Government and Expertise: Specialists, administrators and professionals* (Cambridge, 1988).

emphasised the importance of public officials and expert administrators in devising public health policies in response to public concerns about the general consequences of urbanisation and industrialisation. The pressures for state intervention stemming from urbanisation also featured in Jose Harris's recent analysis of the changing relationships between the state and civil society between 1870 and 1914.[3] These general influences did not produce a simple expansion of state intervention and regulation, rather there were reversals and inconsistencies so that government influence fluctuated. Harris highlighted the diversity of attitudes toward the state and the capacity of individuals, interest groups and government departments to pursue contradictory objectives and policies, often simultaneously.

Approaches to Regulation

Regulation is most commonly associated with state intervention and its supporting legal framework.[4] The state's coercive power makes it a potentially decisive force in determining and maintaining rules of behaviour, but government operates within, and interacts with, a wider world. Indeed a great deal of the literature on regulation is concerned with the extent, character and consequences of exchanges between the state and other institutions and actors. One general approach is to explain regulation in terms of the pursuit of general social objectives that are in the 'public interest'. This, as McCraw notes, is a vague, even 'indefinable' concept, but one which consistently features in political rhetoric and legal arguments as a justification for regulation.[5] Such usage reflects its rhetorical value, but in practice there are certain common approaches to 'public interest'. In economics, the theory of perfect competition contends that markets allocate goods and services efficiently through the actions of informed and economically rational individuals intent on maximising their material self-interest. The theory assumes that individual suppliers cannot influence market prices and it emphasises the importance of consumer choice. The legal system establishes property rights and enforces contractual obligations, though the origins of this institutional framework are taken for granted. Perfect competition theory presumes that markets allocate resources efficiently and so obviates the need for state intervention. But even under this ideal type, where one or more of its key assumptions are absent or in question, the theory of perfect competition provides a rationale for intervention to correct market 'failure'.[6] Intervention can be a response to the structure of the market. In the case of monopolies, governments endeavour to re-arrange markets or industries through anti-trust laws, or to approximate competitive outcomes by regulating prices or other aspects of the business. State control may even extend to public ownership to supply goods or services for the general community.

---

[3] Jose Harris, *Private Lives, Public Spirit: Britain, 1870–1914* (London, 1993), chapter 7.
[4] Anthony I. Ogus, *Regulation: Legal form and economic theory* (Oxford, 1994), pp. 1–3.
[5] Thomas K. McCraw, 'Regulation in America: A review article', *Business History Review*, 49, 1975, pp. 160–2.
[6] Ogus, *Regulation*, chapter 1.

If perfect competition represents an ideal type, the actual operation of markets is characterised by uncertainties, limited information and effects that generate 'public-interest'-based calls for government intervention. In these respects, and thus, in the application of regulatory theories, food production and consumption touches on key issues. Transactions may involve externalities, such as pollution, whose costs are borne by third parties and, therefore, are not fully reflected by the operation of the market. A further strand of 'public interest' regulation concerns health, safety and product performance. Harris notes the acceptance in the late nineteenth century of state intervention intended to assist vulnerable groups, such as children and invalids, and to regulate, or even supply, general services, such as water and transport.[7] Regulation may seek to protect consumers where a product or service involves hazards, either inherently or where goods are defective. In the case of food, there may be risks to health from the ingredients or the insanitary conditions of production, distribution or preparation. Under perfect competition price provides the key source of information and producers and consumers are each taken to possess sufficient knowledge prior to an exchange. In practice, individual consumers face considerable difficulty in acquiring and evaluating information about the characteristics of all of their potential purchases.

Price is, at best, only a partial indicator of features such as product quality. Information is elusive, incomplete, costly to acquire and unevenly distributed. Williamson identifies asymmetries in the information available with, for instance, suppliers knowing more than their customers about the nature of any commodity.[8] He also argues that the incentives for opportunistic behaviour are a fundamental constraint on all contracts and exchanges. These insights provide the basis of the new institutional economics, which has been used primarily to explore the boundaries between firms and markets in terms of their relative efficiency in minimising information costs, but the fundamental problems involved in contracting are relevant to regulation. In addition to price, transactions themselves provide information. Where exchanges take place repeatedly, as in the case of foods, past experience establishes routines and common expectations about the nature of the commodity and trust among the parties that simplify future dealings.[9] Producers have incentives to provide safe or acceptable products in order to lower transaction costs, thereby stimulating repeat business and protecting their reputations.[10] Such incentives increase where a firm holds a large share of the market, invests in

---

[7] Harris, *Private Lives*, pp. 196–197.

[8] O.E. Williamson, *Markets and Hierarches: Analysis and anti-trust implications* (New York, 1975).

[9] Richard N. Langlois and Paul L. Robertson, *Firms, Markets and Economic Change: A dynamic theory of business institutions* (London, 1995), pp. 17, 28–9.

[10] G. Akerloff, 'The Market for "Lemons": Quality uncertainty and the market mechanism', *Quarterly Journal of Economics*, August 1970, pp. 488–500; B. Klein and K. Leffler, 'The Role of Market Forces in Assuring Contractual Performance', *Journal of Political Economy*, August 1981, pp. 615–42; Mark Casson, *The Economics of Business Culture: Game theory, transaction costs, and economic performance* (Oxford, 1991).

specialised assets and anticipates long-term growth.[11] Hence Stigler emphasises quality as a competitive strategy.[12] Such assumptions are problematic if it is difficult for producers to distinguish higher-quality commodities from lower-grade goods, a dilemma encapsulated in Akerloff's analysis of the market for 'lemons' which hinges on a lack of information to enable consumers to evaluate qualitative features of products.[13] Under these circumstances, where poor-quality products, or 'lemons', cannot be identified easily, the higher-quality goods will not command premium prices. One response is the use of branding and advertising in order to offer information about the nature of the product, thereby, according to Wilkins, lowering transaction costs and promoting future business.[14] Food and drink were among the leading sectors in applying such marketing methods. Yet brands and advertising involve the dissemination of selective facts and images which, though mediated by the consumers' own interpretation, may mislead by suppressing or distorting other evidence.[15] In terms of the model of perfect competition, state intervention may occur on 'public interest' grounds to supply consumers with additional information about a product or service in order to facilitate consumer choice. Legislation may require the disclosure of specific information on labels or in advertising or else regulate the nature of claims advanced about particular products. Another approach is to rely on an agent with the expertise to collect, evaluate and disseminate information about commodities. Agents will be particularly valuable where potential risks or hazards are hard to detect, though agents also encounter problems of limited knowledge and uncertainties so their influence is by no means straightforward.[16] There is a continuum of possible agents in the food sector from trade associations to professional bodies, consumer organisations and government inspectors and agencies.

In this 'public interest' context the existing literature on the 1875 SFDA is highly plausible. John Burnett's authoritative study of the history of Britain's food, *Plenty and Want*, presents the 1875 legislation as the uncontentious product of several decades of inquiry and debate. The anti-adulteration movement was unambiguously in the 'public interest'. Adulteration of food was defined in terms of a risk to the consumer's health or an attempt to deceive the purchaser about the nature of the product. An inspectorate was put in place to identify and penalise breaches of the law, so consumers received clear and unambiguous legal protection. Burnett concludes that the legislation proved highly effective, ensuring that by the end of

[11] Gary D. Libecap, 'The Rise of the Chicago Packers and the origins of Meat Inspection and Antitrust', *Economic Inquiry*, 30, April 1992, pp. 242–62.

[12] Stigler, G.J., 'Can Regulatory Agencies Protect the Consumer?', in G.J. Stigler (ed.), *The Citizen and the State: Essays on regulation* (Chicago, 1975).

[13] Akerloff, 'Market for "Lemons"', pp. 488–500.

[14] Mira Wilkins, 'When and Why Brand Names in Food and Drink?' in Geoffrey Jones and Nicholas J. Morgan (eds), *Adding Value: Brands and Marketing in food and drink* (London, 1994), pp. 15–40.

[15] Ogus, *Regulation*, pp. 39–41; Mark Casson, 'Brands: economic ideology and consumer society' in Geoffrey Jones and Nicholas J. Morgan (eds), *Adding Value: Brands and Marketing in food and drink* (London, 1994), pp. 41–58.

[16] Mark Casson, 'Brands', pp. 48–9.

the nineteenth century adulteration had ceased to be a significant medical or commercial problem. This interpretation is supported by Ingebourg Paulus's legal and sociological analysis of the 1875 Act which, she emphasises, was firmly in the Victorian 'public interest' tradition, particularly as the legislation was consolidated by an 1899 amendment.[17] Like the 1890 revision to the Public Health Act, this gave central government, in the shape of the Local Government Board in England and Wales and a newly established Local Government Board for Scotland, the power to enforce the law where local councils failed to do so. Paulus also emphasised the significance of judicial activism as courts sanctioned wider interpretations of the food laws, thereby extending their scope and effectiveness.

If the concept of 'public interest' helps to describe and legitimate areas subject to regulation, it leaves open the precise sources of specific policies. The term itself implies broad public support or approval that fits with pluralist theories of interest groups and political power. Pluralist models treat power and influence as widely diffused among different groups, though perhaps on the basis of different resources and to varying degrees according to the issue at stake. 'Public interest' objectives could then be pursued by many disparate groups with regulation emerging as the product of their alliances and rivalries. This image is questioned by Olson's claims that a large group possessing a potential collective interest is unlikely to become an effective lobby. Using a model of rational self-interest derived from economic theory, he argues that in a large group individuals have more incentive to remain 'free riders' than to co-operate in pursuit of collective goals. Any common interest remains latent, inhibiting the emergence of 'public interest' lobbying. According to Olson, large economic pressure groups appear only as a by-product of organisations, such as unions or professional bodies, established for other narrower purposes. Effective interest lobbies are more likely to be small groups which must co-operate to achieve a common objective and where each individual's participation affects the outcome and each stands to reap a significant portion of any benefits.[18] Olson concluded that as 'a general rule' business would be organised at least along industrial or sectional lines, where groups would be sufficiently small to create the incentive for organisation.[19] Peak associations designed to represent all business would become too large and, thus, encounter barriers to organisation.

Whereas Olson concentrated on certain determinants of the membership of interest groups, the 'public interest' explanation of state intervention has been subject to more fundamental criticism. The earliest critic, perhaps, was Karl Marx who claimed that any propertied class will advocate satisfying its needs as the best way to ensure the general public good.[20] From this perspective, 'public interest' rhetoric merely conceals private ambitions, and competing or shifting definitions of the

---

[17] Ingeborg Paulus, *The Search for Pure Food: A sociology of legislation in Britain* (London, 1974).
[18] Mancur Olson, *The Logic of Collective Action: Public goods and the theory of groups* (Cambridge, MA, 1965).
[19] Olson, *Logic of Collective Action*, pp. 141–4.
[20] Karl Marx, *The Eighteenth Brumaire of Louis Bonaparte* (Moscow, 1934), p. 40.

concept afford insights into the nature of economic and social changes.[21] Other social science disciplines developed the notion of 'capture' to evaluate the influence of interest groups on regulation. From the premise that any regulatory rules will redistribute wealth in favour of some groups, Stigler asserts that 'as a rule, regulation is acquired by the industry and is designed and operated primarily for its benefit'.[22] The extent of influence is a product of the degree of self-interest as well as the size and homogeneity of the interest group. In these terms, producers constitute a relatively small coherent group, possessing relevant expertise, information and financial resources, plus a keen interest in the outcome of regulations touching on their business affairs. Effective mobilisation becomes more likely as the importance of the issue at stake increases and where the consequences of regulation are clear. Regulatory 'capture' has been used in two principal ways. One scenario is that a particular interest group decides on its regulatory objectives and lobbies successfully for suitable legislation. A second sequence offers a more defensive image of 'capture', where an interest group encounters calls by others for regulations and then reacts to ensure that the final character of any measures suits its purposes rather than those of the original advocates of intervention. While these two forms of 'capture' could result in identical outcomes, they involve rather different processes in terms of how regulation is initiated and the relationships between different lobbies.

The first form of capture involves a conscious strategy by a particular interest group. Since state regulation is only one of many forms of governance, its selection over other options requires explanation. Business or producers might be expected to operate through non-regulatory avenues, such as markets or trade associations, where their economic powers exert greatest influence or have little reason to engage in politics because their interests were accommodated already. Campbell *et al* suggest that changes in technology or market conditions promote a search for new institutional arrangements.[23] If private arrangements cannot be established or produce unsatisfactory outcomes, state regulation becomes an appealing source of fiat. Those adversely affected by technological change may seek to use the state to control or limit the uses of that technology. Stigler noted that industry typically seeks subsidies, control of entry, and price agreements to undermine substitute products or promote related activities to their own. Wood identified regulation as one potential competitive strategy for obtaining barriers to entry, controlling markets for raw materials or finished goods or generally enforcing rules of behaviour.[24] Such defensive strategies may be easier to organise among existing businesses, but are predicated on disadvantaging actual or potential rivals. In these areas com-

---

[21] McCraw, 'Regulation in America', pp. 159–83

[22] George J. Stigler, 'The Theory of Economic Regulation', reprinted in George J. Stigler (ed.), *The Citizen and the State* (1975), p. 209.

[23] John Campbell *et al.* (eds), *Governance of the American Economy* (Cambridge, 1991).

[24] Donna J, Wood, 'The Strategic Use of Public Policy: Business support for the 1906 Food and Drug Act', *Business History Review*, 59, Autumn 1985, pp. 403–32; *Strategic Uses of Public Policy: Business and government in the Progressive era* (Pittsburg, 1986).

petitive tensions or sectional, functional and regional differences are likely to be to the fore with regulation providing a further arena for rivalry.

Some interpretations claim that business or producer interests enjoy a privileged political status.[25] Their control over employment, investment and other economic levers provides direct powers in addition to the organisational advantages of financial resources, expertise and self-interest.[26] If their welfare is perceived as essential for the efficient operation of the economy, business views carry added weight and features such as property rights may be treated as unquestioned elements of the status quo. Miliband and Lindblom both identified such features as the basis of the uniquely privileged position held by business.[27] In the same vein, Kolko depicted the Progressive era in the United States as one of conservative reform because the prerogatives of business were not challenged.[28] The idea of business privilege is helpful in drawing attention to sources of power and the parameters within which regulation operates. On the other hand, it risks denying significance to any reformist measures short of revolution or assuming that the capacity to accommodate regulations is equivalent to advocating them. And its implications are also unclear; does business privilege mean that business is the most effective pressure group or that its interests will somehow be recognised and accommodated without any need for lobbying? Again, the precise meaning of 'capture' is at issue. The existence of divisions, paradoxically, increases the prospects that business interests will pursue political influence, but also that rivalries diminish their overall effectiveness. Again the meaning or extent of 'capture' is likely to vary according to the balance of competing business forces and the strengths of other pressure groups rather than being a product of business privilege.

'Public interest' and 'capture' interpretations concentrate on those who demand or benefit from regulation and then treat the state as a relatively unproblematic supplier of rules and laws, in effect reflecting the relative strengths of competing pressure groups. In a pluralist version the state is a crowded arena within which outside forces struggle over policy while in 'capture' models dominant interests simply pull the levers of power. Neither image reflects the diversity, complexity and inner logic of government, with its different levels of power and policy making. Politicians, civil servants or law officers may pursue different, even conflicting, objectives, including electoral calculations, bureaucratic ambitions and their own notions of 'public interest'. Kitson Clark regarded experts and officials as the prime movers behind public health policies in Britain during the 1850s and 1860s, describing measures as 'devised by experts, appealing to experts, to be executed by

---

[25] For a summary see Wyn Grant, *Business and Politics in Britain* (Second edition, 1993), chapter 2.
[26] Olson suggests that the economic powers of business provide additional leverage or influence and Stigler assumes that producer groups hold the best organisational cards.
[27] Ralph Miliband, *The State in Capitalist Society* (London, 1969); Charles Lindblom, *Politics and Markets: The world's political economic systems* (New York, 1977).
[28] Gabriel Kolko, *The Triumph of Conservatism: A reinterpretation of American history, 1900–1916*, (Chicago, 1967).

experts'.[29] In the second half of the nineteenth century, Harris noted the emergence of a generation of civil servants that identified with the ideal of an 'impartial' state, balancing different interests, but subservient to none. Thereafter Harris detects varying degrees of activism and attitudes towards state intervention across the range of departments. Rather than acting neutrally or following orders, governments may seek to incorporate interest groups into policy making in order to achieve consensus or, in forms of state corporatism, to use them to disseminate or implement government policies. They have incentives to accommodate other, less influential, groups in order to minimise criticism and maximise satisfaction.[30] Moreover, regulation may give discretion to officials in the implementation of policy, and their access to information makes them a source of potential influence. Skocpol argues that the scope for bureaucratic initiatives increases when interest groups are divided or discredited by crises.[31] Such conditions may prompt all parties to search for new institutional arrangements with politicians and officials gaining greater autonomy. The evolution of the food laws in the UK is characterised by scares with regulatory changes on more than one occasion made in response to crises. And the role of public concern was particularly relevant with food, given the potentially severe, even fatal, consequences of unfit foods. In this respect the food story validates, in part, the various state-centred theories which suggest that government is a complex institution whose different elements possess some autonomy in their relationship to pressure groups and the wider society.

With the state and pressure groups both characterised by diversity, regulation threatens to become a highly fragmented and unwieldy process, especially in a pluralistic political system. In an attempt to broaden the boundaries of regulation and make different levels of influence more manageable, political scientists identify more structured interactions between government and interest groups in the form of loose networks or more stable communities that determine a specific aspect of government policy making in particular areas.[32] The concepts of networks and communities assume restricted access to policy making, but allow for varying degrees of influence by the state and interest groups and direct attention to the dynamics of specific regulatory processes. Networks may be closed, that is confined to a few members, or relatively open; they may involve formal contacts, informal relationships, and the flow of information and even personnel to and fro between groups. It is clear that the various theories of regulation offer diverse perspectives, in part because the subject can be approached at various points or levels. This

---

[29] George Kitson Clark, *The Making of Victorian England* (Oxford, 1962), pp. 110–111.

[30] Sam Peltzmann, 'Toward a More General Theory of Regulation' reprinted in George J. Stigler (ed.), *Chicago Studies in Political Economy* (Chicago, 1988), pp. 234–66; Harris, *Private Lives*.

[31] Theda Skocpol, 'Political Responses to Capitalist Crisis: Neo-Marxist theories of the state and the case of the New Deal', *Politics and Society*, 10 (2), 1980, pp. 155–202; P. Hall, *Governing the Economy: The politics of state intervention in Britain and France* (Cambridge, 1986).

[32] David Marsh and R.A.W. Rhodes (eds), *Policy Networks In British Government* (Oxford, 1992); R.A.W. Rhodes, *Understanding Governance: Policy networks, governance, reflexivity and accountability*, (Buckingham, 1997), chapter 2.

complexity places a premium on historical studies that can address the dynamic character of regulation, particularly any changes in the relationships or relative influence of different interest groups and state bureaucrats. At the same time it should be noted that much of the regulatory literature has been developed and applied in the United States and, thus, in relation to specific economic and political systems. Within this US literature there has been a considerable focus on the origins of the food and drugs laws.[33] It is within this framework that this book undertakes a historical analysis of regulation in the UK by examining the food laws. The book is guided by the various US perspectives on regulation, but is sensitive to the influence of the different economic, social and political context of the UK.

The study is divided into three parts. This first part, setting the scene, continues with chapter 2, which provides the detailed background to the regulatory processes by describing the structure of the food industry and the principal trends between 1870 and 1938. Its main sectors – farming, food processing and the wholesale and retail trades – were all characterised by a certain dualism. On the one hand, there was a trend toward greater concentration and the emergence of new technologies, advertising and marketing methods. Such processes led to the appearance of large-scale manufacturing companies and multiple retailers. Yet, on the other hand, each sector retained a large number of small units, whether farms, factories or shops, whose scale and business practices altered little. Britain's commitment to free trade, though questioned and ultimately compromised between 1890 and 1938, ensured that its food industry operated within an international market, facing competition from imported produce, adding a further dimension to the potential factors shaping regulation of quality. Food producers and distributors shared the Victorian and Edwardian appetite for organisation in pursuit of common interests and the final part of chapter 2 outlines the main pressure groups from landowners to manufacturers and grocers. The period from 1870 to 1938 offers a fertile period for evaluating the growth and activities of pressure groups concerned with a wide range of economic, especially trade, issues and social problems. By 1914 the British state had extended and developed its responsibilities in a piecemeal, fluctuating and at times contradictory fashion.[34] Central government widened its gaze, primarily through the appointment of new inspectorates and the collection of statistical information, though the implementation of social programmes still depended largely on local authorities. The business community organised itself, sometimes along industry lines or more broadly in employers' associations or around specific issues, notably tariff reform. The overall picture was one of great associational activity, but much fragmentation and even a sense of division between the economic and political spheres.

---

[33] Jack High (ed.), *Regulation: Economic theory and history* (Ann Arbor, 1991); Clayton A. Coppin and Jack High, 'Umpires at Bat: Setting food standards by government regulation', *Business and Economic History*, 21, 1992, pp. 109–19; Kolko, *The Triumph of Conservatism*; Wood 'Strategic use of the public policy', pp. 403–32; James Harvey Young, *Pure Food: Securing the Federal Food and Drugs Act of 1906* (Princeton, 1989).

[34] Harris, *Private Lives*, pp. 28–41.

The second part of the book (chapters 3 and 4) discusses the actual evolution of the food laws from the landmark 1875 Sale of Food and Drugs Act to the introduction of national standards for milk (1901) and butter (1907). In this period the food laws were enforced at the local level with limited national oversight by the Local Government Board (LGB). The sources of pressure for greater central direction are examined, with some food processors and traders shifting from resistance to regulation to an appreciation of its potential advantages. Reformers and business groups each presented 'public interest' cases for and against intervention. By the 1880s a strand of agrarian interests turned to regulation as one part of its attempt to use national government to reduce the costs of local administration and to provide a form of protection against imported and new products, notably margarine. Chapter 4 shows how food scares over arsenic in beer and American meat resulted in greater intervention, in part due to the influence of key officials, by the Local Government Board. At the same time there was continuity, in that government proceeded cautiously. The outbreak of war stalled proposals for further legislation, though state direction of food production and distribution was extended on a considerable, if only temporary, basis between 1914 and 1918.

The final part (chapters 5, 6 and 7) takes a thematic approach by examining key debates about food preservatives, general food standards and milk between the 1890s and 1938. This approach allows an evaluation of the views and interactions of pressure groups in relation to specific regulatory issues and spans the transition from nineteenth-century debates to the interwar economy and society. Discussion of food preservatives deals with important questions about food additives, revealing the uncertainties involved in analysing and interpreting the effects of chemicals and determining what type of information should be available to regulators and consumers. The newly formed Ministry of Health introduced Preservatives Regulations in 1925, the major new item of food legislation between the wars, and the background to this measure reveals the interaction between different pressure groups and officials and Ministers. There was a parallel debate about general food standards that led to more limited intervention and chapter 6 considers the factors that promoted and constrained policy making. It emphasises the capacity of certain business interests to initiate regulation, often in alliance with reformers, but also the wider resistance of business groups to any scheme of general standards. Again the attitudes and ambitions of government officials contributed to the timing and character of regulation. Milk featured as a major commodity in the general debates over adulteration, preservatives and standards and its central place is discussed in chapter 7. It was a commodity for which public health concerns and the commercial interests of producers and distributors were distinct and influential. The farming community supported regulation in certain respects, but waged a largely effective campaign to limit the extent and form of intervention. Finally the conclusion uses the case of the food industry, 1870–1938, to assess the value and limitations of regulatory theories for understanding the evolution and character of Britain's food laws.

2

The food business and interest groups, 1875–1938

From the late nineteenth century onwards food occupied a central position in British social and economic life. A central aspect of the state's commitment to free trade was its capacity to deliver cheap food as well as raw materials in order to minimise the cost of living. The production and distribution of food was a major economic sector; along with housing costs it constituted the basic item of family budgets. This important sector was extremely diverse, comprising an array of large and small producers, wholesalers and retailers, and involving a significant range of competing as well as interlocking interests. Its economic and social significance and the variety of manufacture and provision were reflected in debates about food regulation. In March 1899 the President of the Board of Agriculture, Walter Long, argued that the manufacture and sale of margarine had to be conducted 'on honest and honourable principles' because of its very popularity, especially 'among the poorer classes'. Critics of the President retorted that in placing restrictions on margarine producers he was more interested in increasing the comparative attraction of butter, responding to pressure from dairy farmers, than defending the interests of working-class margarine consumers.[1] This brief exchange of views highlights the two basic themes of this book: that regulation emerged from a combination of public and private interests, and that different groups of food traders sought different things from the regulatory process. The outlawing of fraudulent trade in margarine, which in the nineteenth century was commonly sold as butter, clearly operated in the interests of consumers who thought they were buying one article but were actually receiving the other. At the same time it worked in the interests of butter producers whose sales were undermined by the fraudulent trade in a rival product. Indeed, the 1887 Margarine Act, which required margarine producers to register with local authorities and allowed local authorities to take samples from margarine factories, was introduced by Irish MPs with a personal or constituency interest in dairy farming and butter production.[2] Margarine was regulated, in other

---

[1] Parliamentary Debates, Fourth Series, vol. 67, 1437, 1464, 6 March 1899.
[2] See chapter 3.

words, not just because it was a large business with many customers, but because its operations interfered to some extent with another business, butter production, which enjoyed greater political strength.

The competing interests and contrasting influence of butter and margarine producers reflected the wider diversity of the food industry as it developed between the 1870s and 1930s. This chapter explores the key features of this period, which witnessed agricultural restructuring in the face of cheap imports, the establishment by manufacturers of larger-scale operations, and the 'retailing revolution', with the appearance of new multiple stores and a greater emphasis on advertising and branding. These features signalled a strengthening of large-scale enterprise, operating in an increasingly mass market, but there were important aspects of continuity as well as modernity. Much of the food industry's business continued to be transacted by small manufacturers and traders, which reinforces the fundamental importance of structural and sectoral diversity in assessing the character of regulation. As with the detailed case of margarine, the evolution of general food regulation reflected the comparative characteristics and influence of a whole host of different trading sectors. The chapter is divided thematically. The first section assesses the scale, structure and character of the food trades – aspects which indirectly informed debates about food regulation. The second and third sections examine two factors which had a more direct impact on these debates, the extent of political and interest group activity within the trades, and the increasing application of scientific knowledge to food production.

Scale, structure and character

Per capita consumption of food expanded from the mid nineteenth century and patterns of distribution developed in accordance with the impact of urbanisation, the completion of the railway network and the expansion of overseas supplies. The flow of cheap imports escalated from the 1870s with grains from North and South America, and from the 1880s with cargoes of frozen and chilled beef from the United States and Argentina. These were accompanied by imported frozen lamb and mutton, predominantly from Australia and New Zealand. Early American domination of the pork trade was challenged by Canadian and other suppliers, including the Danish, who established niche markets in premium quality bacon and butter. In terms of volume, between 1872 and 1913 wheat imports increased their share of home consumption from 48 per cent to 81 per cent, while meat imports increased their share from 14 per cent to 42 per cent, averaging 53 per cent in the 1930s. Other foods imported on a large scale included refined sugar, much of which came from Central Europe, and more exotic items like tea, coffee and chocolate, drawn primarily from Africa and South-East Asia.[3]

[3] Philippe Chalmin, *The Making of a Sugar Giant. Tate and Lyle 1859–1989* (New York, 1990), pp. 26–7; Richard Perren, *Agriculture in Depression, 1870–1940* (Cambridge, 1995), p. 8; Richard Perren, 'The Retail and Wholesale Meat Trade, 1880–1939' in Derek J. Oddy and Derek S. Miller (eds), *Diet and Health in Modern Britain* (London, 1985), pp. 48–9, table 3.1.

By reducing demand for British produce, food imports directly affected the scale and structure of domestic agriculture. Under the impact of steadily falling grain and land prices, and the coincidental growth of urban employment opportunities, Britain moved decisively away from being a rural society. While farm labouring was by far the most common male occupation in 1871, by 1914 only 8 per cent of the population was employed in agriculture.[4] In structural terms, many grain farmers responded to the depression by removing themselves from the threat of foreign competition. In the consequent shift from grain to dairy production, the combined acreage under crops fell from 13.76 million in 1875 to 10.43 million in 1914, and the dairy cow population rose from 2.25 million to 2.94 million. Milk's share of total farm output increased as a result, from 14 per cent in 1870 to 25 per cent in 1910. In reducing the economic and political strength of grain producers, while promoting the growth of a large interest group of more than 200,000 dairy farmers by 1914, the flow of food imports was to have a considerable bearing on regulatory developments, as chapters 4 and 7 indicate.[5] Milk was not the only area of agriculture that was less vulnerable to foreign competition, and other farmers diversified into fruit and vegetables, produce that found markets in the expanding jam and preserves trade.[6]

With rising real incomes and increasing imports, people consumed a greater volume and variety of foodstuffs and drinks. Staples were cheaper and O'Rourke estimates that imports of cheaper grain raised urban real wages by around 5 per cent between 1870 and 1913.[7] More discretionary income was available to purchase newer luxuries, although, given falling prices, food sales actually declined as a proportion of all retail sales from around 60 per cent in 1900 to about 47 per cent in 1938.[8] Between the 1870s and 1930s changes in the composition of the average diet included declining consumption of cereals and increasing consumption of fats, meat, milk and fruit. Consumption of tea and sugar doubled, that of butter and margarine trebled, and that of ham and bacon increased six-fold.[9] Drinking habits were also changing. The growth of tea sales was accompanied by rising demand for cocoa, but per capita consumption of spirits and beer, having stabilised in the final third of the nineteenth century, fell after 1900, especially during and after the First World War.[10]

Changing patterns of consumption were not uniform. Household expenditure on food varied inversely with income, so that between half and two-thirds of

[4] Harris, *Private Lives*, pp. 41–3.
[5] Keith A. H. Murray, *Agriculture* (London: HMSO, 1955), p. 371; Peter Mathias, *The First Industrial Nation* (1983), pp. 316–18.
[6] John Burnett, *Plenty and Want* (Third edition, London, 1989), pp. 116–18.
[7] Kevin O'Rourke, 'The European Grain Invasion, 1870–1914', *Journal of Economic History*, 57 (4), December 1997, pp. 775–801.
[8] James B. Jeffreys, *Retail Trading in Britain, 1850–1950* (Cambridge, 1954), p. 45, table 10.
[9] Gareth Shaw, 'The European Scene: Britain and Germany', in John Benson and Gareth Shaw (eds), *The Evolution of Retail Systems, c. 1800–1914* (Leicester, 1992), pp. 26–7.
[10] A. E. Dingle, 'Drink and Working-Class Living Standards in Britain, 1870–1914', *Economic History Review*, 35 (4), November 1972, pp. 608–10.

working-class income went on food, compared to perhaps 30 or 50 per cent of middle-class income and 20 per cent among the really wealthy.[11] New products tended to be popular first among the social classes with greater amounts of discretionary income. Hence, according to Hamish Fraser, lower-middle-class families were the main original consumers of new factory-produced soups, meats, biscuits and jams.[12] In the case of biscuits, Corley identifies the first rise in popularity among wealthy consumers, followed by entry into middle-class and then affluent working-class diets.[13] Breakfast cereals, which began as niche products, sold primarily as health foods, and only reached a truly mass market through growing middle-class consumption in the 1920s and 1930s.[14] Yet from the late nineteenth century there was increasing room in working-class budgets for the purchase of sugar, jam, pickles, cocoa, treacle, condensed milk and tea.[15] Even in small amounts these items added flavour or novelty to basic meals, like the thrice-daily 'tea and two slices' which George Orwell, visiting northern England in 1936, grimly recorded as the norm in many unemployed households. Orwell noticed that even these households were occasionally able to supplement these basic items with cheap and tasty luxuries like fish and chips and ice cream.[16] Nonetheless, his general observations about food consumption in communities of high unemployment indicate that the interwar depression, with its uneven geographical and social impact, prevented many people from participating in the emergence of a mass market in food.

The growing scale of food production and distribution had a significant bearing on debates about regulation. The food trade was highly conscious of its expanding economic importance, and sought to shape these debates accordingly. One measure of the industry's increasing strength was employment. In overall terms, employment in the food trades grew steadily before 1938, contrasting with the declining workforce in brewing. Table 2.1, based on the Census of Population, shows the extent of employment in food production and distribution between 1891 and 1931.

With bread remaining the basic dietary item, baking and milling were major sectors.[17] More rapid growth of employment was apparent in the sugar refining and chocolate and cocoa sectors from 1911, and in milk during the 1920s, when

---

[11] B. E. Supple, 'Income and Demand, 1860–1914' in Roderick Floud and Donald McCloskey (eds), *The Economic History of Britain since 1700; vol. II* (Cambridge, 1981), pp. 128–31.

[12] W. Hamish Fraser, *The Coming of the Mass Market, 1850–1914* (London, 1981), pp. 40–1.

[13] T. A. B. Corley, 'Nutrition, Technology and the Growth of the British Biscuit Industry, 1820–1900' in Derek J. Oddy and Derek S. Miller (eds), *The Making of the Modern British Diet* (London, 1976), pp. 22–4.

[14] E. J. T. Collins, 'Brands and Breakfast Cereals in Britain', in Geoffrey Jones and Nicholas J. Morgan (eds), *Adding Value: Brands and Marketing in Food and Drink* (London, 1994), pp. 237–42.

[15] Dingle, 'Drink and Working-Class Living Standards', pp. 608–22.

[16] George Orwell, *The Road to Wigan Pier* (London: Penguin reprint, 1962), pp. 80, 86.

[17] Burnett, *Plenty and Want*, pp. 258–9.

Table 2.1 Food employment by sector, 1891–1931[a]

	1891	1901	1911	1921	1931
Milk and dairies	49,683	72,525	93,517	78,172	102,499
Meat	108,841	121,208	149,022	132,470	176,784
Bakery	155,700	181,138	230,502	194,090	258,117
Fish and poultry	33,471	35,987	49,537	54,413	60,734
Milling	25,988	32,757	28,704	54,339	41,992
Corn and flour	13,255	18,117	22,006	32,203	28,496
Sugar refining	4,920	3,175	4,537	13,410	20,877
Jam and preserves	N/A	24,564	34,919	22,491	N/A
Cocoa, etc.	N/A	8,002	19,257	44,985	N/A
Groceries	208,509	226,582	244,167	303,351	330,501
Fruit and veg.	44,540	57,771	78,410	91,651	115,265
All Food	676,063	692,354	991,247	1,175,560	1,401,715

Note: [a] Cocoa includes chocolate; milk and dairies includes butter and cheese.

Source: Census of England and Wales, 1891, Vol. 3, C. 7058; *ibid.*, 1901; *ibid.*, 1911, Vol. 10, C. 7018 and C. 7019; *ibid.*, 1921, Industry Occupations and Workplaces; *ibid.*, 1931, Occupations. Census of Scotland, 1891, c. 6390; *ibid.*, 1901, Cd. 644; *ibid.*, 1911, Vol. 3, Occupation, Cd. 7163; *ibid.*, 1921, Vol. 3, Occupations and Industries; *ibid.*, 1931, Vol. 3, Occupations and Industries.

large distributors were consolidating their market share by emphasising the medical safety and nutritional value of milk.[18] Sectoral changes contributed to an expansion in the proportion of female employees: from 20 per cent in 1881 to 26 per cent in 1911, rising to 38 per cent by 1938. In 1901, for example, women already constituted the overwhelming majority of the workforce in sweet confectionery, jam and preserves, and chocolate and cocoa. As these sectors developed rapidly during the next four decades, the numbers and proportion of female employees in the food trades as a whole expanded.[19]

Further indicators of the trade's developing strength from the 1870s were innovations in food production and distribution. Food manufacturing was part of the 'second industrial revolution', the response to expanding urban markets and transport improvements in the late nineteenth century. Food was one of several consumer industries where older forms of small-scale artisan or workshop production encountered competition from larger-scale enterprises using new machinery and

---

[18] P. J. Atkins, 'White Poison? The social consequences of milk consumption, 1850–1930', *Social History of Medicine*, 5, 1992, pp. 207–27; Ben Davies, 'The Nation's Milk Supply: its hygienic production and control' (London, 1933); copy in PP/JPH Box No. 14, A147, Contemporary Medical Archives Centre, The Wellcome Institute for the History of Medicine.

[19] Miriam Glucksman, *Women Assemble: Women workers and the new industries in inter-war Britain* (London, 1990), pp. 57–66, 95–110.

factories. Brewers led the way – investing in larger plants, promoting branded ales and developing control of distribution through the acquisition of public houses – and food manufacturers followed. According to John Burnett, the transformation of bread making began in the 1870s, with greater mechanisation and advances in scientific knowledge and technical training contributing to the spread of larger-scale operations.[20] Technological innovation, in the shape of canning, facilitated the growth of Moir & Son, Aberdeen fish canners from the 1820s, and Crosse & Blackwell, canning salmon in Cork from 1849, although the main expansion in canned goods occurred with imported products, particularly North American meat. Only in the 1920s did an indigenous British canning industry develop.[21] New technology, along with more intensive marketing, contributed to the expansion of biscuit producers like Peek, Frean, Huntley & Palmers and McVitie & Price, and the growth of cocoa and confectionery manufacturers such as Fry, Rowntree and Cadbury. Cadbury's story also illustrated the manner in which the introduction of state regulation could actively benefit business. Most nineteenth-century cocoa was mixed with starch to mask the bitter taste of its natural oil. In the late 1860s Cadbury acquired from Holland a machine press which extracted most of this oil, allowing him to pioneer the sale of unadulterated powder with his branded item, Cocoa Essence. The 1872 Adulteration Act and the 1875 Sale of Food and Drugs Act, which required labelling of mixed items, gave Cocoa Essence a competitive advantage over its rivals: Cadbury promoted it as a superior brand, distinct from cocoa blended with sago or other starchy additives.[22]

The growth of these major enterprises made the food and drink trades highly prominent in the ranks of the largest British industrial companies by 1919; more so, indeed, than was the case in the USA or Germany.[23] Rubinstein has highlighted the much higher profile of industrialists from the food and tobacco sectors from the 1880s alongside a consolidation of the already prominent brewing fortunes.[24] In some cases food producers, along with tobacco barons and big brewers, came to enjoy national as well as local eminence.[25] Among these the most notable, perhaps, were the Colmans of Norwich, the Frys of Bristol, the Cadburys of Birmingham and the Blackwells of London. Long-term patterns of industrial leadership were established in the chocolate, tobacco and brewing sectors by 1900 or 1914. A number of these large-scale enterprises, having gained first-mover advantages through the application of technological change, reinforced their market strength by grasping the value of the new techniques of advertising and brand-name pro-

---

[20] John Burnett, 'The Baking Industry in the Nineteenth Century', *Business History*, 5 (1/2), 1962–3, pp. 98–108.

[21] Alfred Plummer, *New British Industries in the Twentieth Century* (London, 1937), pp. 229–46.

[22] David J. Jeremy (ed.), *Dictionary of Business Biography* (*DBB*), vol. I (London, 1984), pp. 547–54.

[23] Alfred D. Chandler, *Scale and Scope: The dynamics of industrial capitalism* (Cambridge, MA, 1990), pp. 239–40, 666–72.

[24] W.D. Rubinstein, *Men of Property: The very wealthy in Britain since the industrial revolution*, (London, 1981), pp. 68–70, 86–91, 182–3

[25] John Stevenson, *British Society 1914–1945* (London, 1984), p. 336.

motion. Oxo, Rowntree and Bovril were early users of poster advertising for brands, while pioneers of advertising in the popular press included Colman's, the mustard and starch manufacturer, which established a dedicated advertising department as early as the 1870s, and Peek, Frean, which also posted free offer schemes directly to individual households.[26] Rowntree took a similarly novel approach, sending free samples to customers who returned newspaper coupons. Hovis deployed arguably the most integrated advertising strategy from 1891, supplying bakers with loaf tins bearing the brand-name so that it appeared on the sides of the finished bread.[27] Even within these pioneering firms, however, change was gradually applied. Fitzgerald's study of Rowntree reveals that executives were initially sceptical about new marketing approaches, regarding the firm's name and reputation as sufficient promotion and associating advertising with sharp practices and patent medicines.[28] More generally, Corley has shown that most manufacturers took a fairly limited approach to advertising and marketing before 1914.[29]

The application of new technology intensified in the food trades after the First World War. The factory-wrapped loaf made its first appearance in the 1920s, and was quickly followed by ready-sliced bread.[30] Popular initially with caterers, by the early 1930s the sliced loaf had begun to achieve significant general household sales, offering significant advantages in terms of economy as well as convenience: no slicing meant less wastage through crumbs. Reflecting on these advantages in 1930, Edmund Bennion of the National Bakery School in London described sliced bread as 'the path of progress', although he was unsure about the correct thickness of slice. While most working-class consumers favoured three-eighths of an inch, 'with a certain class of trade a quarter-inch slice would be still more acceptable'.[31] The Midland Vinegar Company, which later became HP Foods, began selling sauces in the 1890s, but its diversification and expansion were stimulated with important improvements in the manufacture of glass bottles in the 1920s. Smoother glass and threaded necks allowed for greater automation, helping the company to supplement its pre-war HP and Daddies sauces with tomato ketchup, salad cream and mayonnaise from 1933 onwards.[32] The canning industry which developed in the 1920s was based on wartime government-sponsored co-operation between fruit growers and fishermen, canners and Welsh tin-plate makers. This involved the

---

[26] Fraser, *Mass Market*, p. 135; Jeremy, *Dictionary*, pp. 750–2; Thomas Richards, *The Commodity Culture of Victorian England: Advertising and spectacle, 1851–1914*, (Stanford, 1990).

[27] E. J. T. Collins, 'The "Consumer Revolution" and the Growth of Factory Foods: changing patterns of bread and cereal-eating in Britain in the twentieth century', in Oddy (ed.), *Modern British Diet*, pp. 29–30.

[28] Robert Fitzgerald, *Rowntree and the Marketing Revolution, 1862–1969* (Cambridge, 1995), pp. 90–126.

[29] T. A. B. Corley, 'Consumer Marketing in Britain, 1914–60', *Business History* 29 (4), October 1987, pp. 66–8.

[30] Burnett, *Plenty and Want*, p. 259.

[31] *Food Manufacture*, March 1930, pp. 77, 90.

[32] Louise Wright, *The Road from Aston Cross: An industrial history 1875–1975* (Leamington Spa, 1975), p. 74.

establishment of large canneries near the Tayside fruit fields and in Fraserburgh and Aberdeen, the principal north-east Scottish herring ports. The foundation of the Metal Box Company in 1921, an amalgamation of 12 separate companies, provided a major force in this business.[33] It came to supply 90 per cent of cans used in British canneries, and used one-third of all British-made tin-plate. Buoyed by the advance of this industrial giant, the quantity of canned vegetables consumed increased from 24,000 tons per year in 1920 to around 193,000 tons per year in 1937–8.[34]

The Metal Box Company was a prime example of the manner in which large-scale enterprise was promoted through merger and acquisition as well as through the application of new technology. There were other important mergers in the food trade. Lever Brothers, the soap and oils manufacturer, entered margarine production at the government's request during the First World War, to fill the gap left by the absence of Dutch imports. At the end of the war imports resumed and the resulting excess capacity increased competition. Following a short but apparently damaging price war between Lever and the Dutch Margarine Union in the mid 1920s, both sides agreed on the merger which gave rise to Unilever in 1929.[35] Merger activity occurred in other sectors. Two of the leading chocolate and cocoa producers, Cadbury and Fry, amalgamated in 1920, while the following year witnessed the formation of Tate & Lyle in sugar refining and the union of Peek, Frean and Huntley & Palmers as Associated Biscuit Manufacturers. In 1922 Crosse & Blackwell secured James Keiller and Sons, the Dundee confectioner and jam and marmalade producer. Later, in 1935 Allied Bakers was formed, and Colman's merged with another mustard and starch manufacturer, Reckitt, in 1937.

Mergers in the food trades contributed to the process of greater industrial concentration between 1870 and 1939, characterised by Eric Hobsbawm as 'the rise of an economy composed of a handful of great lumps of rock – trusts, monopolies, oligopolies – rather than a large number of pebbles'.[36] At least as far as the food trades are concerned, however, it is easy to exaggerate the extent of this concentration. Before the First World War bread-making remained largely the province of independent local bakers, and as late as 1937 factory bakeries accounted for no more than 12 per cent of bread production.[37] Even mergers frequently resulted in the survival of separate enterprises rather than co-ordination so that Cadbury's did not stop competing with Fry's, and Keiller's and Crosse & Blackwell still operated independently. Moreover, an expanding market offered opportunities for smaller enterprises so that food manufacturing continued to encompass firms of many shapes and sizes, even towards the end of the period. Table 2.2, based on the Census of Production, captures some of this diversity, with more than 5,000 firms,

---

[33] W. J. Reader, *Metal Box: A history* (London, 1976), pp. 34–43.
[34] Sidney Pollard, *The Development of the British Economy 1914–1980* (London, 1983), p. 64.
[35] Charles Wilson, *The History of Unilever, Vol. I* (London, 1954), pp. 157, 227, 283, 297–311.
[36] E. J. Hobsbawm, *Industry and Empire* (London, 1968), pp. 172–7.
[37] Collins, 'The "Consumer Revolution"', p. 27.

excluding those with ten workers or less, active in the food trades. Of these 4,465 employed between 11 and 99 staff, absorbing about 30 per cent of the total workforce and accounting for 24 per cent of net output.

Table 2.2 Distribution of employment and output by size of firm, 1930

Size of firm	Number of firms	% share of workforce	% share of net output
11–99	4,465	30.4	24.2
100–199	439	13.2	13.5
200–299	164	8.6	8.5
300–399	75	5.5	6.3
400–499	36	3.5	3.9
500–749	54	7.1	7.4
750–999	31	5.9	5.5
1,000–1,499	23	6.0	6.3
1,500 plus	29	22.0	24.0

Note: Total percentages exclude firms with ten employees or less.

Source: Figures extrapolated from the Final Report of the Census of Population, 1930 (HMSO, 1935), Vol. 3, p. 10 and Vol. 5, pp. 26–7.

Comparing these relative shares of employment and net output by firm size suggests modest economies of scale once the workforce exceeded 300 and for firms employing more than 1500 workers. This provides some support for the notion that technology and increased demand favoured larger enterprises. The limited degree of concentration also had important implications for debates about regulation, particularly during the 1920s and 1930s when the state tended to assume that manufacturing conditions in the minority of large enterprises were representative of those in the industry as a whole. The implications of this assumption, which ensured that a minimum of new regulations were introduced after the First World War, are explored in chapter 6.

Like manufacturing, food distribution underwent substantial changes in structure, scope and business practices after 1850, though earlier forms of small enterprise displayed considerable resilience. The survival of small shops had a significant bearing on regulatory developments, for the 1875 Sale of Food and Drugs Act was aimed at detecting and punishing malpractices among retailers rather than producers. In the mid nineteenth century food was sold by a variety of traders, ranging from itinerant hawkers to market stall holders and shopkeepers of varying levels of sophistication. At their best, grocers practised a highly skilled trade, purchasing items in bulk and undertaking the key tasks of sorting, grading, weighing and packaging before sale. They were also responsible for blending tea, roasting coffee and mixing or preparing spices and other commodities. This central mixing and packing role partially explains the fact that the early adulteration legislation, including the 1875 SFDA, was aimed directly at grocers rather than producers. These skilled practices remained important to the self-image of many grocers and survived widely after 1914. The vast bulk of retail trade remained in the hands of small shopkeepers, and the small shop continued to provide most people's daily contact with the food business after the war. In England and Wales in 1939 there were still 80,000 grocers, 40,000 butchers, 30,000 bakers and 30,000 greengrocers.[38] The business strategy of the small shop was based on convenience for working-class consumers: selling in small quantities, remaining open after normal working hours and providing credit to cover weekly shortfalls or tide families over in periods of unexpected unemployment or sickness. Skilful operation of credit was crucial to the financial health and very survival of such retailers.[39] Broader changes in manufacturing and retailing were not entirely without benefit for these more marginal operators. While increased standardisation, in the form of packaged and branded articles, clearly helped the multiples, it enabled small retailers to draw on the investments made by larger firms in packaging and advertising.[40] At the same time, however, increasing demand and improved communications were giving rise to changes in the functional character of retail outlets. Some specialist operators began selling a wider range of goods; others, conversely, became more specialised, like butchers who ceased slaughtering and simply sold meat obtained from wholesalers. Frozen meat shippers pursued a different strategy, moving into retailing in order to overcome the existing vendors' resistance to the new product.[41]

The imported meat distributors, a number of whom came together in the Union Cold Storage merger in 1923, were one component in the rise of the multiple stores. Their appearance signalled a retailing revolution in urban markets in terms of the size of retail businesses and the adoption of business strategies based on cash dealing and the use of special offers, advertising and shop-window displays. Among the pioneers, Lipton's and Maypole Dairy concentrated on a handful of lines like tea, butter and margarine; their lower prices were accompanied by a strict policy of cash sales only. Another early multiple, Sainsbury's, retained some traditional retail features, concentrating on a few departments and sub-dividing bulk items for sale. A further important branch of the retailing revolution was the growth of Co-operation, a movement adopting similar business methods but organised around a distinct ideology with an unambiguous commitment to fair trade. Guaranteed non-adulteration of produce was a strong element in the Co-operative movement's promotion of fair trade, and assisted in the growth of its membership, from 600,000 in 1880 to 3 million in 1914 and 8.4 million in 1938.[42]

---

[38] Burnett, *Plenty and Want*, p. 260.

[39] Christopher P. Hosgood, 'The "Pigmies of Commerce" and the Working Class Community: Small shopkeepers in England, 1870–1914', *Journal of Social History*, 22, 1988–9, pp. 439–60.

[40] Jeffreys, *Retail Trading in Britain*, p. 81.

[41] Michael J. Winstanley, *The Shopkeeper's World, 1830–1914* (Manchester, 1983), pp. 36–9; Benson and Shaw, *Evolution of Retail Systems* (Leicester, 1992), pp. 155–6.

[42] Peter Gurney, *Co-operative Culture and the Politics of Consumption in England, 1870–1930* (Manchester, 1996), pp. 205–6, 241–2.

The trend towards concentration, Hobsbawm's 'rocks', was more distinct in retailing than in manufacturing, although even here it was far from complete. Multiples accounted for 12–14 per cent of the grocery trade in 1914 and 22–25 per cent in 1939; in the meat trade there was little change, the multiples holding 9–11 per cent of sales in 1915 and 11–13 per cent in 1939.[43] In addition, Co-op stores supplied 17–19 per cent of groceries in 1915 and 22–4 per cent in 1938, with their share of meat sales rising from 5–8 per cent to 9–11 per cent in the same period.

Political and interest group activity

The proliferation of associations and organisations of all shapes and sizes was a pervasive feature of late Victorian society. Some enjoyed brief lives; in time others produced celebratory volumes chronicalling their founders, achievements and pedigree. Some operated at a local level or within a limited sphere of co-operation among individuals, societies or enterprises for specific purposes. Other associations aimed to shape public policy. Such political activity was usually just one element of a group's broader social or professional functions, which included promoting the identity and self-image as well as defending the material interests of their members. The food trades were no exception with political and interest group activity apparent at all stages of the food chain through numerous local and several national organisations.

The multiplicity of societies and associations is rather at odds with Olson's classic analysis of organisational activity which emphasised potential obstacles to effective organisation. Olson's economic logic highlighted the resources required for collective action and the incentives for individuals to leave the task to others in the hope of avoiding the costs, while still reaping the benefits of any effective co-operation. Given these incentives for 'free riders', Olson concluded that co-operation was most likely where there was a small number of similar groups or individuals whose common interests could be pursued through a clearly identifiable programme.[44] The prospects for organisation were increased if a policy was likely to reward all participants, thereby ensuring commitment and reducing the likelihood of 'free rider' problems. He recognised, however, that once an organisation was established for any purpose, the cost of extending its collective action into other areas was reduced significantly. Olson's emphasis on the incentives for, and constraints on, collective action provide insights into the character of associations in the food trades, with the most frequent and effective organisation occurring at the level of local groups or in relation to specific commodities or trades, although broader national associations and campaigns were evident. The various institutions in the food sector often broadened or changed their activities from their original remit so that a society might combine cultural activities with political campaigning. If the capacity for collective action cannot be taken for granted, its

[43] Jeffreys, *Retail Trading in Britain*, pp. 163, 201.
[44] Mancur Olson, *The Logic of Collective Action* (Cambridge, MA, 1965).

precise form and aims also require consideration. Influencing public policy via regulation may be only one of many possible means of achieving an organisation's aims, especially in the context of Victorian assumptions about the limits of government responsibilities, which extended to the notion that the state and society occupied entirely separate spheres of activity.

Agricultural societies were well-established by the middle of the nineteenth century. For large landowners and farmers the local Chambers of Agriculture supplied an institutional base that was extended further with the establishment of a national co-ordinating organisation, the Central Chamber of Agriculture, in 1865. Its focus on national politics reflected a concern with minimising local rates, in part by seeking concessions and national expenditure to the benefit of rural areas.[45] The Central Chamber operated through various committees, usually designated by commodity, and had a general Parliamentary committee. This helped landowners to maintain a substantial presence in local and national politics, providing them with direct access to policy making. The scope for national influence was increased by the establishment of the Board of Agriculture in 1889 and its elevation to cabinet status in 1895. Class divisions and changing social attitudes within the rural community were emphasised with the formation in 1908 of a new national body, the National Farmers' Union (NFU), to represent tenant farmers. By the 1920s the NFU was the leading agricultural organisation in part because its local committees were an integral part of the wartime campaign to increase food production. The NFU and other earlier farming organisations have been depicted as ineffectual and divided by class, commodity and region. Consequently the establishment of a powerful agricultural policy community able to shape public policy has generally been located in the 1940s, and attributed to state initiatives.[46] Such perceptions reflect comparisons with the greater spread of agricultural tariffs in continental Europe. Between 1870 and 1938 farmers and their representatives waged a series of substantial political campaigns, seeking protection from imports, measures to counter rural de-population and general financial assistance, but the impact of these campaigns was limited.[47] Although state support was forthcoming after the First World War for marketing and grading schemes for commodities like milk, bacon and potatoes, British farmers failed to secure the degree of state protection enjoyed by their European competitors. This arguably reflected the increased economic and political influence of the expanding urban electorate, though this leaves open the question of how agricultural interests were later successfully incorporated into

---

[45] Avner Offer, *Property and Politics, 1870–1914: Landownership, law, ideology and urban development in England*, (Cambridge, 1981), pp. 173–5, 210.

[46] Charles P. Kindleberger, 'Group Behaviour', *Journal of Political Economy*, 59 (1), 1951, pp. 30–47; Peter Self and Herbert J. Storing, *The State and the Farmer* (London, 1962), pp. 17–18; Wyn Grant, *Business and Politics in Britain* (First edition, Basingstoke, 1987), pp. 156–61.

[47] A. H. H. Matthews, *Fifty Years of Agricultural Politics: Being the history of the Central Chamber of Agriculture, 1865–1915* (London: 1915); Self and Storing, *The State and the Farmer* pp. 37–9; Niek Konig, *The Failure of Agrarian Capitalism: Agrarian politics in the United Kingdom, Germany, the Netherlands, and the USA, 1846–1919* (London, 1994), p. 9.

policy making.[48] While the impact of the Second World War and the post-war 'dollar gap' were critical in this respect, when food shortages gave farmers renewed economic and political strength, and commodity groups had clear influence, the framing of policy from the late 1940s on indicates that there was no decisive urban political bias against agricultural or rural interests in general. Arguably the seeds of future farming influence were gradually laid before 1939 in the development of milk policies. The waning political influence centred more with those farmers who were most exposed to competition from imported produce. Hence the failure of the 'pure beer campaign', examined in chapter 4, which was mounted by English barley producers from the 1880s onwards in an attempt to promote demand for domestic produce by confining the legal ingredients of beer to grain, hops and yeast. Dairy farmers were free from international competition and this helped them to be far more successful when lobbying the state on regulation of milk and dairies, as chapter 7 indicates.

Merchant and manufacturing interests had a long tradition of organisation, usually along sectional or local lines, in pursuit of economic, social and political aims.[49] There were general business organisations, notably the local Chambers of Commerce of which the largest, such as Manchester or Liverpool, enjoyed good access to national political institutions. By 1900 some 90 Chambers were affiliated to the Association of British Chambers of Commerce (ABCC), then celebrating its thirtieth anniversary.[50] The ABCC and individual Chambers dispatched resolutions, memorials and delegations to Westminster over issues such as patents, trade marks and the bankruptcy laws as well as advocating the creation of a Ministry of Commerce. At the local level the Chambers provided a common forum for merchants and manufacturers in the food trades. However the London Chamber of Commerce (LCC), established in 1881, enjoyed a special prominence given the significance of imported foods and provided a central forum for dealers in the substantial metropolitan commodity markets. The diverse trading interests were recognised in the LCC's structure with its separate trade sections with their own committees, and an overarching central council.

In manufacturing, the most effective organisations appeared at industry level, especially where government exerted a considerable influence on trading conditions, as in the textile and railway sectors. Equally there were significant divisions within the general business community. These were apparent in the debate about tariff reform in the 1890s and 1900s as industrialists adopted varying stances

---

[48] A.J. Marrison, 'The Tariff Commission, Agricultural Protection and Food Taxes, 1903–1913', *Agricultural History Review*, 34, 1986, pp. 171–87; Graham Cox, Philip Lowe and Michael Winter, 'The Origins and Early Development of the National Farmers' Union', *Agricultural History Review*, 39, 1991, pp. 30–47.

[49] A.R. Ilersic, *Parliament of Commerce: The story of the Association of British Chambers of Commerce, 1860–1960* (London, 1960), pp. 2–8; for a valuable survey see John Turner, 'The Politics of Business', in John Turner (ed.), *Businessmen and Politics: Studies of business activity in British politics, 1900–1945* (London, 1984).

[50] Wyn Grant, *Business and Politics in Britain* (Second edition, Basingstoke, 1993), pp. 118–19.

towards free trade and protectionism, which at times cut across industrial lines. The numerous employers' associations testified to the primary area of mutual self-interest. While manufacturers were clearly organised, their relationship with the state has been a matter of debate. Trentmann portrays business as poorly organised politically, reflecting a deliberate preference for remaining outside the political sphere in return for autonomy within its own economic realm.[51] This functional and ideological divide was, according to Trentmann, progressively renegotiated, so neither its terms nor scope were set in stone. Indeed the involvement of the various business groups in Parliamentary activity and the direct lobbying of central government emphasises the mingling of the economic and political spheres. The establishment in the 1890s of an Employers' Parliamentary Council was followed in the unique conditions of war by new groupings, primarily as tools for negotiating with government on employment and raw materials. By 1918 there was the prospect of unprecedented business influence with the creation of new peak level organisations, namely the Federation of British Industries and the National Confederation of Employers' Organisations, as well as the greater presence of businessmen in government and Parliament.[52] Indeed, Middlemas identifies the war as the beginnings of a 'corporate bias' in British politics with policy shaped by employers' associations, unions, and the state. In the event, business directed its efforts mainly to dismantling wartime controls and resisting new forms of government intervention. Business–government relations still operated chiefly at the industry level, whether in terms of rationalisation schemes, price collusion or even the formulation of tariff policies. Peak organisations expanded and were consulted, but without possessing any special status.[53] Indeed industry's preference for its own forms of governance and its suspicion of government were so powerful that in 1935 the FBI opposed a bill to establish industrial self-government, in contrast to the corporatist rhetoric of its own founders.[54] Turner, Grant and Block all emphasise the political and organisational weakness of business before 1945, a product of an individualistic ethos which inhibited agreement.[55] Yet the state too is portrayed as a feeble institution, so that Turner describes business–government relations as 'bargaining between two weak entities which often did not know their own minds'.[56]

---

[51] Frank Trentmann, 'The Transformation of Fiscal Reform: Reciprocity, Modernisation and the fiscal debate within the business community in early twentieth century Britain', *Historical Journal*, 39, 1996, pp. 1005–48.

[52] John Turner, 'The Politics of 'Organised Business' in the First World War', in Turner (ed.), *Businessmen and Politics*, chapter 3.

[53] Keith Middlemas, *Politics in Industrial Society: The experience of the British system since 1911* (London, 1979); Jim Tomlinson, *Public Policy and the Economy since 1900* (Oxford, 1990), pp. 24–5.

[54] Daniel Ritschel, *The Politics Of Planning: The debate on economic planning in Britain in the 1930s* (Oxford, 1997), pp. 209–20.

[55] Turner (ed.), *Businessmen and Politics*; Grant, *Business and Politics in Britain*, pp. 18–20, 193–4; Stephen Blank, *Industry and Government in Britain: The Federation of British Industries in politics* (Farnborough, 1973).

[56] Turner (ed.), *Businessmen and Politics*, p. 3.

The food industry followed this general pattern with local and sectoral co-operation initially focused on pricing and industrial relations. In the nineteenth century, the main national body in the food industry was the Manufacturing Confectioners' Alliance, based in part on the networks of Quaker business families, including Cadbury. Other groups, like the Margarine Manufacturers' Association or the Condensed Milk Defence Association, were formed to rebut criticism of their products or counter threats of regulation. By 1914 there were at least 166 employers' associations in the food, drink and tobacco industries.[57] In line with manufacturing generally, the First World War prompted greater national organisation in food manufacturing. The Confectionery and Preserved Food Manufacturers' Federation was established by a number of firms in 1913 to conduct discussions with the Board of Trade on the industry's behalf. This expanded during the war and was reconstituted in 1917 as the Food Manufacturers' Federation (FMF), with a number of major firms among its founders, including Peek, Frean, Keiller's and Rowntree. The FMF expanded to 750 members in 1934 with a combined workforce exceeding 150,000. Operations also extended into exchanging information, promoting improved business practices, supporting research and organising social activities. The focus of the Federation's associational activities, including lobbying, remained largely at the industry level, although food processors were involved in peak level organisations, including the FBI, with which it shared a preference for self-regulation. The FMF enjoyed a close relationship with the Manufacturing Confectioners' Alliance, which was chaired for most of the interwar period by Paul Cadbury, and established a Parliamentary presence with the Food Group of MPs in 1932. Both trade associations maintained an important lobbying role in the 1920s and 1930s, enjoying a significant amount of influence on the regulatory framework, especially during the Ministry of Health's inquiry into standards and definitions which is discussed in chapter 6.

Britain's shopkeepers have been perceived as highly individualistic which, in addition to differences of status and an antagonism to government intervention, impeded organisation and limited their desire for any state regulation.[58] Local trade associations, many of which had been established by the 1880s, reflected the insecurities and interests of owners of large shops and specialist retailers rather than small shopkeepers. The larger operators tended to assert their skill, standing and moral worth as 'legitimate' traders, distinct from smaller shopkeepers, stallholders and itinerant traders. A variant of this distinction was regularly offered in *The Grocer*, a trade weekly founded in the 1860s, which routinely defended the integrity and skill of 'honest' traders. According to Michael Winstanley these sectional interests were behind the support which some shopkeepers gave in the late nineteenth century to the campaign for food adulteration laws. Such regulation

---

[57] Arthur J. McIvor, *Organised Capital: Employers' associations and industrial relations in Northern England, 1880–1939* (Cambridge, 1996), p. 60, table 3.1.
[58] For a discussion see John K. Walton, *Fish and Chips and the British Working Class, 1870–1940* (Leicester, 1992). pp. 111–13.

would help to eliminate what they regarded primarily as an unfair trade practice, allowing dishonest rivals an immoral competitive advantage, rather than an affront to food consumers.[59] Similar sentiment, springing from the distinction between honest and dishonest traders, certainly informed *The Grocer*'s campaign for tougher laws in the 1900s against the fraudulent sale of margarine as butter.[60] While damning the dishonesty of small rivals, grocers' trade associations also fulminated against the emerging threat from the multiples, and reserved particular spleen for the Co-operative movement, which combined conventional commercial rivalry with an alternative ideal of trading.[61]

For retailers, according to Geoffrey Crossick and Heinz-Gerhard Haupt, the most appropriate form of lobbying was conducted through local government: state regulation of food, drink and retailing were all administered by local authorities, and grocers were greatly affected by locally determined rates and taxes.[62] Shopkeepers and grocers were an important force in local politics in many towns and cities, being elected as mayors, JPs and representatives on councils, vestries and other local authorities. Crossick and Haupt suggest that the lower-middle-class shopkeeper–councillor was most prevalent in smaller and medium-sized towns, diminishing in numerical frequency and influence in greater cities where wealthier classes dominated local politics. Yet even in the smaller cities, judging by Hosgood's study of Leicester, shopkeepers were moving away from direct participation in local government by the end of the nineteenth century, favouring instead greater lobbying through trade associations.[63] In 1903, however, Board of Agriculture officials in England and Wales noted that in some areas, including urban localities, trader influence on councils was hindering the enforcement of the Sale of Food and Drugs Act.[64] A similar perspective was offered in Scotland as late as 1912, where the presence of grocers on local councils was still presenting an important potential problem. According to the public analysts who were charged with monitoring food quality and safety, the direct involvement of so many councillors in food retailing was interfering with the effective operation of the adulteration act.[65]

The Grocer was one form of national focus for retailers' interests. Another was the National Federation of Grocers' Associations, established in 1891, which enjoyed Parliamentary links through MPs with retail interests like Hudson Kearley, later Lord Devonport, the founder of the International Tea Company's stores – a multiple that in size exceeded Lipton's and the Home and Colonial Stores in the

[59] Winstanley, *Shopkeeper's World*, pp. 64–5.
[60] *The Grocer*, 23 February 1907, p. 483.
[61] Gurney, *Co-operative Culture*, pp. 199–202.
[62] Geoffrey Crossick and Heinz-Gerhard Haupt, *The Petite Bourgeoisie in Europe, 1780–1914: Enterprise, family and independence* (London, 1995), pp. 115–21, 128–31.
[63] C. P. Hosgood, 'A "Brave and Daring Folk"? Shopkeepers and trade associational life in Victorian and Edwardian England', *Journal of Social History*, 36, 1992, pp. 285–308.
[64] Board of Agriculture (Intelligence Division), Annual Report (1903), p. 5.
[65] John Biggart, Association of Public Analysts in Scotland, to the Secretary, the Local Government Board in Scotland, April 1912, HH 64/191, Scottish Record Office.

1890s.[66] Despite this national presence, Crossick and Haupt state that in comparison with their European counterparts British shopkeepers, along with the lower middle class generally, were a feeble political force before 1914.[67] Shopkeepers' anti-co-operative campaigns were sometimes counterproductive. Boycotts and attempts to prevent Co-op stores from obtaining supplies merely prompted the Co-operative Wholesale Society to enter manufacturing which, in turn, persuaded private manufacturers to continue to supply the Co-op in the hope of averting a similar response. As subsequent chapters of this book make clear, the limited lobbying power of grocers is also suggested by the character of the 1875 Sale of Food and Drugs Act. Despite the efforts of the Grocers' Federation and other retailer groups, throughout the 1875–1939 period the law continued to focus on retailers rather than manufacturers.

Science and technology

The lobbying strength of different trading groups had a direct impact on debates about food regulation, quality and safety; so too did the increasing application of science and technology to food production. These influences were evident in the case of Liebig's Extract of Meat, a new product marketed in 1865 in terms of its nutritional value and the scientific reputation of its inventor.[68] When these claims were subjected to critical examination by other scientists, Liebig's marketing shifted to emphasising the product's convenience for consumers. The gradual introduction of adulteration laws, culminating in the 1875 and 1899 Sale of Food and Drugs Acts, gave manufacturers a powerful incentive to monitor the composition and quality of their raw materials and finished products. Accustomed to relying on the experience and skill of their workers and management, manufacturing firms began to employ analysts and chemists on a consultative basis and then, as Sally Horrocks has demonstrated, some began to employ scientists directly, equipping them with basic laboratories.[69] The pioneer in this respect appears to have been Colman's, which employed two chemists to monitor incoming mustard seed from 1893. Many others followed. When a London Medical Officer of Health alleged in 1905 that a sample of Rowntree's eucalyptus pastilles was 'chemically impure', the company defended itself by pointing to the work of its specialised chemical and bacteriological staff, insisting that such well-equipped experts would

---

[66] Jeremy, *Dictionary*, pp. 561–4.

[67] Crossick and Haupt, *Petite Bourgeoisie in Europe*, pp. 136–7, 156–60.

[68] Mark R. Finlay, 'Early Marketing of the Theory of Nutrition: The science and culture of Liebig's extract of meat', in Harmke Kamminga and Andrew Cunningham (eds), *The Science and Culture of Nutrition, 1840–1940* (Amsterdam, 1995) pp. 48–74.

[69] Sally M. Horrocks, 'Quality Control and Research: The role of scientists in the British food industry, 1870–1939', in John Burnett and Derek J. Oddy (eds), *The Origins and Development of Food Policies in Europe* (Leicester, 1994), pp. 131–3; and 'Nutrition Science and the Food Industry in Britain, 1920–1990', in Adel P. den Hartog (ed.), *Food, Technology, Science and Marketing: European diet in the twentieth century* (East Linton, 1995), pp. 7–18.

not have allowed 'impure' products to enter the market. The London official dropped his charges.[70] By 1914 companies like Cadbury, the Co-operative Wholesale Society, Keiller's, Huntley & Palmers and Fry's also had chemists working within the firm. The pioneers were joined by a growing number of manufacturers between the wars, including Lever Bros., United Dairies, Heinz, Horlicks, Chivers, Crosse & Blackwell and Tate & Lyle.[71] By this point the photograph of the company's research laboratory, complete with chief chemist, was becoming an emblem of modernity and corporate ambition, on a par with the nineteenth-century depiction of factory or mill. In 1939 Crosse & Blackwell's Bermondsey factory had bacteriological and analytical departments as well as a technical research centre responsible for quality control. The analytical department reportedly examined 40,000 samples of raw materials and products annually.[72] While the first function of these scientists was to ensure that the ingredients, quality and safety of food complied with government regulation, a more extensive role was developing. Scientists were expected to find cheaper ways of producing a product which, in physical appearance and taste, seemed unchanged. Here Horrocks presents as typical the case of Crosse & Blackwell, which on many occasions changed both the recipe and method of production of its Branston's Pickle, but managed to maintain consistencies of flavour and colour through chemical innovation. Other forms of manufacturing innovation were facilitated by advances in nutrition science and the discovery of vitamins.[73]

For the average small or even medium-sized company any investment in laboratories was well out of reach, but the creation of industry and government research establishments offered alternative, low-cost sources of information and guidance. In 1925 the Food Manufacturers' Federation established a Research Association to work with a similar body that had been set up by cocoa, chocolate, sugar confectionery and jam producers in 1919. The two bodies shared a Research Director and a laboratory in North London.[74] Flour millers had their own research association, and the Society of the Chemical Industry formed a Food Group in 1932.[75] In agriculture central government support for research expanded substantially from 1910, providing 20 separate specialist research centres by 1925, largely based in colleges and universities. The Campden Research

---

[70] T. H. Appleton to Butler Hogan (MOH for Tottenham), 6 May 1905, R/DH/SR 19, Rowntree Mackintosh Archive, Borthwick Institute.

[71] D. E. H. Edgerton and S. M. Horrocks, 'British Industrial Research and Development before 1945', *Economic History Review*, 67, 1994, (2) pp. 213–38.

[72] *Food Manufacture*, April 1939, pp. 115–20.

[73] Sally M. Horrocks, 'The Business of Vitamins: Nutrition science and the food industry in inter-war Britain', in Harmke Kamminga and Andrew Cunningham (eds), *The Science and Culture of Nutrition* (Amsterdam, 1995), pp. 235–58; 'Quality Control and Research', pp. 130–45.

[74] British Food Manufacturers' Research Association, Memorandum and Articles of Association, 31 December 1925; copy in DSIR 16/71, Public Record Office.

[75] *Food Manufacture*, January 1933.

Station in Gloucestershire, for instance, made a significant contribution to developments in canning and preservatives in the 1920s.[76]

This growth in the supply of domestic canned foods was overseen by a producers' organisation, the National Food Canning Council (NFCC), established in 1926. The same year witnessed the foundation of *Food Manufacture*, a monthly trade journal which emphasised the technological modernity of the industry and the high quality of the goods which it produced. A key word in *Food Manufacture*'s editorial matter was 'progress': the journal encouraged readers to develop sales by adopting new methods of production and marketing. Smaller producers, unable to invest in laboratory space or a qualified chemist, were advised in December 1927 to pick out from the shopfloor a 'young, intelligent hand', finance his instruction in junior technical classes at the local night school, 'give him a chance of gaining experience in each stage of factory operations, and put FOOD MANUFACTURE into his hand every month'.[77] The aspect of technological innovation promoted most vigorously by the new journal was canning, which combined several of its most prominent interests: production, science, preservation and packaging. *Food Manufacture* was highly enthusiastic about the work of the NFCC and its chairman, the one-time Ministry of Munitions civil servant and Liberal MP, Edgar Rees Jones, who it described as canning's 'dominant genius ... who is doing for Preserving and Canning what Lord Melchett did for another industry'.[78] This allusion to ICI, the giant of chemical production, was telling, a vivid example of the journal's insistence that food manufacturing was as reliant on the application of science as any other branch of modern industry. And to bring the point home *Food Manufacture* carried regular bulletins on the NFCC's annual conventions and site visits, to places like Chivers' laboratories at Histon and Smedley's pea factory at Wisbech, all of which were designed to convey the trade's involvement in research and development.[79]

Food Manufacture's rhetorical praise of the industry's modernity finds echoes in the use that the trade made of scientific expertise and imagery in the promotion of new and developing products. One such product in the interwar period was ice cream. In February 1926 a number of manufacturers formed the British Ice Cream Association, in order to promote increased sales by emphasising that ice cream was a year-round nutritious item rather than a mere summer refreshment. The new association set up a monthly journal, *Ice Cream Industry*, to articulate its aims and values. Uncannily similar to *Food Manufacture* in its physical lay-out and editorial structure, *Ice Cream Industry* pressed similar claims on behalf of producers to

---

[76] C. J. Holmes, 'Science and Practice in English Arable Farming, 1910–50', Derek J. Oddy and Derek S. Miller, *Diet and Health in Modern Britain* (London, 1985), pp. 5–31; J. P. Johnston, 'The development of the food canning industry in Britain during the Inter-War Period', in Oddy and Miller, *Modern British Diet*, pp. 174–83.

[77] *Food Manufacture*, December 1927, p. 201.

[78] *Ibid.*, May 1929, p. 139.

[79] For examples see *Ibid.*, December 1931 and November 1935.

modernity and skilful exploitation of the latest technology. Its first edition ran articles in praise of 'Modern Methods', 'The New Season', (new) 'Flavourings in Ice Cream' and show-cased 'A Model Factory' at Stoke and 'Model Showrooms' in the City of London.[80]

While the industry was generally positive about the growing involvement of professional scientists in food production, disquiet was expressed in some quarters from a relatively early stage. When giving evidence to a Commons Select Committee in 1895, John Innes Rogers, a representative of London Chamber of Commerce, commented on the increasingly sophisticated nature of adulteration. 'In the old days', he said, 'the adulterators worked on a small scale and were more or less bunglers. They are now men of science and work wholesale, and, having microscopic and chemical analysis to dread, they use their knowledge to defeat the checks which science places on their criminal practices.' He concluded, 'you have to set science to catch science'.[81] Two decades earlier the Sale of Food and Drugs Act had established a group of professional scientists dedicated to this very pursuit, the local public analysts who formed their own association, the Society of Public Analysts (SPA), in 1875. Analysts participated in related bodies, notably the Institute of Chemistry which supervised qualifications in the emerging chemical profession. And there was a notable division among analysts from 1899 when Charles Cassal, previously an active figure in the SPA, established his own *British Food Journal* (*BFJ*). As editor to 1915 Cassal used the *BFJ* to promote the British Analytical Control, a scheme for manufacturers to subject their products to regular inspections by analysts.[82] This scheme, an extension of the analysts' fundamental role, emphasised the value of expert scientific analysis and Cassal remained highly influential. However, the SPA was recognised by government as the voice of public analysts. Its representatives were invited to give evidence at successive inquiries from the 1880s to the 1930s. Among the SPA's more prominent figures was Otto Hehner, German-born and educated at Anderson's University in Glasgow. Hehner held numerous public analyst posts during his long career, which began in the 1870s and included wartime service, refereeing glycerine contracts between soap manufacturers and the War Office. Appointed to a Ministry of Health Departmental Committee on preservatives in 1923, Hehner pre-empted its proceedings with a lengthy letter to *The Times*, outlining his views on the extent to which food manufacturing had changed during the 50 years of his career. Instead of arriving in the kitchen directly from the farm, according to Hehner it now passed 'through factories in which it is prepared, preserved and beautified, and, incidentally, made dearer'.[83] This attack on the use of preservatives and

---

[80] *Ice Cream Industry*, 1 (1) April 1926; thanks to Sally Horrocks for supplying this reference.

[81] Report on Food Products Adulteration, Parliamentary Papers, 1895 (363), p. 249.

[82] Involvement in the British Analytical Control was voluntary and, in return for the periodic inspections, manufacturers could advertise their participation as a sign of the quality of their products. For details see the *British Food Journal*, 1900 and 1901.

[83] *The Times*, 20 September 1923.

colourings led to Hehner's removal from the Departmental Committee, and he died a few months later in South Africa after a malaria attack,[84] but other public analysts broadly shared his views from the 1870s to the 1920s. Through the pages of the SPA's journal, *The Analyst*, and in testimony to the periodic investigations of the Sale of Food and Drugs Acts, public analysts argued the case for precise definitions of foods in order to monitor the growing use of chemicals and other additives. Analysts also debated the merits of new and rival methods of scientific analysis, notably microscopical versus chemical approaches, believing that the establishment of agreed and precise tests for food ingredients held the key to ensuring quality and safety. At the same time they were always anxious that manufacturers were devising new and less easily detectable substances. In 1930 the President of the SPA, addressing his members' annual meeting, referred to the increasingly 'more subtle' forms of food adulteration.[85] This perspective was shared by Sir George Newman, Chief Medical Officer at the Ministry of Health. Although usually reticent on potentially controversial matters, in his 1932 Annual Report Newman included a lengthy passage on 'A New Problem in Food Adulteration'. This cast doubt on the medical safety and nutritional value of food that had been subjected to 'scientific "treatment"', including the addition of vitamins and chemical preservatives.[86] Producers responded to such criticisms and misgivings by emphasising that public health and safety were guaranteed by their deployment of chemical and bacteriological expertise, as in the case of Rowntree's and the London Medical Officer of Health in 1905. Such also was the later optimistic judgement of *Food Manufacture*, which insisted that the industry was essentially fit to police its own standards, advising that these could best be improved through the employment of analytical chemists and other scientific experts.[87]

The debate about standards and definitions, prompted by the growing involvement of scientists in food production, is discussed in chapter 6, and formed a major part of the broader debate about food quality and food regulation. By assessing the changing character and structure of the food trades from the 1870s to the 1930s, this opening chapter has sought to introduce two significant features of this debate. First, as the food trades constituted a large and increasingly important economic sector, they attempted to exert some influence on patterns of regulation. Second, given that food production and distribution were characterised by extreme diversity, business demands on the regulatory process were not uniform. In some cases, indeed, as with the different legal obligations on producers and retailers under the Sale of Food and Drugs Act, they were even conflicting. The SFDA, focusing the law on retailers rather than producers, was a measure of the contrasting political and economic influence of different parts of the food business. Even within the production sector, however, there were clear points of

[84] For Hehner's obituary see *The Analyst*, 49, November 1924, pp. 501–5.
[85] *The Analyst*, 1930, vol. 55, p. 237.
[86] Ministry of Health, On the State of the Public Health. Annual Report of the Chief Medical Officer (1932), pp. 135–42.
[87] *Food Manufacture*, March 1935.

heterogeneity. The limited degree of industrial concentration was immensely significant in terms of debates about standards and quality, for the state was to base its understanding of manufacturing conditions on evidence gathered from big firms alone, at a time when small enterprises still provided the vast bulk of domestically produced food.

3

The evolution and operation of the Sale of Food and Drugs Acts, 1875–1907

Public interest in food regulation in Britain stemmed initially from a developing perception, from the 1820s onwards, that dangerous and fraudulent food posed a potentially serious threat to public health and the commercial operations of legitimate traders. In common with much Victorian public health legislation, however, the 1872 Adulteration Act emerged only after a lengthy period of gestation, involving a mixture of medical activism, scientific publicity, official investigation and an ineffective first attempt at legislation.[1] The most influential campaign for regulations against adulteration of food and drink appeared in the 1850s as an extension of the social reform concerns of Thomas Wakley, a medical doctor and publisher of the *Lancet*. Wakley commissioned a series of investigations by Arthur Hill Hassall, physician at the Royal Free Hospital in London, who analysed some 2,400 samples, making extensive use of the microscope.[2] Between 1851 and 1854 Hassall's series of articles in the *Lancet* supplied an unprecedented degree of systematic, scientific information which exposed the extent of food adulteration and its implications for public health. This information, and its challenge to perceptions about food, were taken to a wider audience through books and articles in the popular press and stimulated the formation of anti-adulteration pressure groups, with doctors prominent. The resulting lobbying finally led to the establishment in 1856 of a Parliamentary Select Committee on food and drugs adulteration.[3] Medical Officers of Health, government chemists, analytical chemists and business representatives, primarily grocers, provided the bulk of the testimony in hearings that revealed further evidence of adulteration.[4] Business interests were largely on the defensive in the hearings, although Paulus argued that business supporters from all

---

[1] The evolution of late-nineteenth century public health legislation in general is one of the subjects examined in the collection of essays edited by Roy Macleod, *Government and Expertise*.

[2] On events surrounding Hassall and adulteration in the 1850s see John Burnett, *Plenty and Want*, pp. 216–27.

[3] Christopher Hamlin, *A Science of Impurity: Water analysis in nineteenth century Britain* (Bristol, 1990), p. 104.

[4] Ingeborg Paulus, *The Search for Pure Food: A sociology of legislation in Britain* (London, 1974), pp. 24–5.

parties mobilised effectively against sanitary reformers, notably John Simon. The resulting 1860 Act for Preventing Adulteration in Food and Drink was a permissive rather than a compulsive measure, allowing rather than instructing some local authorities to appoint food analysts, and this, plus the lack of any clear definition of adulteration, ensured that the Act had little practical effect. Nor had a second Adulteration Act in 1862, which allowed local authorities to appoint inspectors to procure samples for analysis, and extended the right to appoint analysts to a large number of local authorities.[5] In 1868 the Pharmacy Act added drugs to the food and drink laws. In 1872 the Adulteration Act at least advised that applicants for public analyst positions come equipped with relevant 'medical, chemical and microscopical' knowledge. It also defined adulteration in terms of health risks by making it illegal to 'admix, with any article of food or drink, any injurious or poisonous ingredient or material to adulterate the same for sale'.[6] These provisions signalled the type of information to be used to gauge adulteration and the terms of the subsequent debates about 'public interest'.

The government established a second Select Committee to consider strengthening the law in 1874. The short life of the 1872 Act is explained by John Burnett in terms of its patchy local implementation and contradictory judgements by magistrates' courts that displeased some local authorities.[7] Ingeborg Paulus has offered a slightly different explanation, emphasising that the prompt review occurred primarily because appeal court judges interpreted the retailers' responsibilities to customers as including full knowledge of the composition of foods sold; in effect judges exercised their legal discretion to extend the scope of the 1872 Act. She also suggested that commercial pressures were important, identifying the Tea Dealers' and Grocers' Association of Metropolitan London as a particularly significant group.[8] They demanded government inspection of imported tea at the port of entry to safeguard them against impure supplies. Business interests certainly displayed a new vigour in criticising the 1872 Act, signalling a less-defensive strategy. According to the President of the Local Government Board who appointed it, George Sclater-Booth, the Select Committee was charged with investigating complaints – the 'many memorials' – which the government had received from producers and retailers about the alleged damage to trade which the 1872 Act had caused.[9] Sclater-Booth's explanation suggests that for the first time some manufacturers and traders looked to shape regulation more in line with their commercial requirements, an impression strengthened by the character of the legal changes, embodied in the Sale of Food and Drugs Act (SFDA), which followed the Select Committee's report in 1874.

The Select Committee was chaired by Clare Sewell Read, Parliamentary Secretary

[5] Colin A. Russell, *Chemists By Profession* (Milton Keynes, 1977), pp. 103–5.
[6] Clause I, Adulteration of Food and Drink and of Drugs Act, 1872, Public General Acts, 1872, chapter 74.
[7] John Burnett, *Plenty and Want*, pp. 229–30.
[8] Paulus, *Search for Pure Food*, pp. 32–8, 66–8.
[9] Parliamentary Debates, Third Series, vol. 218, 627, 16 April 1874.

to the Local Government Board in Disraeli's recently elected Conservative government. Sewell Read shared the new Prime Minister's enthusiasm for 'progressive Conservatism', but as a Norfolk farmer – a calling followed by his ancestors for 300 years – he was also committed to securing 'fair play for British agriculture', which led him to assume a prominent role during later debates about beer ingredients.[10] On the Select Committee, supported by food-processing MPs Jeremiah Colman, a Norfolk neighbour of Read's, and Sir Henry Peek, Read appeared equally keen to ensure 'fair play' for food manufacturers and retailers, extending a sympathetic hearing to the several prominent industrialists who gave evidence at the hearings which were held in April and May of 1874. With retailers anxious to escape censure for perhaps unknowingly selling adulterated produce, the manufacturers also attempted to have their own responsibilities more clearly defined. The essence of the manufacturers' evidence was that retailers were being prosecuted under the 1872 Act for selling food which, having been processed, mixed or otherwise altered from its original 'pure state', was adjudged to have been 'adulterated'. Analysts were portrayed as incompetent, over-zealous or unreasonable. Colman's influence was neither subtle nor secretive since he also appeared as a witness in his capacity as the mustard and starch producer from Norwich, describing cases where retailers had been fined for selling his mustard because it was not purely mustard seed, but also contained turmeric, chillies and other ingredients that he described as making the finished article more palatable. Colman emphasised that these fines, along with the threat of further legal action under the 1872 Act, had involved 'a very disturbing effect' on trade, with hundreds of retailers refusing to stock his mustard.[11] Colman was adamant that there was nothing offensive or fraudulent about his mustard, which was sold 'absolutely and positively' as a manufactured condiment rather than as an article in its original state. A similar sentiment was expressed by Joseph Storrs Fry, who mixed his cocoa with sugar and starches like arrowroot and sago. These made cocoa powder more soluble and offset the bitter flavour of cocoa butter, rendering the mixed article more palatable and popular than the pure form which he also sold. Like Colman's labelling of the mustard 'condiment', Fry attempted to obviate the difficulty presented by the Adulteration Act, which had materially affected his business too, through labelling; his mixed cocoa was 'most decidedly sold as distinct preparations, and distinctly acknowledged to be preparations'.[12] Both Colman and Fry, claiming to speak for their wider trades, insisted that manufactured items – where distinctly labelled – should be excluded from an amended law, implying that regulation should be concentrated on the covert adulteration of foods sold as being in their natural state, like diluted milk or tea mixed with iron filings.

A further important business perspective on the impact of the 1872 law was

[10] M. Stenton and S. Lees (eds), *Who's Who of British Members of Parliament. vol. I, 1832–1885* (Brighton; Harvester Press, 1981), p. 324. In an obituary notice Sewell Read was described as 'the distinguished authority on agricultural questions'; *The Times*, 23 August 1905.

[11] Report from the Select Committee on Adulteration of Food Act (1872). Proceedings and Minutes of Evidence, Parliamentary Papers, 1874 (262), VI, 243, pp. 54–63.

[12] Ibid., pp. 65–9.

provided by George Cadbury, who had pioneered the manufacture and sale of pure cocoa in Britain with the launch of his unadulterated Cocoa Essence in the late 1860s. The 1872 law had actually given Cadbury a competitive advantage over rival producers, allowing him to promote Cocoa Essence as a superior brand, distinct from cocoa blended with sago, sugar or other additives.[13] While this advertising implicitly claimed a purity for Cadbury's cocoa that was not present in the mixed products of other firms, he was prepared to defend the wider trade against charges of harmful adulteration. Prompted by Colman, acting this time in his capacity as a member of the Parliamentary Select Committee, Cadbury asserted that 'leading manufacturers' had not been forced to change their methods or ingredients as a result of the Adulteration Act. In fact, they had never 'been guilty of anything like dangerous adulteration' in the first place, and did not, therefore, need to be regulated.[14]

The Committee did not gather evidence from business representatives alone. Alfred H. Allen, Public Analyst for the City of Sheffield, urged that the permissive laws against adulteration be made compulsory. He added that consumers should be protected against fraudulent as well as simply dangerous adulteration; he objected, in other words, to the mixture in food of harmless ingredients that added to the bulk but not the nutritional value of a commodity. Both of these recommendations were later effected in the 1875 SFDA. Allen also gave the analysts' seal of approval to the suggestion which Colman and Fry had already placed on the Committee's agenda. Asked for his view on mixed articles, Allen said that many prosecutions since 1872 had been unjust, and that such articles should be rendered legal if distinctly labelled. Allen's evidence was important. The Committee recommended, in a report published on 3 July 1874, that the law be made compulsory. But the evidence of the business witnesses, especially that of Cadbury, was arguably even more influential. The report observed that the 1872 law had led to the unwarranted punishment of many respectable and honest tradesmen and concluded that, in the way of adulteration, the public was being 'cheated rather than poisoned'. In other words, dangerous adulteration had already been largely eradicated from the food supply, and with little or no evidence that 'injurious' – as opposed to merely fraudulent – items were actually on the market, there was no justification for introducing tighter regulations that would only 'hamper or fetter trade'.[15]

Business objections to the existing law were duly met in the 1875 Sale of Food and Drugs Bill, which was introduced on 12 February and attained the Royal Assent on 11 August.[16] The SFDA placed the regulatory emphasis firmly on retailers rather

[13] Iolo A. Williams, *The Firm Of Cadbury, 1831–1931* (London, 1931), pp. 39–42, 71; David J. Jeremy (ed.), *Dictionary of Business Biography (DBB)*, Vol. I, (1984) pp. 547–54; James Walvin, *The Quakers: Money and morals* (London, 1977), chapter 10.

[14] Report from the Select Committee on Adulteration of Food Act, pp. 111–16; A.G. Gardiner, *Life of George Cadbury* (London, 1925), pp. 26–7, 32–3. Gillian Wagner, *The Chocolate Conscience* (London, 1987), pp. 34–7.

[15] Report from the Select Committee on Adulteration of Food Act, pp iii–viii; for Hill's evidence see pp. 171–90.

[16] Sale of Food and Drugs Act, 1875, Public General Acts, 1875, chapter 63.

than food processors, allowing local authority officials to inspect and take samples for analysis from retail outlets but not places of manufacture. Of equal importance, given the thrust of Colman's and Fry's evidence, the Act gave legal protection to producers of 'compound' foods, provided these items were adequately labelled and contained nothing that was dangerous or designed to increase bulk. This provision was in accord with the self-confident tone of Colman, Cadbury and Fry, and provided added momentum to their enterprises' promotion of company brands. The 1875 Act, given unqualified support in Parliament by Sir Henry Peek on behalf of food processors, contained important 'public interest' elements too.[17] First, it sought to establish a compulsory system of inspection and analysis, administered by local authorities. Food traders would be obliged to sell formal samples of their wares to various categories of local officialdom – Medical Officers of Health, Inspectors of Nuisances or Weights and Measures, and Police Constables – who in turn were to submit the samples to a public analyst, an official post which all local authorities were now required to fill. Second, the Act provided more accurate definitions of adulteration, deemed as the addition of anything which rendered food 'injurious' to health, or which altered – 'to the prejudice of the purchaser' – its 'nature, substance and quality'. This second definition of adulteration reflected the concern which Allen had expressed to the Select Committee. But it also confirmed the impression which producers had conveyed, namely that the processes and ingredients of food manufacturing were essentially safe, and that the real target of regulation should be fraudulent retailers who tampered with manufactured products before selling them. Colman and Peek, the food-producing MPs who sat on the 1874 Select Committee, were certainly keen to distinguish between dangerous and merely fraudulent adulteration, and they accepted, as Read put it, that the state should protect the public's pockets as well as its health.[18]

Returning to the theoretical explanations for regulation, this fair trade aspect of the law was clearly in the 'public interest': individual consumers stood to gain from the criminalisation of fraudulent yet physically harmless exchanges, such as the dilution of milk with water. But as the focus on fraudulent – as opposed to dangerous – adulteration came from manufacturers, who had a clear interest in promoting the idea that 'cheating' was a much greater danger than 'poisoning', the regulatory process also involved a strong element of business capture. Burnett has said that the 1875 Act persuaded manufacturers to put their 'own houses in order before they were compelled to do so'. In other words, to obviate the need for further and more stringent legislation, producers themselves assumed responsibility for actively improving methods and ingredients.[19] But this is at odds with the sworn position of a number of manufacturers during the 1874 Select Committee hearings. George Cadbury, it will be remembered, remarked that the Adulteration Acts had not forced him to change anything. By the end of the 1860s he had already

---

[17] Parliamentary Debates, Third Series, Vol. 222, 605–6, 19 February 1875.
[18] Report from the Select Committee on Adulteration of Food Act, p. 174.
[19] Burnett, *Plenty and Want*, pp. 229–30.

installed the machine press which enabled him to extract cocoa butter, negating the need for additions that masked this butter's unpleasant flavour.[20] Cadbury used advertising and public comment to compare his cocoa favourably with rival products, such as Fry's, which contained non-hazardous but additional ingredients like sago or sugar; he also deployed scientific imagery and favourable comments from the medical press to promote his own cocoa as pure and nutritious. Such claims prompted vigorous public rebuttals from Fry's and other competitors into the early 1900s.[21] Perceptions of product quality were a key issue since Fry, Rowntree and Cadbury collaborated over discounting policies from 1889 and prices from 1895. Regulation was then one element of a wider blend of co-operation and rivalry. In other words, to paraphrase Burnett, as the state believed that the houses of Cadbury and other producers were already in order in 1875, subsequent regulation was not designed to have a significant direct impact on the manufacturing process. Colman, Cadbury and others admittedly endeavoured to integrate their business strategy and the regulatory regime, using branding and advertising to supply consumers with additional information. Yet through the 1875 SFDA, they had obtained the type of minimum legal framework that allowed market mechanisms to operate as freely as possible.

Evolution of the law, 1875–99

The same mixture of capture and 'public interest' informed subsequent amendments to the SFDA. As demonstrated earlier, Britain's food industry experienced significant changes during the last quarter of the nineteenth century. The rising volume of imports were a competitive threat to some manufacturers, farmers and distributors who looked to state regulation for protection. Milk, butter and coffee traders all hoped to use regulation to gain a competitive market advantage for their 'premium' products over 'budget' rivals – skimmed, separated or condensed milk, margarine and coffee 'mixtures'. Debates about regulation of these products, which took place principally during a Parliamentary investigation on food adulteration in the 1890s, produced competing definitions of 'public interest', with producers of both 'premium' and 'budget' items claiming to be operating in the interests of consumers. 'Premium' producers argued that the public had a right to protection against fraudulent imitations, and 'budget' producers countered that they were serving the public by providing affordable and perfectly nutritious goods.

In the face of these conflicting business interests, doctors and public analysts, who were the original organisational core of the anti-adulteration reform movement, saw themselves as the true guardians of the 'public interest'. Additional support was forthcoming from the Royal Society of Arts, the National Association for the Promotion of Social Science and other specialised pressure groups including

---

[20] Jeremy, *Dictionary*, pp. 547–54.
[21] Wagner, *Chocolate Conscience*, pp. 34–37.

the Bread and Food Reform League in the 1880s, described by Burnett as 'middle-class vegetarians, socialists and ascetics'.[22] The Co-operative movement was also important, emphasising purity, especially in flour and basic foods, and its expansion testified to the wider demand for unadulterated foods. In common with other new inspectorates, public analysts and Medical Officers of Health based their influence on professional expertise used in an official capacity in their policing role in the administration of the SFDA.[23] Consequently the food reform movement combined elements of 'capture', local bureaucratic discretion and professionalism. Analysts had commercial roles too, providing consultancy services to food processors, traders and agricultural societies and in some cases held academic and hospital posts. Analytical chemistry had the potential to act as the forum for food regulation, but the processes of professional specialisation slowly compartmentalised analysts. This might have been expected to make analysts more effective lobbyists in line with Olson's emphasis on the advantages of smaller, specialist groups, and the establishment of the Society of Public Analysts (SPA) in 1874 certainly strengthened their organisational basis. The Society's meetings and the pages of its journal, *The Analyst*, disseminated information about analytical techniques, court cases and reform initiatives. Most leading analysts were members, and often past office-holders in the SPA, and the Society's current President was usually invited to testify before official inquiries. In other respects, though, public analysts were on the defensive. Not all local authorities appeared to take the SFDA seriously, and provided their analysts with very few samples to examine. Every year the SPA spent some time discussing the low esteem with which some local authorities regarded the work of public analysts. One illustration of the profession's low status was the alleged inadequacy of the flat rate (10s 6d) which analysts received per sample. In 1889 Charles Cassal, initially one of the Society's more prominent and influential figures, advised colleagues that the minimum fee failed even to cover laboratory and material costs. He claimed that 'every public analyst knew that the majority of local authorities looked upon "the analyst" as a sort of necessary nuisance, who was paid the smallest possible sum for doing the smallest possible number of samples. This was occasionally varied by the payment of the smallest possible sum for the largest number of samples.'[24] Cassal later abandoned the SPA, criticising it for admitting chemists who were not public analysts, and organised a rival system of analysis around the publication, the *British Food Journal* (*BFJ*), from 1899. This focused on the proposed British Analytical Control scheme discussed in chapter 2. Some analysts were involved with both the *BFJ* and the SPA. A further organisation, the Institute of Chemistry, was the principal source of professional qualifications for analysts and, like the SPA, admitted industrial and other chemists. Nonetheless throughout the 1875–1938 period the SPA

[22] Burnett, *Plenty and Want*, pp. 229, 236.
[23] Paulus, *Search for Pure Food*, pp. 68–9. On other inspectorates see Macleod, *Government and Expertise*.
[24] *The Analyst*, 15, January 1890, p. 5.

was the recognised professional association, whose representatives were called to give evidence at various official inquiries.

In the short term, however, the authority of Public Analysts generally was undermined by the system of appeal established in 1875, where defendants could have a third part of the offending sample examined by chemists at the Inland Revenue Laboratory at Somerset House in London. Much publicity was attached to the fact that condemnatory findings of local Public Analysts were often contradicted by the Inland Revenue chemists, leading to accusations that many analysts were actively malicious or simply incompetent. The dispute between Somerset House and the Society of Public Analysts was not resolved until after the Inland Revenue Laboratory merged with its Board of Customs equivalent to form a new Government Laboratory in 1894.[25] The status of public analysts was also undermined by the practice, observed by many local authorities, of delegating large areas of analytical responsibility to the Medical Officer of Health. Medical Officers of Health were equally dependent on the extension of social policy, but, having become a legally required appointment by 1872, were a larger group than the analysts with closer links with local and legal authorities and greater prestige as part of the medical profession. Although several individuals held posts jointly as public analyst and Medical Officer of Health, the SPA disliked such combined appointments.[26] They regarded it as a false economy given the responsibilities and technical difficulties of the two posts, but also as something which undermined their professional status. In 1893 the SPA president claimed combined appointments were 'intelligible from the "Vestry" point of view, but cannot be fair to the chemical or medical professions'. Perhaps more important, analysts did not believe that Medical Officers possessed enough chemical knowledge to discharge the duties of chemical analysis competently.[27]

The first significant alteration in the law after 1875 was the 1879 Sale of Food and Drugs Act Amendment Act. This carried two important 'public interest' refinements. First, it was no defence, in cases of adulteration, to allege that where a sample of food had been bought explicitly for analysis, the sale had not been to the prejudice of the purchaser. This was designed to safeguard the operation of the 1875 Act after an English magistrate had found in 1878 that such a defence was valid.[28] Second, samples of milk were allowed to be taken from the place of delivery as well as original distribution. This eased the task of urban authorities, which in some cases were monitoring the quality of milk that was being produced hundreds of miles away. The other main object of the 1879 Amendment, defining an acceptable minimum strength for alcoholic spirits (fixed at 25 per cent 'under proof' – about 36 per cent alcohol, in other words), combined 'public interest' and capture.

---

[25] 'Inland Revenue Laboratory, History and Functions', 207/6/1, *Current Guide*, Public Record Office (PRO).

[26] Paulus, *Search for Pure Food*, pp. 67–8.

[27] Otto Hehner's presidential address, 4 January 1893, *The Analyst*, 18, February 1893, p. 31; F. Gowland Hopkins, 'The Analyst and the Medical Man', *The Analyst*, 31, December 1906, p. 385.

[28] *The Analyst*, 4, February 1879, p. 19.

While drinkers of spirits were protected from dishonest publicans and tradesmen, increased sales of undiluted spirits were clearly going to benefit established producers, as James Bell, Principal of the Inland Revenue Laboratory at Somerset House in London, recognised in evidence to a Commons Select Committee.[29]

The second chief amendment to the 1875 legislation came with the Margarine Act of 1887.[30] This targeted one of the most frequent methods of fraudulent dealing in food, the covert sale of margarine as butter, an issue partially highlighted by the Danish Margarine Act of 1885, which was part of a state-sponsored strategy to aid farmers and butter-makers in promoting Danish butter as a high-quality product. The 1887 Act required margarine producers to register with local authorities and allowed local authority officers to take samples from margarine factories. It will be remembered that no other food factories or producers were subject to registration or inspection. Like the standardisation of alcoholic spirits, the Margarine Act combined elements of 'public interest' and capture. In 'public interest' terms, it clearly benefited consumers to outlaw fraudulent trading. Moreover, at the suggestion of James Bell, the Act allowed inspectors to take samples without having to go through the formal practice of purchasing them. This, it was thought, would ease the task of gathering samples and thereby increase the likelihood of detecting fraudulent trade.[31] Pressure for the new law did not come from the SPA, which simply favoured applying the SFDA, as did the manager of the Manchester Co-operative Wholesale Society's butter department.[32] Neither was there central government pressure for new regulations: characteristically the Local Government Board was content to rely on local enforcement of the SFDA. Margarine manufacturers and distributors defended the commodity as nutritious, cheap and well-known among consumers as different from butter, thereby constituting neither a health risk nor fraud. George Barclay, a Manchester wholesaler, criticised the demands for controls as 'harassing and unnecessary' attacks on a 'very useful article of food'.[33] These attacks, and the real pressure for legislation, came from dairy producers who felt that sales of butter were being undermined by fraudulent trade in margarine. The legislation was introduced in the House of Commons in January 1887 by six Irish MPs, five of whom represented constituencies where dairy farming was the main form of economic activity. The sixth, William Lane, stood to gain directly from the proposed regulation: he was a butter merchant from Cork.[34]

---

[29] Report from the Select Committee on the Sale of Food and Drugs Act (1875) Amendment Bill, Parliamentary Papers, 1878–79 (155), X.1, p. 8.

[30] Margarine Act, 1887, Public General Acts, 1887, Chapter 29.

[31] Paulus, *Search for Pure Food*, pp. 39–40; Report from the Select Committee on the Butter Substitutes Bill, Parliamentary Papers (208), 1887, p. 27.

[32] Report from the Select Committee on the Butter Substitutes Bill. Herbert Preston-Thomas testimony, pp, 6–9. Thomas Pearson testimony, pp. 112–18.

[33] Report from the Select Committee on the Butter Substitutes Bill, Testimony of George Barclay, pp. 56–61.

[34] The other five were Thomas Mayne, John O'Connor, James Flynn, Joseph Biggar and either Joseph Kenny or Matthew Kenny. All six were Home Rule Nationalists.

The title of the legislation represented an important additional victory for the dairy trade. Originally presented as the 'Butter Substitutes Bill', the measure was retitled by a Select Committee to provide a clearer distinction between butter and mixtures of butter, other animal and vegetable fats, which were sold under a variety of names. Of these margarine was the most common, although another term used fairly widely was 'butterine'. At the 1887 hearings, the SPA, represented by Alfred Allen, by now its president, and Otto Hehner, its secretary, though opposed to mixtures of butter and margarine as deception, had been content that consumers knew 'butterine' was different to butter.[35] During the Bill's Third Reading Jeremiah Colman and Jacob Bright – both urban Liberals and free traders who were perhaps not disposed to the dispensation of special favours to farmers – sought to substitute the word 'butterine' for 'margarine'. But dairy representatives successfully demanded, as the Select Committee had recommended, that such combinations be sold under the name of margarine alone. Explaining to fellow peers why the term 'butterine' had been prohibited, Viscount Cranbrook, Lord President of the Council in Lord Salisbury's Conservative government, said that it was calculated to mislead people into believing that the substance which it described was 'of the nature of butter'. And by insisting on the term 'margarine' the government would help consumers to distinguish the 'well-manufactured article' from the 'bad and unwholesome mixture': butter from margarine, in other words.[36]

Milk producers had also sought changes to the law after 1875, concentrating on the need for a minimum standard that would be recognised by all analysts – an absolute definition, in effect, of milk adulteration. In 1877 the Secretary of the Manchester and Salford Milk Dealers' Association, George Jackson, pressed Sclater-Booth on the matter, pointing out that analysts differed in their interpretation of what constituted adulteration. Jackson suggested that a 'universal standard' of 8 or 8.5 per cent non-fatty solids would reduce legal uncertainty and provide honest traders with a degree of protection.[37] Sclater-Booth referred the letter to the Inland Revenue Laboratory, which since 1875 had been examining the milk of more than 300 cows from 24 separate dairy herds in different parts of England. As this research indicated that the composition of milk varied widely, with some samples rich in one constituent and deficient in another, James Bell advised the Manchester and Salford Association that it would be 'injudicious' to fix a required standard of fats or non-fat solids.[38]

The debate about milk standards involved a strong element of 'public interest'. In March 1877 the newly appointed Public Analyst for Falkirk, Robert McAlley, had asked Bell whether the Inland Revenue Laboratory, in its capacity as referee under the SFDA, had any standards in mind, on fatty and non-fatty solids, when

---

[35] Report from the Select Committee on the Butter Substitutes Bill, see Hehner's testimony, pp. 22–5.
[36] Parliamentary Debates, Third Series, vol. 315, 475–84, 1579.
[37] Jackson to Sclater-Booth, 13 July 1877, DSIR 26/118, PRO.
[38] Bell to Jackson, 13 August 1877, DSIR 26/118, PRO.

deciding whether milk was genuine. McAlley received the same reply as Jackson, Bell insisting that the variety of composition of genuine milk meant that it would be impossible to fix standards without inflicting 'serious hardship on honest vendors'.[39] Bell's inflexibility on this issue appears to have precipitated the long conflict between his department and the SPA. In 1878 the SPA invited Bell to address its members on the analytical methods and standards which his department used to determine whether items of food, including milk and butter, were adulterated. In extending the invitation the Society's Secretary and President hinted at early problems in their relationship with the refereeing body. 'There are', they wrote, 'differences between us but we have no means of judging, either the amount of these differences, or what the reason for them is.' This appears to have been a reasonable call for clarification, but Bell refused to speak to the SPA as a body on general issues and principles, admitting only that he would speak to individual analysts about individual analyses.[40]

The SPA was disappointed by Bell's response, and abhorred the 'absurd' secrecy in which Somerset House shrouded its analytical standards and methods.[41] Without central guidance a number of Public Analysts inevitably found themselves in conflict with the Somerset House Laboratory. Milk was the source of much of this conflict. Between 1875 and 1888 the Laboratory received 194 samples of milk which had been condemned by Public Analysts, mostly on the grounds that they contained too much water or too little cream or fat. In 91 of these cases the findings of the analyst were significantly qualified or flatly contradicted by Somerset House. In all of these 91 disputed cases the Inland Revenue analyst found the trader to have been harshly treated by the Public Analyst.[42] These differences, given considerable publicity in the trade and daily or weekly local press, did much to undermine the credibility of Public Analysts as a professional body. 'The Analysts Again!' was a characteristic headline in *The Grocer* in February 1876, above an account of a dispute between London Public Analysts and Somerset House over a sample of butter purchased in Southwark. Having been convicted on the evidence of an analyst, a vendor had successfully appealed to Somerset House. The editors of *The Grocer* congratulated the vendor, and advised readers to emulate him whenever charged with fraudulent dealings. 'The cost will be trifling, and there will be the satisfaction of having the analysis made by a body of men who have no other purpose to serve than simply arriving at the truth, and who possess the necessary knowledge and skill to discover whether the samples submitted are or are not adulterated.'[43] The dual inference from this was that Public Analysts somehow had a vested interest in catching fraudulent traders, and were in any event not competent to pass sound analytical judgement.

[39] McAlley to Bell correspondence, March 1877, DSIR 26/118, PRO.
[40] Correspondence between Bell and Heinsch and Wigner of the SPA, January–February 1878, DSIR 26/118, PRO.
[41] *The Analyst*, 9, February 1879, p, 19; 5, February 1880, p. 15.
[42] 'Reference: Court Cases', 1875–83, DSIR 26/120, and 1884–8, DSIR 26/121, PRO.
[43] *The Grocer*, 5 February 1876; clipping in DSIR 26/247, PRO.

The Grocer maintained its criticism of Public Analysts in the 1880s and 1890s, dusting down the 1876 headline for an editorial in 1888 entitled, 'The Public Analyst Again!' This relayed another case of a convicted retailer successfully appealing to Somerset House. 'Here was an honest tradesman', the journal noted, 'who, through the blundering of the public analyst, had been involved in great expense, trouble, and loss of time, and for two months had been in painful suspense as to the ultimate issue and its effect upon his business.' The editor expressed great regret that the analyst, by comparison, had not even been reprimanded.[44] Grocers could at least take satisfaction in the fact that the Courts tended to take Somerset House's decision as final in cases of disputed analyses. The SPA found this immensely galling, for under the 1875 Act Courts were supposed to attach equal weight to the evidence of both parties. This had been stipulated by George Sclater-Booth, the Local Government Board President, and supported by a large Parliamentary majority after Sir Henry Peek, during the 1874 Select Committee hearings, had tried to give the decisive word to Somerset House. In reality, however, Somerset House chemists were rarely called to appear in court. A rare exception took place in 1883, during an appeal at the Manchester Sessions Court by a Derbyshire farmer against conviction for selling adulterated milk, when James Bell explained in Court why he believed that the milk had not been adulterated. On the basis of Bell's evidence the Recorder, H. Wyndham West, observed that he was not satisfied 'beyond reasonable doubt' that adulteration had taken place, and upheld the appeal.[45]

The dispute between Somerset House and the SPA rumbled on in the 1880s and 1890s. One area of contention was the wording used by Somerset House to describe doubtful or disputed samples. Bell often used formulations which implied a false degree of certainty, noting of possibly adulterated milk that he was 'unable to affirm that water has been added'. The SPA believed that statements of this kind had 'an erroneous impression' on magistrates and members of the public, and in 1892 asked Bell to use different words when he was unsure about the character of a sample. The SPA even suggested an alternative phrase, where adulteration of milk with water was probable but not certain: 'the results of the analysis are compatible with the presence of X per cent added water'. Having obtained the advice of the Board of Trade's Solicitor, Bell simply informed the SPA that he had 'serious objections' to the suggested amendments, and the matter was closed.[46]

At the end of the 1890s the methods and intentions of 'parochial analysts' were still being compared unfavourably in *The Grocer* with 'the more extended experiences and elaborate appliances' of the 'undoubtedly impartial' Somerset House.[47] But relations between the SPA and the central reference body were improving. This may have been connected to the establishment of the new Government Laboratory in 1894, with the expertise of the Inland Revenue Laboratory supplemented – and

---

[44] *The Grocer*, 54, 28 July 1888, p. 153.

[45] Verbatim account of the case, *The Analyst*, 8, November 1883, pp. 185–240.

[46] Correspondence between Bell, Board of Trade Solicitor and SPA, September–November 1892, DSIR 26/118, PRO.

[47] *The Grocer*, 73, 19 March 1898, p. 816.

its prejudices possibly diluted – by the presence of chemists from the old Board of Customs laboratory. It could also have been due to the retirement of Bell, who was succeeded as Principal of the new Laboratory by Thomas Edward Thorpe. While Bell had been at the Laboratory since 1854, Thorpe had enjoyed a much wider range of employment experiences, and these appear to have made him more open-minded to changes in policy and practice. Having worked at Anderson's University in Glasgow in the 1870s at the same time as Otto Hehner, one of the country's leading Public Analysts, he certainly enjoyed a far more cordial professional relationship with the SPA. In 1901, in recognition of his work in cultivating a 'better understanding between Public Analysts and Government Departments', the SPA unanimously elected Thorpe as an Honorary Member.[48] Another reflection of these improved relations was the falling number of analyses disputed by the Government Laboratory. Between 1894 and 1897 the Public Analyst's findings were only challenged in 36–23 per cent of the 158 milk samples submitted. To the SPA this represented a considerable improvement on the 47 per cent of milk analyses which had been challenged by Somerset House in the 1875–88 period.[49]

Between 1894 and 1896 a new Parliamentary Select Committee investigated food adulteration, under the chairmanship of Sir Walter Foster, Consulting Physician at Birmingham General Hospital and Parliamentary Secretary to the LGB in William Gladstone's final administration.[50] The business presence on the committee was Hudson Kearley, a leading retailer, and Jeremiah Colman, a manufacturer. Its lengthy hearings reveal the attitudes and ambitions of the key interest groups, all of whom felt aggrieved or disappointed by the existing legislation, though for different and often contradictory reasons. Analysts considered that the SFDA was not applied uniformly or effectively enough, but grocers, resentful about their position of liability, viewed the law as arbitrary and draconian. *The Grocer* had long been expressing its general disapproval of the fact that grocers were 'at the mercy' of malevolent or spiteful inspectors while manufacturers remained undisturbed, and the journal highlighted cases where the use of an invoice as a warranty would have saved grocers from conviction.[51] The Grocers' Federation had been lobbying Parliament for legal changes in the early 1890s, and actually claimed part of the credit for the establishment of a broad-ranging Select Committee inquiry in 1894. Without their pressure, the Federation claimed, the investigation would have confined itself to adulteration of dairy products.[52] Butter producers and retailers as well as landowners from dairying counties desired more stringent regulation of margarine, after the 1887 Act had failed to prevent increasing sales of the rival product. They had previously lobbied the LGB, HM Customs and the Board

---

[48] Edward Bevan and Alfred Chapman to Thomas Thorpe, 9 April 1901, Letters and Papers of Sir Thomas Thorpe, MS. 373, Royal Society Library, London; *The Analyst*, 27, March 1902, p. 81.
[49] 'Reference: Court Cases', 1894–7, DSIR 26/123, PRO.
[50] Report on Food Products Adulteration, Parliamentary Papers, 1894 (253).
[51] *Ibid.*, 65, 9 March 1889, p. 474; vol. LXVI, 13 October 1894, p. 762.
[52] *The Grocer*, vol. LXV, 2 June 1894, p. 1270 and see A.J. Giles' testimony in House of Commons, Report on Food Products Adulteration, Parliamentary Papers, 1895(363), pp. 314–24.

of Trade for more active inspection, especially at the ports, but were dissatisfied at the response. Each of these interest groups, whether organised locally or nationally, believed their ambitions could be secured through regulatory intervention. They constituted a distinct policy network in terms of being the principal parties consulted by government over the SFDA. Although many witnesses testified in their individual capacity as trader, producer or analyst, most represented professions or trades and the various national organisations were more prominent than in the 1874 or 1878 hearings.

The 'public interest' reform movement was led by doctors and public analysts who stated their case for more active and uniform enforcement of the SFDA to ensure consistent implementation of the law and to counter persistent and increasingly subtle adulteration. Consumers, they argued, required the protection of well-supported analysts and the disclosure of additional information through labelling. Above all, the analysts developed their call for a Central Court of Reference that would analyse foods and set precise standards for a variety of commodities. Doctors and analysts highlighted the health risks, including poor nutritional value from products such as skimmed milk. Medical Officers of Health and Public Analysts also had a professional interest in regulations that would strengthen their roles as local enforcers of the food laws. A handful of local authorities supported stricter regulation on similar grounds, though other councils were reluctant to enforce even the regulatory model in existence.

A second source of pressure were agrarian interests, principally landowners, who wanted stricter centralised inspections of imported produce. Already dissatisfied by the Local Government Board's caution, the local and national Chambers of Agriculture proposed creating a new central inspectorate and giving additional powers to the Board of Agriculture. The agrarian organisations' approach to regulation resembled their support for the Fertilisers and Feedingstuffs Act of 1893 which required manufacturers to identify the minimum quantities of the constituents of their products; farmers could submit suspect samples for analysis, though the farmer had to pay the analyst's fee. By 1906 a new Act authorised the appointment of County Analysts and required manufacturers to disclose the actual proportions of all ingredients.[53] The 1901 Adulteration of Seeds Act provided further indication of farmers' concern to ensure the quality of their raw materials and to regulate their suppliers.

Organised lobbying was evident among food distributors. With the Select Committee proceeding slowly, in 1895 the London Chamber of Commerce passed a resolution in favour of extending the SFDA to cover manufacturers or wholesalers with invoices being treated as warranty, and *The Grocer* awaited Sir Walter Foster's findings with confidence.[54] 'Members of Parliament', it predicted, 'who have the old-fashioned notion of the retail grocer sanding the sugar before prayers will learn

---

[53] Report of the Departmental Committee on the Working in Great Britain of the Fertilisers and Feedingstuffs Act, 1893, 1905, Cd 2372.

[54] Report on Food Products Adulteration, 1894 (253), pp. 201.

from this Committee that the boot must be put on quite another leg nowadays'.[55] Limited legal protection for grocers had been advocated by several important manufacturers during the Select Committee hearings. Representatives of Colman's, Fry's and Van Houten's, the cocoa manufacturer, declared their willingness to have the manufacturer's invoice accepted as warranty, especially for propriety or packaged goods, so that action under the SFDA would be brought against the producer rather than the retailer. In assuming direct legal responsibility for the safety and quality of their branded products, these manufacturers of mixed articles were arguably more confident than they had been when seeking to evade regulation in the 1870s. Indeed, several producers had attempted to gain a market advantage from the 1875 legislation by invoking its legal guarantees in packaging or marketing materials. In labelling its cocoa mixture, required under the 1875 Act, Fry's stated: 'Contains cocoa combined with other ingredients, the perfect purity and wholesomeness of which is guaranteed in accordance with Act of Parliament.'[56] Cadbury's and Colman's invoked the 1875 and then the 1899 legislation in their advertising matter. In the 1900s *The Grocer* regularly carried the following copy, cheek by jowl on its editorial page:

CADBURY'S COCOA ESSENCE
GUARANTEED ABSOLUTELY PURE
AND THEREFORE MAY BE SOLD WITH PERFECT SAFETY
UNDER THE NEW ACT

COLMAN'S STARCH
GRAND PRIX, PARIS UNIVERSAL EXHIBITION, 1900
WARRANTED FREE FROM ADULTERATION
IS AS GOOD AS COLMAN'S MUSTARD

The various demands for further reform elicited little support from within the LGB which continued to interpret its responsiblities narrowly. The Ministry was concerned in the 1890s that in some areas of the country the SFDA was 'practically a dead letter', because local authorities were failing to enforce it, with many consumers and 'honest traders' enjoying inadequate legal protection as a result. Attempts to shame errant authorities into action were made by singling them out in the LGB's Annual Reports, but in England and Wales in 1898–9 there were still 26 districts, ten large counties and 16 large boroughs, where the authorities had 'almost entirely failed' to invoke the law.[57] Yet such conclusions did not automatically prompt initiatives for stricter regulation. The existing constraints and obstacles to greater central government intervention were apparent in the testimony of

---

[55] *The Grocer*, 69, 28 March 1896, p. 792.
[56] Report on Food Products Adulteration, 1894 (253), pp. 256–71.
[57] Local Government Board, Annual Report, 1890–1, C. 6460, p. cli; Annual Report, 1894–5, C. 7867, p. cxlviii; Annual Report, 1898–9, C. 9444, p. cxxxiii.

the two principal official witnesses, Herbert Preston-Thomas and Richard Bannister, who resolutely opposed any changes. Preston-Thomas, who had recently headed the Public Health department, emphasised the LGB's limited remit of collecting and publishing adulteration statistics and rejected any more active role or responsibilities.[58] Enforcement was, he argued, an exclusively local matter. Bannister, the deputy-principal of the Government Laboratory, described competition as the primary guarantee of product quality and any further intervention as unnecessary interference.[59] There was then no evidence of support, far less initiative, in two key departments for more interventionist central government or 'bureaucratic discretion', rather the preference was for the status quo based on local responsibilities.

Manufacturers still lacked any general organisation, but, as in the 1870s, certain industries defended their specific interests. The 1890s Select Committee hearings had revived discussion of whether a generic name – mustard or cocoa being the two prime examples – should be allowed for a commodity which contained added ingredients. Jeremiah Colman again sat on the Committee, and listened as the general manager of his Carrow works argued that the public, including members of the Royal family, preferred 'mustard' mixed with turmeric and other spices. Another veteran of the 1874 hearings, Joseph Storrs Fry defended his products by countering the Public Analysts's claims that mixing cocoa with arrowroot amounted to adulteration. He also neutralised the testimony of one of his competitors, Hahnemann Epps, who had argued that only cocoa mixed with arrowroot and sugar merited the description 'pure cocoa', to distinguish it from preparations which used additional starches to increase solubility. No change to the law on mixtures resulted in 1899.

Epps had been trying to secure a trading advantage for his superior brand of cocoa, much in the way that butter producers had obtained through the 1887 Act an advantage over their 'budget' margarine rivals. The 1890s hearings included a related discussion on coffee and mixtures which contained chicory. This debate had a lengthy history. The 1856 Select Committee on adulteration had taken evidence from advocates and opponents of coffee mixtures. Advocates believed that mixtures were wholesome, cheap and therefore completely justifiable alternatives to coffee, and also insisted that there was a public demand for the lighter flavour which the addition of chicory brought to coffee. Opponents argued simply that such blending constituted adulteration and fraudulent trade. From the 1850s onwards the Treasury duly issued several separate orders stipulating that mixtures were to be labelled, although these labels were not required to indicate the proportions of ingredients used. The debate before the 1894–6 Select Committee revolved around similar issues. James Sanderson, honorary secretary of the Coffee Association of London, described all mixtures as 'unfair trading', and argued that in the interest of consumer protection any product containing chicory should not be sold

[58] Report on Food Products Adulteration, 1894 (253), pp. 3, 23–7, 29, 49.
[59] Ibid., pp. 49–52, 94–6, 136, 138–9.

as 'coffee'.[60] Sanderson added that mixtures had impaired public taste, suggesting people would have to be educated into drinking 'pure coffee and pure cocoa, in the same way that they like good port wine'. Increased coffee consumption appealed to Sanderson's constituencies in the London Chamber of Commerce's coffee section and among Mysore coffee planters, but the limits of their ambition were apparent in his rejection of the idea of legal standards for grades of coffee. General traders were divided on the issue. The coffee section of the London Chamber of Commerce believed that labelling mixtures with the proportions of coffee and chicory was impractical, but the full meeting of the Chamber disagreed, supporting full labelling of mixtures in the interests of traders and consumers. And while one London wholesaler described chicory in coffee as 'legalised fraud', proposing that mixtures with more than 33 per cent of chicory should be sold as 'coffeine', another argued that consumers were afforded sufficient protection by the then widely used term for such mixtures, 'French Coffee'. As with the debate about cocoa and other mixtures, these disagreements about precisely what information should be available to consumers led to no change in the law.

The combination of price competition, disputed ingredients, and rival trade interests was most apparent in the dairy sector where various organisations looked for regulatory suppport. The campaign which secured the 1887 Margarine Act had been continued by dairy producers into the 1890s. Landowners, wholesalers and grocers assumed responsibility for sampling privately and even initiating prosecutions of fraudulent dealers where they considered local authorities to be insufficiently active. In 1891, for example, the Metropolitan Grocers' and Provision Dealers' Association led the prosecution of a margarine factory owner who had been supplying grocers with margarine as butter. The prosecuting counsel described the Association as a 'useful society for the protection of the trade and the public', and highlighted the fact that the factory owner had compounded his felony by failing to register under the terms of the 1887 Margarine Act. He was convicted in Lambeth Police Court and fined 40s and £1 5s costs.[61] The Danish government endeavoured to protect the reputation of Danish butter by having their representative in Britain, Harald Faber, purchase butters advertised incorrectly as Danish and then initiate prosecutions under the UK Merchandise Marks Act.[62] Elsewhere a group of Gloucestershire landowners had formed a Dairy Produce Defence Association, merchants had financed a London Butter Association after failing to persuade the Local Government Board to appoint travelling inspectors, and in 1892 the Manchester Grocers' Association had established a 'vigilance committee' directed against market stalls suspected of selling butter and margarine mixtures. Each of these groups favoured the appointment of a travelling central inspectorate as a mechanism to prompt, or supersede, inactive local authorities and, thereby, provide a less expensive means for action against dishonest or rival businesses.

[60] Report on Food Products Adulteration, 1895 (363), pp. 239–43.
[61] *The Grocers' Chronicle*, 20 June 1891; clipping in DSIR 26/247, PRO.
[62] Report on Food Products Adulteration, 1894 (253), pp. 71–80.

Thomas Ling, a member of the Council of the Metropolitan Grocers' Association, was even willing to meet the costs of sampling by a central agency in return for being able to complain anonymously. Ling noted: 'We do not want to prosecute our neighbour; we do not want to appear in any way. Give us the means of prosecuting a dishonest man, and dishonesty, in my opinion must cease, at any rate in larger towns.'[63] A Staffordshire farmer called for a central inspectorate for all imported foods by drawing a parallel with controls on animals with contagious diseases, citing the public health benefits of stringent controls as sufficient to overcome his admitted distaste for strong central powers.[64]

These local details were placed before the 1894–6 Select Committee hearings on Food Adulteration, evidence of the butter trade's determination to resist what it perceived as unfair competition from margarine.[65] The trade was highly vocal during these hearings, with representatives generally agreeing that margarine factories and retailers should be licensed as well as registered, that a third conviction for selling mixtures should result in imprisonment, and that there should be a prohibition on any brand names, packaging or appearance which suggested margarine to be butter. There were even calls for margarine to be coloured red, for the two products to be sold at separate counters and for margarine sales to be confined to specialist shops. In advancing this call for increased protection, butter traders were anxious to emphasise their 'public interest' credentials: stamping out the fraudulent sale of margarine or mixtures of margarine and butter as 'butter' would serve the consumer as well as the butter merchant. A Yorkshire farmer summarised his aim as: 'Principally to protect my industry, and, to a certain extent, to protect the public.'[66] The margarine trade's response to these attacks was also couched in 'public interest' terms. Its defenders argued that margarine was a wholesome, nutritious and cheap food which was popular with consumers who were well aware of the differences between butter, margarine and mixtures.[67] Although margarine producers had opposed the 1887 Act, they now emphasised the effectiveness of its enforcement in order to deter further intervention. Henry Van Den Bergh, a leading manufacturer, cited scientific evidence in support of the nutritional value of margarine.[68] According to William George Watson, owner of the Maypole Dairy Company, a leading multiple stores company, consumers recognised that the quantity of margarine present in a mixture varied according to its price.[69] The existing labelling was adequate in Watson's view in 'these days of board schools', and he thought it should be permissible to wrap purchases in brown paper to save customers any embarrassment from carrying margarine in public. The notion that price is a proxy for quality is consistent with the theory of perfect competition, and

[63] Ibid., pp. 159–60.
[64] Ibid., p. 179.
[65] Ibid., pp. 8–9, 59–61, 299–306.
[66] Ibid., p. 121.
[67] Ibid., pp. 49–58, 149–51.
[68] Report on Food Products Adulteration, 1896 (288), pp. 139–49.
[69] Report on Food Products Adulteration, 1894 (253), p. 173.

this logic was used by opponents of regulation such as Joseph Fry. He rejected calls for compulsory labelling of ingredients on the grounds that price conveyed sufficient information to consumers.[70] Compulsory labelling or, more precisely, the actual information to be provided, was a controversial issue since manufacturers feared that consumers might be deterred by knowledge of ingredients. Analysts wanted labels to disclose, for example, the presence of starch in cocoa and other foods, but manufacturers feared that consumers would believe this indicated the presence of washing powders. The analysts' preference for labelling using chemical descriptions was similarly an anathema to some food processors, concerned that the public would interpret such formuli as a threat to their health.

The Select Committee's report appeared in 1896 and, after tentative proposals in 1897 and 1898, a new Food and Drugs Act was passed in 1899. Paulus concluded that the Act signalled a 'workable truce' between farmers, grocers and manufacturers, and government experts.[71] Although the law continued to concentrate on retailers rather than producers, this focus, established in 1875, was slightly modified by giving retailers partial legal protection in cases where the true offender was a manufacturer or a wholesaler. A vendor charged with an offence was able to use a manufacturer's or wholesaler's warranty or invoice as defence, so long as this was passed to the prosecution within seven days of charges being made. This would then require the charges to be dropped or transferred to the warrantor – the manufacturer or wholesaler, in other words. Many grocers were duly disappointed by the 1899 Act's limited provision on invoice as warranty, having sought to obtain absolute legal indemnity against prosecution for selling any adulterated articles that had been directly supplied by wholesalers and manufacturers.[72]

The margarine regulations incorporated in the 1899 SFDA reflected the views of farmers and butter rather than margarine producers. For home-produced and imported margarine alike, these included new guidelines on labelling and the taking of samples from manufacturing premises by Board of Agriculture inspectors, and a ban on the sale of margarine which contained more than 10 per cent butter fat. The transfer of authority from the LGB to the Board of Agriculture signalled the emergence of a new policy community and the dairy farmers' hopes for a more sympathetic and active response. Walter Long, President of the Board of Agriculture, offered a curious explanation for these measures, claiming they were not really intended as protection for butter producers. But then he added that butter producers were entirely justified in their complaints, saying that the regulations were meant to ensure that the competition between butter and margarine was conducted 'on honest and honourable principles'. In other words, by limiting the potential quality of margarine, and thereby exaggerating the distinction between the two products, the regulations were clearly intended to increase the relative attraction of butter. This was certainly the view of Sir Walter Foster, who regarded

[70] *Ibid.*, p. 201.
[71] Paulus, *Search For Pure Food*, pp. 42–3.
[72] *The Grocer*, 76, 22 July 1899, p. 238.

the 10 per cent limitation on the use of butter fat in margarine as particularly unfair. Observing that margarine which contained 20 or 30 per cent butter fat would be a far more wholesome product, Foster said that there should actually be no limit on the proportion of butter fat used in margarine, so long as this was clearly labelled. This was, after all, the principle which the 1875 Act had applied to other manufactured food products.[73]

The 1899 Act put into effect one of the Select Committee's main recommendations, that the law be transformed from a permissive to a compulsory measure, with the LGB allowed to intervene and enforce the regulations wherever local authorities continued to neglect the law. This satisfied both analysts and farmers. The latter were accommodated further as the Board of Agriculture was given new interventionist powers to sample products where the 'general interests of agriculture' were affected.[74] The 1899 Act strengthened central administrative powers in Scotland as well as in England and Wales, consolidating the position of the Scottish Local Government Board, which had only been established in 1894. As in England and Wales, in Scotland from 1875 the SFDA had been simply a permissive measure, with central responsibility for monitoring local operations residing with the Secretary of State for Scotland. The 1899 Act transferred this responsibility to the Scottish LGB which, like its English and Welsh counterpart, was given the power to compel reluctant local authorities into enforcing the law. The young Scottish department also saw itself as having a distinct duty under the SFDA to monitor 'matters affecting the general interests of the consumer as distinguished from the interests of agriculture'.[75] The implied threat of central government intervention pleased the SPA, and proved to be a sufficiently effective stimulus to local action without LGB officials having to involve themselves in the daily operation of the law. In 1902–3 the LGB noted that, for the first time, every single local authority had submitted a report outlining its activities under the SFDA.[76]

This comprehensive coverage arguably ensured that the law became far more effective in eradicating adulteration. According to John Burnett, by the early decades of the twentieth century food no longer posed a significant threat to public health.[77] A measure of the law's impact on the trade is found in table 3.1, which summarises officially-recorded food adulteration from 1899 to 1938. Adulteration, it will be remembered, was defined as anything which rendered food 'injurious' to health, or which altered – 'to the prejudice of the purchaser' – its 'nature, substance and quality'.

---

[73] Parliamentary Debates, Fourth Series, vol. 67, 1437, 1471, 6 March 1899.

[74] Sale of Food and Drugs Act, 1899, Public General Acts, 1899, chapter 51; Board of Agriculture (Intelligence Division), Annual Report (1900), pp. 4–6.

[75] Local Government Board for Scotland, Annual Report, 1899, Cd. 182, p. xxxi.

[76] President of the SPA, Annual Address, 24 January 1900, The Analyst, 25, 1900, p. 61; Local Government Board, Annual Report, 1902–3, Cd. 1700, p. clxxiii.

[77] Burnett, Plenty and Want, pp. 222–30.

Table 3.1 Level of adulteration of formally purchased food samples in England and Wales and Scotland (%), 1899–1938

Year	England and Wales	Scotland
1899	9.4	14.4[a]
1902	8.7	11.0
1905	8.2	9.2
1908	8.5	10.8
1911	8.7	9.7
1913	8.2	9.9
1920	7.1	9.2
1923	6.1	7.5
1926	5.8	6.5
1929	5.4	8.4
1932	5.1	7.4
1935	5.5	7.0
1938	5.7	7.7

Notes: [a] Figure for 1900.

Source: Figures compiled from the published annual reports of the Local Government Boards in England and Wales and Scotland (1899–1913), the Ministry of Health and The Scottish Board and Department of Health (1920–1938).

Since the number of samples showing up as adulterated almost halved in this period, the figures can be interpreted positively, confirming the impression that the law was successful. But as an accurate picture of overall food quality they are not entirely reliable, measuring only the standard of food which retailers knowingly sold for analysis to local authority inspectors. In the 1900s many local authorities suspected that dishonest traders were supplying officials with genuine products while selling adulterated items to ordinary customers, and so began taking informal samples.[78] Table 3.2 shows the substantial discrepancy between adulteration of formal and these 'informal' samples in Edwardian Scotland (separate figures were not published in England and Wales).

Table 3.2 Adulteration (%) of formal and informal samples in Scotland, 1904–13

	1904	1908	1913
Formal	9.0	10.8	9.9
Informal	20.3	21.0	18.4

Source: Annual Reports of the Local Government Board for Scotland, 1905, Cd. 2541; 1909, Cd. 4679; 1914, Cd. 7327.

[78] Local Government Board, Annual Report, 1905–1906, Cd. 3105, p. c.

This discrepancy was partly caused by inspectors targeting informal sampling among traders suspected of fraudulent trade. But in assessing the true level of adulteration, it is worth reiterating that informal sampling only arose because traders, in England and Wales as well as in Scotland, frequently supplied officials with different items from those which regular customers received. In 1900 the Board of Agriculture recognised a developing trend, observing that in 'many small towns the fact that the inspectors are well-known to shop-keepers, and not unnaturally on terms of intimacy with their neighbours, must be recognised as more or less hindering the general adoption of measures which are essential to effective sampling'.[79] In 1905 Fulham's Medical Officer of Health noted that some traders reserved adulterated goods only for regular customers, while providing occasional or unfamiliar customers, suspected as being officials or paid agents of officials, with the genuine article. An agent of the Fulham official visited the same shop regularly in a short period, requesting butter on each occasion. Genuine butter was sold during the first five visits, but on the sixth and two subsequent visits margarine was fraudulently offered.[80] In the same year in Lanark a food inspector's attempt to entrap a dishonest grocer through using a young boy as an agent was foiled by the vigilance of the grocer's wife. The boy was sent in to the shop to ask for butter, which the grocer started to serve. Suspecting a trap, the wife stepped outside, saw the inspector on the threshold, and re-entered to warn her husband who immediately advised the boy – and the inspector when he entered the shop – that there was in fact no butter on the premises.[81] Another tendency was identified by a director of the Maypole Dairy Company, one of the major early multiples, who claimed that new branches were inspected regularly at first, but then rarely visited.[82] With practices like this in mind it seems reasonable to conclude that the actual scale of adulteration was probably below the informal figure, but almost certainly above the formal, and, though ambiguous, the figures do offer a valuable perspective on the SFDA's impact on food quality. They do not necessarily contradict Burnett's view that the law reduced the amount of dangerous adulteration, like the addition of lead filings to tea leaves, but they do suggest that adulteration in more benign forms, such as the dilution of milk with water, remained a significant problem long after the First World War.

Whatever its limitations, the downward trend in adulteration might have been expected to weaken the 'public interest' case for further regulation. But analysts and doctors could point to the discrepancy between formal and informal sampling or voice their suspicions that some local authorities were too lenient due to the influence of local traders. The tendency for a particular product to become the subject of publicity and, thus, an increased level of sampling, created its own momentum in which short term, often localised, findings played an important role in

[79] Board of Agriculture (Intelligence Division), Annual Report (1900), pp. 6–9.
[80] Local Government Board, Annual Report, 1905–6, Cd. 3105, p. c.
[81] Annual Reports of County Medical Officers, 1905, Report to the County of Lanark, p. 53, HH 62/30, Scottish Record Office (SRO).
[82] Report on Food Products Adulteration, 1895 (363), pp. 176.

raising wider concerns. Two other factors were even more influential. First, reformers argued that although fraud remained a significant problem, as with dangerous forms of adulteration it could be overcome by rigorous sampling and enforcement. A second, and potent, interpretation was that older forms of adulteration had been superseded by new, more subtle techniques so that constant and even increasing vigilance was required. By implication, the fall in official adulteration rates duly included an unknown element of successful deception. The term 'Sophistication', a common alternative name for adulteration, encapsulated such suspicions. In 1891, responding to a *Daily Telegraph* article on the decline of adulteration, the *Lancet* announced the refurbishment of its laboratories to allow more analytical work because foods still contained harmful or sub-standard ingredients.[83] An article in *The Times* in 1903 identified scientific 'sophistication' by manufacturers as the principal problem.[84] In 1906 Bernard Dyer, a leading analyst, described the relationship between adulterators and analysts as a 'constant duel'.[85]

Cassal's establishment of the *British Food Journal* signalled a division among the public analysts in 1899, based partly on personalities and partly on the strategy for tackling adulteration. Cassal supported the British Analytical Control, a system by which manufacturers could voluntarily submit their products for scientific analysis. Their goods and advertising could then carry an official control label indicating for consumers their participation and that products were subject to periodic sampling as well as testing on demand.[86] The intention was to persuade manufacturers, distributors and consumers of their common interest in high-quality products since Cassal and others regarded legislation as limited and liable to promote the lowest common denominator. The scheme operated in five countries in 1900 involving 169 manufacturers and importers, but the only British based firms were two wine importers, a chutney firm, two flour producers and an importer of butter and cheese. Bovril joined the scheme in 1901, but its limited scale indicates that manufacturers felt little need to seek such scrutiny or marketing tactics.[87]

Butter and milk, 1901–7

In Paulus' view, the debates and compromises leading to the 1899 Act marked the point at which food and drug adulteration became the province of a closed policy community of agriculturalists, traders, processors, retailers and government experts, that excluded consumers or other external influences. But little attention has been paid to the subsequent evolution of the regulatory system either in terms of the relative strengths of the pressure groups or their ambitions. The most immediate developments in the Edwardian era concerned the authority granted under the 1899 SFDA to the Board of Agriculture to set minimum standards for milk,

---

[83] *Lancet*, 1 August 1891, p. 235.
[84] See reprint in the *British Food Journal*, January 1903, p. 2.
[85] Dyer testimony, Report from the Select Committee on the Butter Trade, 1906 (245), p. 238.
[86] See *British Food Journal*, September 1900, pp. 267–74, July 1900, p. 177 and January 1901, p. 34
[87] *British Food Journal*, December 1901, p. 400.

butter, cream and cheese. Dairy producers enjoyed a close working relationship with Board of Agriculture officials, and thus influenced the character of the standards which were subsequently introduced. The 1901 Sale of Milk Regulations fixed a minimum standard of 3 per cent fat solids and 8.5 per cent of non-fat solids.[88] The 1902 Sale of Butter Regulations fixed an upper limit of 16 per cent water content.[89] Both the milk and butter regulations were generally regarded as undemanding or realistic levels, rather than major departures from existing practice. Although apparently precise specification standards, in reality the milk and butter regulations fixed presumptive levels from which any deviation was prima facie evidence of adulteration that required explanation from the retailer. If the suspect sample could be shown to be untampered with or if the consumer had been informed, either verbally or in writing about the true nature of the product, then the retailer could escape prosecution or conviction.

During 1900 the Board of Agriculture held hearings on milk which illustrated the existence of the policy community identified by Paulus, though with more involvement by the medical profession than had been the case in the 1894–6 hearings on the SFDA.[90] There was testimony from 17 dairy farmers, including representatives of the Dairy Trade and Can Protection Society and local associations, and from 12 representatives of dairies and milk distributors. Charles Lehmann, a director of the leading Dutch manufacturer, appeared on behalf of the Condensed Milk Defence Association, a body formed by overseas manufacturers to counter public attacks on machine-skimmed condensed milk. The committee saw 14 analysts, of whom four represented dairying associations or creameries and others testified on behalf of the SPA, the Incorporated Society of Medical Officers of Health and the Sanitary Inspectors Association.

The Committee's remit was to determine whether standards should be set and, if so, at what level. Throughout, the debate about standards was in terms of the proportions of fat and non-fat solids in milk, reflecting existing *de facto* standards which were applied to milk. Around 1875 the Government Laboratory had established 2.5 per cent fat and 8.5 per cent non-fat solids as a minimum level below which milk was presumed to be adulterated. In 1886, after evaluations of a new analytical method, the SPA had recommended a higher level of 3.25 per cent fat and 8.5 per cent of non-fatty solids. This was applied by many analysts and some courts and adopted by some dairy companies. The Government Laboratory remained the final arbiter and raised its 'standard' to 2.75 per cent fat in 1894 and then to 3 per cent in 1899.[91] There was no discussion of bacteriological tests, then being developed by doctors who were examining milk-borne infections, so health

---

[88] Sale of Milk Regulations, 1901, Statutory Rules and Orders, 1901, No. 657.
[89] Sale of Butter Regulations, 1902, Statutory Rules and Orders, 1902, No. 355.
[90] Departmental Committee on Milk and Cream Regulations, Report, 1901, Cd. 491.
[91] Departmental Committee on Milk and Cream Regulations, Minutes of Evidence, 1901, Cd 484, pp. 1–3, 10, 45–53, 71, 120–1.

issues were raised in relation to nutrition rather than disease, and this limited the scope of the debate.

The SPA advocated a minimum standard of a 3 per cent fat and 8.5 per cent non-fat content. A vocal minority within the SPA favoured even higher standards; the Incorporated Society of Medical Officers of Health simply called for the highest possible standard to improve milk's nutritional value. Although their membership was divided, the representatives of elite agricultural organisations generally supported standards as a means of exposing dishonest distributors. Since 1895 the Central and Associated Chambers of Agriculture had advocated a level of 3 per cent and 9 per cent; F.J. Lloyd, analyst to the British Dairy Farmers' Association, accepted this level too, providing there was some allowance for sampling variations.[92] The milk trade also contained supporters of standards, primarily the Aylesbury Dairy Company, whose contracts already required farmers to supply milk that met the Government Laboratory's standards.[93] Henry Droop Richmond, the firm's trade analyst, regarded a standard of 3 per cent fat and 8.5 per cent non-fat solids as broadly reasonable. For such companies, regulation would consolidate existing *de facto* standards at a level corresponding to their established business practices, and disadvantage those of their competitors, presumably at the cheaper end of the trade, who had not operated in line with the Government Laboratory's standards. Thus, although the Committee eventually concluded that creameries and milk dealers were the main opponents of standards, trade opinion was divided and the trade associations' lobbying required them to determine the balance of opinions among their members. Dealers and farmers who disliked standards claimed that they were impractical or would depress the average quality of milk. On behalf of the Dairy Trade and Can Protection Society, Alfred DeHailes, an analyst, argued that legal standards would depress quality by becoming a maximum level. He claimed that only the dishonest trader would prefer a fixed standard and that such a standard would simplify life for analysts and magistrates without resulting in any improvement for consumers.[94] But, since the 1899 SFDA had approved the principle, the debate in 1900 was less about the desirability of regulation than about exactly where the criteria would be set. As a result, opponents of regulation simply argued for undemanding or variable standards that would legitimise existing practices. Much discussion centred around factors, such as the time of year, breed of cow, or local conditions, that might affect the composition of milk. For instance, one suggestion was that summer milk was richer than winter milk, so standards should vary according to the season. For the condensed milk producers, Lehmann defended their product as nutritious, emphasising the manufacturers' self-interest in maintaining quality and his own firm's practice of analysing milk supplies and cancelling contracts

---

[92] Final Report of the Departmental Committee, Minutes of Evidence, 1904, Cd. 1750, pp. 333–40; 434–41.
[93] Report on Food Products Adulteration, 1894 (253), pp. 28, 169.
[94] Departmental Committee on Milk and Cream Regulations Report, 1901, Cd 491, pp. 20–1.

where fat content was consistently low.⁹⁵ Having rejected criticisms on health grounds, Lehmann addressed possible allegations of fraud with the argument that the public were knowledgeable and discriminating consumers.

Within a year the Board of Agriculture reported in favour of standards for milk and cream as a means of reducing adulteration. It proposed a national scheme applied throughout the year rather than one that distinguished between areas or seasons. The Committee used the public analysts and their evidence as the basis for deciding between the competing arguments of farmers (pro-regulation) and milk traders (anti-regulation), though this portrayal ignored the differences of opinion within each group. The analysts were pictured as experts whose lack of commercial self-interest lent weight to their view compared to the farmers and milk dealers. For a committee report this was an unusually positive reference to the analysts' authority and highlighted their greater status in food matters, but its isolated character suggests that there was a rhetorical value in buttressing the highly commercial motivations of farmers and some dairy companies. The final regulations were set at the level of 3 per cent fat and 8.5 per cent other solids, which was the minimum proposed by the SPA and fully acceptable to farmers' organisations and leading dairy companies as consistent with established practice. Yet the immediate impact of the regulations disappointed their supporters, failed to achieve the uniformity expected by the Committee and indicated the blurred line between *de facto* and legal standards. The hearings had publicised conflicting evidence and opinions about the variables affecting milk, possible analytical techniques and preferred standards. Since the regulations only set a presumption of adulteration, the hearings effectively provided defendants with information and arguments which could be used to dispute prosecutions and make courts hesitant.⁹⁶

Butter regulations were devised by a Board of Agriculture Departmental Committee, chaired by Horace Plunkett, a leading figure in the rural co-operative movement in Ireland and Vice-President of the Irish Department of Agriculture. The committee included Robert Anderson, a close associate of Plunkett, as well as Hudson Kearley and Christopher Dunn, chairman of the Cork Butter Market. There was a scientific presence with Professor Thorpe of the Government Laboratory, Sir Charles Cameron, who was Dublin's Medical Officer of Health, and Professor Thomson, president of the Institute of Chemistry. The committee leant heavily on advice from industry analysts including Henry Droop Richmond and Frederick Lloyd. The alliance of convenience between public analysts and farmers re-emerged in the debates and official reports about butter standards, but in contrast to the milk standard debate, doctors were not consulted, indicating the different composition of this policy community. The butter debate was more protracted, and it revealed differences, based on alternative methods of produc-

---

⁹⁵ Departmental Committee on Milk and Cream Regulations, Minutes of Evidence, 1901, Cd 484, pp. 336–48.

⁹⁶ Board of Agriculture and Fisheries (Intelligence Division), Annual Report of Proceedings under the SFDA for 1903, 1904, Cd 2187, pp. 8–10.

tion, both betweeen British and Irish butter producers and traders and within Ireland. The Committee attached significant weight to the temper of the Irish butter trade, gathering evidence in Cork and Dublin before issuing an interim report in January 1902.[97] It proposed a standard based on a maximum water content of 16 per cent. The Irish butter trade was divided between farm-produced butter, the proprietary creameries, generally controlled by merchants, and the newer co-operative creameries which Plunkett had done much to promote since 1889.[98] Both types used the recently developed cream separator, but the Irish trade, especially the farm-produced salted butters, had lost ground to Danish and Australian imports from the 1880s. The co-operative movement and the Cork market aimed to improve the quality and marketing methods, and thus prices, of farm butters by copying the Danish system of co-operatives and investment in new cream separating equipment. The strategy provoked hostility from the proprietary creameries and disinterest among farmers, especially smaller producers whose cheap 'salt firkin' butter had the highest water content. But the support of the co-operative movement and leading merchants was sufficient for Plunkett to press ahead in April 1902. The 16 per cent limit was confirmed, but salt firkin butter was permitted a higher water content, providing it was labelled appropriately.

As with milk, the immediate results disappointed the pro-standards lobby. New products appeared, notably milk-blended butter as an alternative to butter mixed simply with water. In response to complaints from local authorities and all sections of the butter trade, the Board of Agriculture promoted a succession of Bills to extend the butter regulations. A 1903 Bill proposed that any butter containing added water, even in the form of extra milk, be labelled as 'adulterated butter'. Despite the Board of Agriculture's active support, these Bills failed due to disagreements among even the business supporters of regulation, further resistance from Irish MPs and the lack of interest among other Parliamentarians. A new Select Committee was appointed to investigate the state of the butter trade in 1906.[99] In his testimony, Thomas Elliott, secretary of the Board of Agriculture and Fisheries, acknowledged lobbying from the Butter Association, a group of metropolitan wholesalers, and by the Grocers' Federation. Elliott commented that the 'consumers, of course, have no associations. The consumers are represented, and I think properly represented by the Local Authorities under the Public Health and Sale of Food and Drugs Acts'.[100] This view was contested, however, by trade supporters of tighter regulation who presented themselves as representatives of the otherwise silent public: the treasurer of the Butter Association emphasised that it

---

[97] Interim Report of the Departmental Committee Appointed by the Board of Agriculture to Inquire and Report upon the Desirability of Regulations for Butter, 1902, Cd. 944.
[98] Patrick Bolger, *The Irish Co-operative Movement: Its history and development* (Dublin, 1977), pp. 61–76, 183–213; Cormac O'Grada, 'The Beginnings of the Irish Creamery System, 1880–1914', *Economic History Review*, 30(2), May 1977, pp. 284–305.
[99] Report of the Select Committee on the Butter Trade, 1906 (245), pp. 1–2.
[100] Elliott testimony in Ibid., p. 5.

had been formed for the 'protection of the public'.[101] The Association initiated prosecutions against retailers selling adulterated butter.[102] The intermingling of roles and definitions of 'public interest' were evident in the appearance of Bernard Dyer, a future office-bearer and historian of the SPA, who proclaimed analysts to be 'one of the official guardians of the public in regard to its food supply'.[103] Yet, in these hearings, Dyer spoke on behalf of the Central Chamber of Agriculture and in his professional capacity was a public analyst in four rural counties and consulting chemist to three county agricultural societies.

For the Board of Agriculture, Elliott justified regulation as a response to fraud since he accepted that mixing butter and water was not hazardous.[104] He argued that a complete ban on milk-blended butter was required because butter adulteration had increased and its practitioners were too ingenious at circumventing current measures through 'scientific adulteration' and cunningly worded advertising. Elliott advocated extending the inspection powers available under the Margarine Act to butter factories to allow the Board of Agriculture to protect the 'security of the public'. When challenged about the interference with private property rights, Elliott cited Inland Revenue powers as a precedent where inspection co-existed with profitability in brewing and distilling. He also portrayed further regulation as a necessary response to technological change, partly in terms of the notion of 'scientific adulteration' and partly in response to a transition from small-scale farm butter-making to new factory methods. The state's role, Elliott believed, was to establish the boundaries of legitimate competition in defence of consumer interests and reputable butter producers and traders. This reasoning corresponds to Campbell's view that the destabilising effects of major technological changes are one factor that can prompt a search for new forms of governance, including state regulation.[105] The important technological development here was the advent of margarine which prompted dairy farmers and butter producers to seek regulations intended to distinguish their product from the new, cheaper substitute. The debate about butter standards in the early 1900s was a further stage in this process. Equally Elliott's concern with consumer protection fits with Wilkins' interpretation of the new food laws as a response to a greater physical and cultural distance between consumers and the processes of food production and marketing.[106] Consumers, Wilkins argues, were no longer able to purchase commodities locally, relying on their own knowledge of the reputations of suppliers. Manufacturers now catered for more distant markets and increased the scale of their operations; their brands offered a new source of information and reputation designed to maximise

---

[101] Page testimony in Ibid., pp. 103–106.
[102] *British Food Journal*, April 1904, pp. 83–6.
[103] Dyer testimony in Report from the Select Committee on the Butter Trade, p. 238.
[104] Elliott testimony in Ibid., pp. 1–20.
[105] Campbell *et al.*, *Governance*, pp. 336–40.
[106] Mira Wilkins, 'When and Why Brand Names in Food and Drink?' Geoffrey Jones and Nicholas J. Morgan (eds), *Adding Value: Brands and Marketing in food and drink* (London, 1994), pp. 17–23, 25–30.

sales and, thus, the volume of production in the new factories. In this context adulteration laws can be seen as a further response to new uncertainties about the information available and the reputation of suppliers. The bulk of butter sold to consumers consisted of blends of imported butters so there was certainly a physical distance between producers and consumers. Yet Elliott's stress on the significance of new factory methods was misleading in terms of the impetus for regulation. Rather than protecting a more traditional product, the butter regulations were perceived as threatening by smaller farm butter makers.

The demand for further intervention came from one of the larger creamery companies. As the only major manufacturer to testify, Reginald Butler of Wiltshire United Dairies claimed that, without factory inspections and stricter regulation, competitive pressures would lead to honest producers supplying inferior products. He had even requested inspection of his own factory as a way of buttressing the firm's reputation. The remaining testimony was marked by inter-regional disputes among the representatives of Irish creameries, traders and butter markets. A County Clare faction continued to advocate a more relaxed standard of up to 20 per cent water to safeguard sales of Irish salt firkin butter. But representatives of the larger creameries and butter markets in south-west Ireland supported the existing 16 per cent level on the basis that it assisted their educational and marketing initiatives to promote improved quality and uniformity in the farm butters. Such testimony suggested that the introduction of a standard had altered production methods, away from heavily salted butters and accelerated the trend to factory methods that Elliott used to justify intervention.

The retail trade had a close interest in these regulations. After all, grocers were frequently convicted under the Margarine Act for selling adulterated butter. In offering a clearer definition of butter adulteration, the 1902 regulations were supported by *The Grocer*, but in the period which followed it pressed for a tightening of the Margarine Act. Reflecting the general retailing view that adulteration had to be tackled at the point of production (this had been witnessed during the debate about invoice as warranty), the journal urged the government to assume increased powers of inspection of margarine factories. Increased vigilance against the 'butter fakers', it insisted in July 1905, would benefit the 'honest grocer and the unwary consumer' as well as the dairy farmer. *The Grocer* duly pointed out that dealers in faked butter forced honest grocers to accept unremunerative prices for genuine butter or sell the adulterated article themselves.[107] During the butter hearings, in contrast to the milk regulations, butter distributors were vocal advocates of regulation. Supporters of tighter controls included the London Chamber of Commerce, and local grocers' associations. Government representatives from Canada, New Zealand and the state of Victoria all wished to see milk-blended butters prohibited as a contribution to improving the general image of butter and to allow their own producers to gain a reputation for quality. The manager of the Manchester CWS's butter department also advocated factory inspections and

---

[107] *The Grocer*, 82, 6 September 1902, p. 541; 88, 15 July 1905, p. 139; 91, 16 February 1907, p. 417.

prohibiting milk-blended butters as well as calling for more extensive labelling to distinguish different grades of butter.

The butter hearings of 1906 were enlivened by robust questioning of the pro-regulation case by James Dalziel, Liberal MP for Kirkcaldy and proprietor of *Reynolds News*. He attacked 'paternal and grandmotherly' state interference based on arbitrary criteria designed to satisfy commercial self-interest. The public were, in Dalziel's view, satisfied with milk-blended butter and perfectly capable of determining its quality without further regulations that would only restrict choice and raise prices. His questioning compelled the advocates of regulation to justify their case more fully. For Thomas Elliott, the exercise of consumer choice was tainted by misleading advertising and the difficulties of assessing quality, and assistance to the butter producers was needed to defend honest traders. He questioned whether milk-blended butter was nutritious, but relied primarily on the claim that consumers were cheated if they expected the product to be butter.[108] Bernard Dyer also questioned Dalziel's premise of consumer choice in terms of the information and expertise required to evaluate commodities. Milk-blended butter might appear satisfactory, Dyer conceded, to 'even educated people of ordinary average intelligence who have never had to think chemically or to think in proportions', but chemical analysis revealed its true 'impoverished' character and the particular nutritional threat to children's health.[109] Thus, Dyer claimed that regulations would benefit consumers even if they could only afford to purchase less of a genuine product and did not appreciate its merits. It was a clear statement of a 'public interest' case for regulation based on using agents (analysts) and regulation to obtain and interpret information about a product on behalf of consumers.

The importance of fair trade and consumer arguments for legal restrictions on margarine became more pressing at the end of 1905 with the establishment of a Liberal government, committed to free trade and suspicious of any measures which appeared to offer protection to farmers. In these political circumstances it seems reasonable to suggest that the emergence of an unlikely alliance between grocers and English dairy farmers was instrumental to the passage of the 1907 Butter and Margarine Act, despite resistance from some Irish MPs.[110] This applied the 1902 16 per cent limit on water content to margarine as well as butter. Milk-blended butter remained legal subject to a maximum water content of 24 per cent; this provision, a departure from the 1906 report, attracted fierce criticism from representatives of grocers and the Co-operative Wholesale Society as well as Irish MPs during the final reading of the Bill.[111] The critics argued that the measure signalled the death-knell of the Irish salt-firkin butter producers and that the Bill was a conspiracy by powerful corporate concerns. Irish MPs offered 'bastardine', 'milkerdine' and 'Lib-

[108] Elliott asserted that 'I do not believe any man wants butter with more than 16 per cent water in it'; Elliott testimony in Report from the Select Comittee on the Butter Trade, p. 11.
[109] Dyer testimony in Ibid., pp. 238–43.
[110] Butter and Margarine Act, 1907, Public General Acts, 1907, chapter 21.
[111] Parliamentary Debates, Fourth Series vol. 295–365, 26 July 1907. A Londonderry MP claimed that allowing milk-blended butter signalled capture of the Bill by 'wealthy capitalists'.

eralism' as prospective names for milk-blended butter. Liberal Ministers, including Lloyd-George, responded that a perfectly safe food could not be banned outright, an echo of Dalziel's concerns, but they claimed that a 24 per cent maximum was significantly below current levels and so would effectively end the manufacture of milk-blended butter. The government's decision contrasted with the failure of Sir Walter Foster's efforts in the 1890s to have the nutritional merits of margarine accepted. The government portrayed the measure as a compromise that was acceptable to both the Central Chamber of Agriculture and the County Councils' Association.

The Board of Agriculture was permitted to determine a new, unspecified, generic name for milk-blended butter. At the same time the Act strengthened the general regulation of the production and sale of margarine. First, this was brought explicitly under the same legal umbrella as the Sale of Food and Drugs Act, which the Butter and Margarine Act was characterised as being 'as one with'. Second, where Board of Agriculture officials had previously been permitted only to take samples from margarine factories, they were now entitled to inspect 'any process of manufacture, blending, reworking or treatment used therein'. This power was also given to Local Government Board officials, and enabled the Liberal government to claim that the Act would protect innocent retailers as well as consumers, by confronting adulteration at its manufacturing source. Hence the measure was approved by the Grocers' Federation as well as the Central Chamber of Agriculture.[112] *The Grocer* especially admired the 'drastic' powers of inspection which the government had secured.[113] In addition, margarine manufacturers had to obtain Board of Agriculture approval for the names under which they marketed their products: the chosen 'fancy or other descriptive' title could not be suggestive of butter or 'anything connected with the dairy interest' and had to include the word margarine. Such intervention acknowledged the commercial significance and partial nature of the information presented to consumers through advertising and brands; it extended the state's protection of commercial interests in a far more precise and detailed way than the Merchandise Marks Act.

The effects of the regulations were mixed. Through their trade association, butter producers had hoped to share responsibility for approving or rejecting the margarine names, but officials at the Board proved to be vigilant enough defenders of dairy interests.[114] By the end of October 1907 around 600 separate names had been submitted for approval, about 300 of which were disallowed. The Board ultimately decided on several different grounds for exclusion, with most of those failing because they implied some butter or dairy connection. Among these were Avondale, Cremona, Cream of the Valley, Dairymade, Grass, Silver Churn and Strathmore. Others were rejected for 'importing praise or suitability

---

[112] Parliamentary Debates, Fourth Series, vol. 172, 1056–7.
[113] *The Grocer*, 91, 23 February 1907, pp. 483–4.
[114] Haygarth Brown departmental memo, 'Procedure with regard to Fancy Names for Margarine', 9 August 1907, MAF 36/56, PRO.

for any particular purpose', notably X'lent, Best of All, Excellent Puff, King of the Netherlands and Victoria. While the latter regal pair were excluded, officials curiously approved Chief, Queen, Sovereign and The Empress, along with less contentious titles like Acorn, Blossom, Crispo, Golden Fleece, Karma, Pansy, Romance and Roma, and more bizarre selections like Surprise and Victim.[115] In officially recognising these selected brand names the state provided an important degree of legal protection for margarine producers. The original Act of 1887, in offering a definition of margarine, can be seen as having had the same effect. Thus, while the need to regulate margarine was initially identified by butter producers, the longer-term benefits of the regulations were at least partially shared by their 'budget' rivals. Certainly the regulations failed to check the expansion of margarine sales. In Ireland, some butter markets and the co-operative movement, through the Irish Agricultural Organisation, endeavoured to promote improved quality through technical advice and training, prizes, and in 1910 established a private scheme based on the 1906 standards.[116] But the latter, and by implication the butter regulations, attracted limited support and lapsed during the war when the priority was maximising production.

In providing clearer information for consumers about the components of competing products, while broadly satisfying the demands of dairy producers and grocers, the 1907 Butter and Margarine Act comprised elements of both 'public interest' and business capture. In this respect it reflected the general character of the 1875–99 Sale of Food and Drugs Acts. Clearly the principle of outlawing the sale of fraudulent or dangerous food benefited the consuming public as a whole. But the essence of the general regulations, focusing on retailers rather than producers, developed after pressure had been exerted by manufacturers on the state, in the first instance through a Parliamentary Select Committee, in 1874, on which two food producers sat and exerted a powerful influence. The concentration on retailers was partially qualified by the 1899 Act, with its provision for the use of warranty as a defence against prosecution, but for law enforcers the premises and processes of manufacturing – other than dairy and margarine production – remained off-limits. The detailed guidelines on alcoholic spirits, margarine, butter and milk, all issued under the broad SFDA umbrella, also benefited the consuming public, and in standardising the definition of adulteration they eased the job of those charged with enforcing the law. But these too were drawn up in response to business pressure. The margarine regulations in particular were specifically intended to offer producers of butter a competitive trading advantage over their margarine rivals. Even when margarine continued to prosper, farmers and butter traders did not lose their faith in regulation, rather they demanded stricter controls. Although comprehensive legislation was delayed, largely because of differences of interest between the English and Irish trades, butter producers ultimately

---

[115] Haygarth Brown, memo on rules for approving and disapproving fancy names, with list of approved and disapproved titles, 7 November 1907, MH 36/56, PRO.

[116] Bolger, *Irish Co-operative Movement*, pp. 202–5.

succeeded because, like every other group of food producers who influenced the regulatory process, they persuaded the state that there was in existence a separate 'public interest', served by the regulations, which happened to coincide with their own commercial interests.

4

Food scares and the Local Government Board

The emphasis in the first three chapters has been on the broad character of state regulation, the food industry and its attendant interest groups, and the evolution of general food laws between the middle and the end of the nineteenth century. In the chapters which follow the chronological focus shifts to the 1900–38 period, examining the regulatory role of central government and the manner in which the state interacted with various interest groups. Subsequent chapters focus on specific commodities and issues, and the new regulatory priorities established by the Ministry of Health from 1919 onwards. But the analysis of central government and its relations with the food industry begins in this chapter with an examination of the Local Government Board's (LGB) attitude and commitments to food regulation.

Historians have rarely cast favour on the LGB, which is usually characterised as having obstructed much-needed social reform through a combination of ideological conservatism and administrative incompetence.[1] The evolution of food policy, especially during the Edwardian era, tends to modify this view slightly. Prompted by two serious food scares, the first at the end of 1900 and the second in 1906, the LGB secured two important changes which strengthened the regulatory powers of central government significantly. First, a dedicated Foods Section was established within the LGB's Medical Department in 1905; and, second, Campbell-Bannerman's Liberal government passed the 1907 Public Health (Regulations as to Food) Act. This enabled the state's bureaucratic representatives to seize and destroy diseased or dangerous food, and to regulate more closely the quality of imported products. The Foods Section was a direct response to the fatal poisoning by arsenic of at least 70 English beer drinkers in the winter of 1900–1. This was the most serious food or drink poisoning epidemic of the entire 1875–1938 period. The 1907 legislation was designed to eliminate the potential dangers highlighted by the 'revelations' in Upton Sinclair's novel, *The Jungle*, about dangerously unhygienic conditions in the stockyards and meat-packing plants of Chicago in 1906. Yet these changes, although innovative, did not entirely meet the demand for closer forms of

---

[1] Kenneth D. Brown, 'John Burns at the Local Government Board: A reassessment', *Journal of Social Policy*, 6 (2) 1977, pp. 157–70.

regulation generated by the scares. In the case of beer, the barley producers of southern and eastern England, who were struggling in the context of increasing imports and falling domestic prices, used the arsenic crisis to press for tighter regulation of beer materials, seeking the elimination of sugar and other 'substitutes' which brewers used in place of more expensive grains. Brewers were an important interest group and used their political as well as economic weight to resist the introduction of new beer materials legislation. It should be emphasised that there had been an earlier debate, from the 1850s to the 1880s, about the presence of arsenic in manufactured articles, including foods, wallpapers and clothing. An intermittent 'public interest' campaign, mainly driven by doctors and through the pages of the *Lancet*, had emphasised the need for closer government regulation of the substance. According to P. W. J. Bartrip no changes in the law actually materialised, although some manufacturers modified their practices as a result of the adverse publicity and replaced arsenic with other colouring substances.[2] The conflict between grain producers and brewers over beer is explored in the first half of the chapter, emphasising the relative weakness of the farming lobby. Unlike the earlier pressure over arsenic in food and wallpaper, this failed to draw in consistent support from established 'public interest' campaigners like doctors and public analysts. The second half of the chapter focuses on *The Jungle* episode. This demonstrates the value of comparative history, indicating the extent to which American and British developments mutually interacted, and charts the evolving role of the new Foods Section, culminating in the introduction of the 1907 Public Health Act.

Arsenic poisoning and 'pure beer'

The epidemic of arsenic poisoning among beer drinkers was chiefly centred in Manchester and Salford, where it was first detected by Dr Ernest Septimus Reynolds of Manchester Royal Infirmary in November 1900.[3] Reynolds identified an upsurge in cases of arsenic-induced peripheral neuritis among his patients, some of whom he attended in the city's Crumpsall Workhouse, and suspected that contaminated beer was the cause. This belief was supported by Charles Tattersall, Medical Officer of Health for Salford, who traced the epidemic to beer supplied by a brewery in his locality. Tattersall analysed the original ingredients of this beer and found that the arsenic was contained in two brewing sugars: the glucose, derived from starch and used in the mash; and the invert cane sugar, used in priming. Tattersall's investigation revealed that the brewer's supplier, Bostock & Co. of Garston in Merseyside, had used a large amount of sulphuric acid in preparing the sugars. Bostock's acid and sugars, which had been supplied to many brewers across the north and midlands, were found to be highly arsenical on 23 November. Reynolds outlined these

[2] P. W. J. Bartrip, 'How Green was my Valance? Environmental Arsenic Poisoning and the Victorian Domestic Ideal', *English Historical Review*, 109, September 1994, pp. 891–913.

[3] For a more detailed account of the epidemic and the pure beer campaign, see Jim Phillips and Michael French, 'The Pure Beer Campaign and Arsenic Poisoning, 1896–1903', *Rural History*, 9 (2), 1998, pp. 195–209.

developments in a letter to the *British Medical Journal*, published on 24 November. The journal's editors affirmed the seriousness and veracity of this report, which prompted correspondence about many similar cases in the north and midlands, particularly from Lancashire and Staffordshire.[4] The Local Government Board responded to the subsequent public anxiety by detailing one of its medical inspectors, George Buchanan, to undertake an informal inquiry.[5] Already in the Manchester area, Buchanan immediately visited the Crumpsall Workhouse and consulted Reynolds, Tattersall and other local medical officials. On 29 November his preliminary report to the LGB confirmed the accuracy of Reynolds' published account, emphasising that all of the contaminated sugar had come from Bostock.[6]

These reports and published correspondence revived a debate about brewing ingredients which had been running since the 1860s, when the newly established Central Chamber of Agriculture (CCA) began campaigning for the abolition of the tax on malted barley used by brewers. The CCA believed that the tax restricted demand for barley, and lobbied for its replacement with a restoration of the beer duty which had been repealed in 1830.[7] The farmers' aim was realised with the 1880 Inland Revenue Act. But to compensate brewers for the introduction of the beer duty, which they opposed, the government framed the legislation to allow for the 'free mash'. This widened the scope for permitted ingredients from barley, hops, yeast and water to anything that could be defined as 'wholesome'. For this reason the 1880 Act was often referred to as Prime Minister William Gladstone's 'compact' with the brewers, and a variety of materials were subsequently introduced: sugar and glucose, as in the Bostock case, to speed up fermentation, but also maize, rice and other items which altered beer's colour and flavour.[8]

The CCA had not anticipated this development, which for farmers meant that in the 1880s and 1890s the Act was having the opposite of its intended effect: brewers were using less rather than more domestically produced barley. This was extremely serious for barley producers, who were already beginning to experience the impact of the severe depression which dominated agricultural production in the closing quarter of the century. Chapter 2 described the long-term restructuring of British agriculture which resulted from this depression, with farmers moving out of grain and other products subjected to international competition, and shifting into dairy or fruit production. There was an important geographical bias in this shift, with the impact of depression felt most severely in the eastern and southern lowland areas of England, where the grain-based economy was less suited to diversification than the pastoral uplands of the north and west.[9]

---

[4] *British Medical Journal*, 24 November 1900, pp. 1492–3, 1520; 15 December 1900, p. 1730.

[5] Buchanan's father, George senior, had been Medical Officer at the Local Government Board, 1879–1892.

[6] Buchanan, 'The "Beer Poisoning" Epidemic', 29 November 1900, MH 56/156, PRO.

[7] A. H. H. Matthews, *Fifty Years of Agricultural Politics*, pp. 254–61.

[8] T. R. Gourvish and R. G. Wilson, *The British Brewing Industry, 1830–1980* (Cambridge, 1994), pp. 221, 251–2.

[9] P. J. Perry (ed.), *British Agriculture, 1875–1914* (Oxford, 1973), pp. xxvi, xxxvii–xl.

The brewing trade's importance as an outlet for grain producers lay in the volume of beer consumed in Britain – an approximate 30 gallons per head from the 1870s to the 1900s.[10] From the 1880s, however, like bakers and other food manufacturers, brewers made increasing use of cheaper imported grains. Grain producers and their political representatives in southern and eastern England sought to arrest this declining demand, compounded by the 1880 Inland Revenue Act, by campaigning for tighter control of beer ingredients, seeking to limit or even prohibit the use of sugar, rice and all other 'substitutes' for barley and hops. In 1881 Colonel Frederick St. John Barne, MP for Suffolk East, introduced in Parliament a Bill to secure 'the purity of Beer' by limiting its constituents to barley, hops, yeast and water. Barne's Bill was withdrawn without attaining a Second Reading.[11] 'Pure beer' campaigners persisted, annually forwarding similar measures with an equal absence of success until 1896 when, with the agricultural depression well into its third decade, a Pure Beer Bill, supported by a 25,000-signature petition raised in Suffolk, East Cambridgeshire and Essex, finally attained a Second Reading. The measure's sponsor, Sir Cuthbert Quilter, MP for Sudbury in Suffolk, claimed that it was designed to protect consumers as well as grain producers. In distinguishing 'pure beer' from 'imitation beer', the Bill would provide the beer drinker with the same 'right to get what he paid for' as the purchaser of coffee or butter enjoyed under the Sale of Food and Drugs Acts.[12] Sir Michael Hicks-Beach, the Conservative Chancellor, had been pressed at meetings with his party's brewing supporters not to concede ground, and offered Quilter an expert inquiry on the subject if he withdrew the Bill. Writing in 1915, the Secretary of the Central Chamber of Agriculture observed that Quilter had accepted this offer in good faith without ascertaining the inquiry's terms of reference or personnel. These, it turned out, were 'not fairly constituted'.[13] The Inland Revenue Departmental Committee included three Treasury officials, who were likely to favour maintaining the 1880 arrangements which secured the Exchequer considerable revenue from the beer duty, and was asked to establish whether 'deleterious substances' were used in brewing and whether beer materials could be legally defined 'without undue interference with the liberty of brewers to use any wholesome materials in brewing'. While this placed the emphasis on establishing whether beer brewed with additional ingredients was dangerous to health, Quilter's Bill was based largely on the idea, to paraphrase the Select Committee which drafted the 1875 SFDA, that drinkers were being cheated rather than poisoned.

In these circumstances it is perhaps unsurprising that the Inland Revenue Committee ultimately took a positive view of the existing legal framework, effectively endorsing evidence provided by brewing trade witnesses. Including chemists like Cornelius O'Sullivan of Bass, Ratcliff & Gretton and Dr G. Harris Morris of the

---

[10] Peter Mathias, *The First Industrial Nation: An economic history of Britain, 1700–1914* (Second edition, Oxford, 1983), p. 419.
[11] Parliamentary Debates, Third Series, Vols 260, 1306 and 265, 608, 27 April and 22 August 1881.
[12] *Ibid.*, Fourth Series, Vol. 39, 89, 25 March 1896.
[13] Matthews, *Fifty Years of Agricultural Politics*, pp. 275–6.

Country Brewers' Society, these witnesses sternly defended the purity and wholesomeness of their products. Senior representatives of the Society of Public Analysts countered by testifying that 'pure beer' legislation was needed to protect consumers and ease prosecutions under the SFDA. This reflected the analysts' general belief in legally enforceable standards, although Otto Hehner, a leading figure in the SPA, also believed his organisation had a vested interest in reshaping the law on beer. In 1887 he advised SPA colleagues that the 1880 Inland Revenue Act, modified slightly in 1885, had undermined the status of their profession by giving relevant powers of inspection and analysis to Inland Revenue officers rather than public analysts.[14] Faced with competing 'expert' testimony from the brewers, on the one hand, and the SPA, on the other, the Inland Revenue Committee eventually concluded in January 1899 that no 'deleterious' materials were used and that therefore legislation was unnecessary. There was, however, one dissenting voice. The inquiry's lone agricultural representative, Clare Sewell Read, chair of the 1874 Select Committee, council member of the Central Chamber of Agriculture and President of the Norfolk Chamber of Agriculture, issued a Minority Report outlining the consumer-protectionist case for legislation.[15]

The government accepted the findings of the Majority Report and ruled out the prospect of legislation, but the arsenic epidemic which followed less than two years later gave the Pure Beer Campaign renewed and entirely unexpected impetus.[16] In December 1900, following publicity in the *Lancet* as well as the *British Medical Journal*, Quilter pressed the government for more public information on the facts of the case.[17] Arthur Balfour, Leader of the House of Commons, said that the investigation by George Buchanan, the LGB official in Manchester, was now formal and that its findings would shortly be published. This was reiterated several days later by Walter Long, President of the LGB, who added that Manchester brewers had behaved in a highly responsible manner, organising their own investigation and undertaking to destroy all contaminated beer.[18] With the explicit intention of allaying public anxiety, the Manchester Brewers' Central Association (MBCA) had indeed acted quickly, establishing an 'expert committee' to investigate the crisis on 21 November.[19] The committee's first report on 1 December established that no materials in use in Manchester other than Bostock's brewing sugars were arsenical, and made two precautionary recommendations: first, that all beer brewed with Bostock's sugars should be recalled and, if found to be arsenical, destroyed; and, second, that no beer should be sent out unless first tested and certified as being free from arsenic by the MBCA. The same committee issued a second report on 15

[14] *The Analyst*, 12, 1887, pp. 118–21.

[15] Report of the Departmental Committee on Beer Materials Conducted by the Board of the Inland Revenue, 1899, C. 9171.

[16] Parliamentary Debates, Fourth Series, Vol. 66, 469, 10 February 1899.

[17] *Lancet*, 1 December 1900, pp. 1590, 1600–3.

[18] Parliamentary Debates, Fourth Series, Vol. 88, 511–12, 11 December 1900, and 848–50, 14 December 1900.

[19] *The Brewers' Almanack*, 1902, p. 62.

December, confirming that Bostock's sugars were the sole cause of the poisoning and that its previous recommendations had been fully carried out, with all contaminated beer destroyed.[20] Having met representatives of this brewers' committee on 17 December, Buchanan communicated the contents of its second report to the LGB on 18 December, along with important additional information about the origins of the outbreak. Like most brewing sugars, Bostock's contained sulphuric acid. This, it now emerged, had come from a single supplier, Nicholson's of Leeds.[21]

While shocked by the poisoning epidemic, the brewing trade was quick to emphasise the positive response of the Manchester brewers. 'Immediately on the discovery of the possible origin of the trouble', noted *The Brewers' Almanack*, 'the brewers took every possible step to secure a prompt investigation and to stop any chance of contaminated beer getting into consumption. Supplies were recalled and destroyed, and unceasing labour to this end undertaken, no outlay, however heavy, was considered for a moment.'[22] These efforts were matched in Liverpool, where many drinkers died after consuming beer prepared with Bostock's sugars. According to the *Lancet*'s correspondent, many Liverpool brewers responded by emptying 'large quantities of suspected beer down the sewers'.[23] This local activity was supplemented on a national level by the Country Brewers' Society, which advised its members at the end of November to test all brewing sugar for arsenic and withdraw any contaminated beer. But the Society could not compel members to observe these recommendations, and Buchanan's formal report, published on 25 January 1901, indicated that in December and January beer containing Bostock's arsenical sugars was still being sold in Lancashire, notably in Blackburn and Preston, and across the Midlands, in Stone, Nottinghamshire and Market Drayton. This failure to withdraw contaminated stocks compounded the extent of the epidemic.

By mid January, 4,000 poisoning cases had been reported, 70 of them fatal, although Buchanan regarded these figures as an underestimate, given the widely held belief among Medical Officers of Health that many cases had gone unreported. Casualties remained overwhelmingly concentrated in the north-west, with 2,000 in Manchester and 1,000 in Salford.[24] These estimates, including Buchanan's belief that 70 fatalities was definitely an under-estimate, were confirmed as correct in the Final Report of Kelvin's Royal Commission.[25] With Buchanan's research indicating that the problem was spread across broad reaches of the north, Long had announced the appointment of the Royal Commission on 10 January 1901. This was duly constituted on 4 February, instructed to assess the extent and precise

[20] Texts of reports issued by MCBA Expert Committee issued as Addendum in Report to the Local Government Board on Recent Epidemic. Arsenical Poisoning Attributed to Beer (Buchanan), HMSO, January 1901, Cd. 459, pp. 21–3.
[21] Buchanan to Medical Officer, Local Government Board, 18 December 1900, MH 56/156, PRO.
[22] 'The Arsenic Question', *The Brewers' Almanack*, 1902, p. 328.
[23] *Lancet*, 8 December 1900, p. 1682.
[24] Report to the Local Government Bard on Recent Epidemic, pp. 3, 18–19.
[25] Final Report of the Royal Commission to Inquire into Arsenical Poisoning from the Consumption of Beer and other Articles of Food and Drink, November 1903, Cd. 1848, p. 5.

causes of the poisoning, and to advise the government on how to insure against similar future outbreaks. The Commission was chaired by Lord Kelvin, the first 'scientific peer', and George Buchanan was appointed as its secretary.[26]

Pure Beer campaigners were not satisfied by the establishment of the Royal Commission. Quilter told a public meeting at Bury St. Edmunds on 16 January that the facts of the epidemic were already clear, having been 'sufficiently elucidated' in the coroners' courts. He insisted that public health would only be protected by the immediate introduction of pure beer legislation. The Bury St. Edmunds meeting was organised, along with numerous others in Town Halls and Corn Exchanges across southern England, by the Committee to Promote the Purity of Beer, the existence of which had been announced in a letter published by *The Times* on 10 January.[27] This was written by Henry Chaplin, a Lincolnshire landowner, Unionist MP, former President of both the Board of Agriculture (1889–92) and the LGB (1895–1900), and racing enthusiast whose weakness for gambling was later to result in his bankruptcy.[28] Chaplin argued that the outbreak demonstrated the need for a 'pure beer' law, but this old claim was asserted in nakedly populist terms. First, in promoting demand for barley, 'pure beer' would arrest rural depopulation, providing wages and employment for many who would otherwise be forced off the land. Second, it would 'guard the health of the community, especially the workers of society – the artisans in the towns, the agricultural workers in the country, and the poorer classes generally who are the chief customers of the beer which is consumed'. Chaplin justified the need for the new organisation in terms of the need to counter the anticipated opposition of powerful brewers. The Committee to Promote the Purity of Beer consisted of around 30 prominent rural peers and MPs or former MPs, including Quilter and Sewell Read.[29]

Support for the Committee came largely from rural and southern quarters. The Buckinghamshire Chamber of Commerce, for instance, passed a resolution calling for the introduction of 'pure beer' legislation, as did a meeting of 200 working men – mainly miners and agricultural labourers – at Alvely in Shropshire. The arsenic poisoning ensured some degree of localised urban support for 'pure beer' legislation for the first time, although this was confined to Manchester and Salford, where the Trades and Labour Council resolved that it was 'absolutely essential' for the government to prohibit all beer that was not 'pure and wholesome' without awaiting the Royal Commission's findings.[30] The Pure Beer Campaign had initially been welcomed by the *Lancet*, which supported Quilter's initial Parliamentary intervention in December and asked why German purity laws – prohibiting the use of malt

---

[26] First Report of the Royal Commission to Inquire into Arsenical Poisoning from the Consumption of Beer and other Articles of Food and Drink, July 1901, Cd. 692.
[27] *The Times*, 14–17 January 1901.
[28] See Chaplin's entry in the *Dictionary of National Biography, 1922–1930* (Oxford, 1937).
[29] *The Times*, 10 January 1901.
[30] *Ibid.*, 17–19 January 1901.

substitutes – could not be applied in Britain. But in January the paper altered its position, suggesting that pure beer and the Royal Commission were both unnecessary diversions: the former it presumed to be unobtainable, and the latter it regarded as irrelevant because the salient information was already in the public domain. The real priority was to secure legislation which simply outlawed the production and sale of beer containing arsenic.[31] The *British Medical Journal* was also sceptical about pure beer, noting in February that 'the "farmers' friends" have been making rather too much of the risk of contamination of glucose by arsenic'. The journal reinforced this view, and anticipated one of the findings of the Royal Commission, by noting that ingredients were not the only sources of potential contamination: beer could become arsenical through the gas coke which was often used to dry malted barley.[32]

The geographical limitations – and economic interests – of the pure beer campaigners were further emphasised by the nature of the Parliamentary support for the 1901 Beer Bill, introduced in February. Nine of its 12 sponsors were from agricultural constituencies which had traditionally supported the campaign, including six from the barley-growing areas of Lincolnshire, Norfolk and Suffolk. The other three were from urban constituencies that had been affected directly by the poisoning.[33] The Bill differed slightly from its 1896 predecessor, defining two categories of beer: 'malt beer', brewed with malted barley, hops, yeast and water; and 'part malt beer', meaning any beer other than 'malt beer'. Producers of 'malt beer' could only use a small amount of sugar – in practice up to another 3 per cent by volume – to 'prime' the beer once brewing was complete. As a response, presumably, to the particular circumstances of the poisoning epidemic, the Bill proposed that brewers, like margarine manufacturers under the 1899 Sale of Food and Drugs Act, would be required to maintain for inspection by Inland Revenue Officers a full list of consignments sent out. In addition, licensing authorities were permitted to withhold licenses from public houses which did not offer 'malt' beer for sale.

John Brickwood, Chairman of the Country Brewers' Society, provided advanced warning that the trade would oppose any legislation that was 'designed to benefit the barley grower rather than protect the beer drinker', and brewers reiterated this opposition on the Bill's publication.[34] Given the appointment of the Royal Commission, the government reacted coolly to the Bill. Walter Long, who was responsible for food laws as President of the LGB, had already spelt out his opposition to

---

[31] *Lancet*, 8 December 1900, p. 1662 and 19 January 1901, p. 192.

[32] *British Medical Journal*, 9 February 1901, p. 378.

[33] The Bill's sponsors were Sir Robert Purvis (Liberal Unionist, Peterborough), Sir Cuthbert Quilter (Liberal Unionist, Suffolk Sudbury), Kenyon-Slaney (Conservative, Shropshire North), Sir James Fergusson (Conservative, Manchester North-East), Frederick Wilson (Liberal, Mid-Norfolk), James Round (Conservative, Harwich), Henry Broadhurst (Home Ruler Liberal, Leicester), Arthur Griffith Boscawen (Unionist, Tunbridge), Brookfield (Conservative, Sussex Rye), Sir Robert Price (Liberal,Norfolk East), William Younger (Unionist, Lincolnshire – not the brewing William Younger) and Joseph Walton (Liberal Home Ruler, Barnsley).

[34] *The Times*, 11 January 1901.

new definitions for beer, when addressing a dinner for the MP, Albert Brassey, on the day of the Royal Commission's establishment. Long claimed that the government was already doing everything that was necessary to protect the public, and questioned the value of pure beer legislation by pointing out that the ingredients which it proscribed – glucose and invert sugars, primarily – would still be used in sweet meats and 'confectionery jams': they could hardly be condemned in beer alone. Long's speech also included a significant reference to the 1880 Inland Revenue Act. With the introduction of pure beer, Long noted, brewers would be perfectly entitled to renegotiate the terms of their 'compact' with Gladstone, which had brought the Treasury £11.8 million in 1900. Long asked the agricultural lobby to consider how this valued revenue would otherwise be obtained.[35] That the government viewed pure beer as a revenue rather than a public health issue was further illustrated during the Beer Bill's Second Reading, when Hicks-Beach, the Chancellor of the Exchequer, rather than Long, spoke on behalf of the government.[36] The poisoning epidemic allowed advocates of legislation to mount a more convincing consumer-protectionist argument than at any point previously, insisting during the Second Reading that the arsenic epidemic would have been avoided if the 1896 Pure Beer Bill had been adopted. When challenged, however, the pure beer lobby struggled to justify this claim fully. As 'malt' or 'pure' beer could contain up to 3 per cent sugar for priming, Bostock's arsenical sugars could have been used in preparing a 'pure' beer as well as in many other 'imitation' beers which would, in any event, not have actually been outlawed. The case against the measure, it should be emphasised, was also flawed. The Country Brewers' Society characterised the Bill as heavily protectionist, assisting domestic farmers, and simultaneously 'calculated to promote the interests' of foreign barley and beer producers. And while emphasising the 'unnecessary and harassing restrictions, excessive penalties, and heavy expense' which the Bill would impose on themselves, brewers also maintained that the real losers would be the consumers and the farmers themselves.[37] In reshaping these arguments in Parliament, pure beer opponents failed to shake widespread concerns about the perceived threat to public health posed by beer brewed with sugar and other additives. Despite the opposition of Sir William Harcourt, Liberal Leader in the Commons, as well as Hicks-Beach, the Bill comfortably received a Second Reading by 245 votes to 133.

This marked the high tide for the Pure Beer Campaign. By March the sense of public crisis had passed; indeed, since late-January the epidemic, having receded, scarcely rated even a mention in the press, although little of anything was being reported in this period other than Queen Victoria's death, announced on 22 January. Crucially, Parliament and apparently the wider public were reassured by the appearance in mid July of an interim report from the Royal Commission. Kelvin and his colleagues had gathered evidence from 45 witnesses, including Edward

[35] *Ibid.*, 12 January 1901.
[36] Parliamentary Debates, Fourth Series, Vol. 91, 1441–507, 27 March 1901.
[37] *The Brewers' Almanack*, 1902, pp. 91–3.

Williamson, former secretary of Bostock & Co, which had gone into liquidation as a result of the scare, and Joseph Nicholson, the Leeds chemical manufacturer, along with medical practitioners, Medical Officers of Health, public analysts and consulting chemists, a number of whom worked for brewers. To the satisfaction of the brewing trade, the report attached sole responsibility for the poisoning to Bostock and Nicholson, the latter claiming he was unaware that the sulphuric acid was intended for a brewing sugar, despite Bostock having been a customer for several years. Kelvin also emphasised that public casualties had been minimised by the 'commendable rapidity' with which most brewers, especially in Manchester, had responded. This support was good news for the brewing trade, as was the report's indirect contribution to the debate about the proposed beer materials legislation. On the advice of Otto Hehner of the SPA and Alfred Salamon, an analytical chemist representing the Manchester brewers' expert committee, Kelvin noted that brewing sugars were not the only vehicle through which beer could become arsenical, for poison could also enter the malt through some forms of fuel, primarily gascoke, that some brewers used when drying it.[38] This confirmed the position adopted during the crisis by the *British Medical Journal*.[39] Sewell Read, the lone advocate of legislation on the 1896-9 Inland Revenue Committee, appeared before the Commission and restated the need for regulation of beer materials.[40] But this narrow concentration on ingredients ran against Kelvin's general findings, which emphasised that there was actually a much broader range of potential risks. As this obviated the need for immediate action on sugar and other 'substitutes',[41] Parliament was reassured and on 26 July the pure beer campaigners withdrew the Bill.[42]

The campaign for dedicated beer ingredients legislation was finally undermined by the appearance of Kelvin's final report in November 1903. This confirmed the initial 1901 suggestion that beer could become arsenical through poisonous malt as well as brewing sugars. It was contamination by the former method, Kelvin emphasised, which was responsible for a second, much smaller outbreak of arsenic poisoning among beer drinkers in January 1902. Confined to the town of Halifax, this killed two people, and was traced to arsenical gas coke used by several local brewers. Recalled to give evidence for a second time after the Halifax fatalities, Alfred Salamon of the Manchester brewers' expert committee went so far as to advocate the prohibition of gas coke for drying malt. It was, he argued, utilised only for 'economy' and the 'best maltsters' made no use of it.[43] This might be interpreted as an attempt to secure regulation that would undermine low-cost suppliers in order to lend a competitive advantage to rival premium producers. But, reflecting his generally voluntarist approach to the subject of regulation, Kelvin merely

---

[38] First Report of the Royal Commission to Inquire into Arsenical Poisoning, p. 5; Final Report, pp. 61–2, 299–304.
[39] *British Medical Journal*, 9 February 1901, p. 378.
[40] Cd. 1845, pp. 304–7.
[41] First Report of the Royal Commission to Inquire into Arsenical Poisoning, paras. 4–7, 22.
[42] Parliamentary Debates, Fourth Series, Vol. 98, 245, 26 July 191.
[43] Minutes of Evidence and Appendices. Vol. II, 1902–3 (HMSO, 1903), Cd. 1869, p. 71.

offered a firm recommendation that brewers dry their malt with anthracite rather than gas coke.[44] Given the pure beer lobby's emphasis on the importance of ingredients, the finding of arsenic in malt was – ironically, perhaps – something of a comfort to brewers. So too, more directly, was the assertion that brewing sugars could be used safely, so long as analyses of all ingredients were regularly conducted and manufacturers made use of the arsenic-free sulphuric acid that was commercially available. To guide brewers in their own analyses, Kelvin suggested that beer should contain no more than 1/100 of a grain of arsenic per gallon of liquid, or per pound of solid malt barley.[45] Hehner and another Public Analyst, Alfred C. Chapman, who was also a consultant to the Country Brewers' Society, had both advised the Commission that most brewers could easily meet this standard. Salamon had gone further, arguing that brewers could 'well work within' a limit of 1/150 of a grain per gallon or pound.[46] Kelvin's recommendation duly became a *de facto* standard, although it was never enacted in legislation. Chapman's successor, Dr Moritz, later told the Ministry of Food that most brewers kept well below 1/100 of a grain per gallon or pound. Regarding anything less as 'risky material', Moritz personally insisted on no more than 1/350 of a grain.[47]

The Royal Commission's findings removed any realistic prospect of new legislation on beer materials. Pure beer campaigners introduced ten separate Bills to prohibit or limit barley or hop 'substitutes' between 1903 and 1914, only one of which, in 1906, was debated in the House of Commons. The First World War brought some respite to grain producers with the temporary absence of cheap imports. To stimulate the required expansion of domestic supply the government introduced subsidies for wheat and oats, though these were repealed in 1921 and home-produced grain prices resumed their downward trend. The geographical and social successors of Cuthbert Quilter and Henry Chaplin duly emerged to press the case once more for beer regulation in the hope of inflating demand for domestic grain. In 1929 Neville Woodford Smith-Carington, Conservative MP for Rutland and Stamford in Lincolnshire, unsuccessfully sponsored a Pure Beer Bill, and followed this up in 1930 with a British Beer Bill. Under the 1930 Bill, brewers who used a minimum of British ingredients could apply to the Minister of Agriculture for an official mark, along the lines of grading schemes that were emerging for potatoes and other agricultural products. Both Bills were supported by Sir Joseph Lamb, Chairman of the Staffordshire National Farmers' Union, and other agricultural MPs like Lieutenant-Colonel Gilbert Acland-Troyte, a future President of the Central Landowners' Association from Devon, and Lieutenant-Colonel Edward Archibald Ruggles-Brise, a JP from Maldon in Essex. They were opposed by the brewing trade (represented in the House of Commons by Walter Guinness) and the Labour government. The Minister of Agriculture, Christopher Addison, characterised the provisions contained in the 1930 Bill as expensive and

---

[44] Final Report of the Royal Commission to Inquire into Arsenical Poisoning, pp. 8–10, 26–7.
[45] *Ibid.*, pp. 21–2, 36.
[46] Cd. 1869, pp. 72, 78–89.
[47] Moritz to Wightman, May 1920, MAF 101/315, PRO.

difficult to enforce: maltsters and brewers would, he suggested, be subject to constant investigation. In the face of combined trade and government opposition both measures went the way of each of their predecessors, failing to obtain even a Second Reading.[48]

This outcome, with beer subject throughout the 1880–1938 period to the Inland Revenue and Sale of Food and Drugs Acts alone, with no regulations aimed specifically at brewers, owed much to the efforts of brewers. During the crucial 1896–1903 period they mounted a defensive campaign, using their political influence with the Conservative governments to delay legislation until official inquiries had taken place, and then doing much to determine the outcomes of the Inland Revenue Inquiry and the Royal Commission through effectively marshalling evidence and 'scientific' witnesses. The strong influence of these trade witnesses on each of the investigations indicates at least an element of successful business capture. The Royal Commission, along with the government, was particularly impressed by the brewing trade's prompt and decisive response to the arsenic scare, and persuaded that brewers were competent and committed enough to regulate themselves. The failure of the Pure Beer Campaign also reflected its own weaknesses. Its two proclaimed aims of protecting agriculture and public health came together only briefly during the arsenic scare. And once public anxiety had been assuaged by the Royal Commission's initial report, the impetus for reform was lost. The Campaign could have been strengthened if grain producers had tried to build bridges with other 'public interest' advocates of regulation by placing beer materials more firmly within the context of wider food safety. An alliance could have been forged with public analysts and other supporters of general food standards. Otto Hehner, who spoke in favour of pure beer at the Inland Revenue Inquiry, linked the use of additives in beer to other food manufacturing practices which he disapproved of, like the greening of peas and other canned vegetables with copper sulphate.[49] By focusing narrowly on beer materials, the only issue which offered the prospect of inflating demand for their own produce, grain farmers minimised the odds of their campaign's success. In some respects alliances were hard to form. The Co-operative movement regarded the Pure Beer Bill as a step forward, but placed more emphasis on the merits of temperance than on regulation. An editorial in *Co-operative News* described co-operation as a better guarantee of pure food than 'an army of inspectors'.[50] Grain producers were also ineffective politically, unable to establish the type of links with the Liberal party and the temperance movement that might have countered the brewers' influence in the Conservative Party. Sir Wilfred Lawson, President of the UK Alliance for the Suppression of the Liquor Trade, summarised the temperance movement's absence of interest in pure beer during the debate on Quilter's 1896 Bill. Tampering with ingredients would be pointless, he

---

[48] Introduction of the Pure Beer Bill, Parliamentary Debates, Fifth Series, Vol. 231, 479, 1 November 1929; British Beer Bill, Vol. 245, 819–36, 21 November 1930.

[49] C. 9172, pp. 274–92.

[50] *Co-operative News*, 19 January 1901, pp. 71–2; 16 March 1901, p. 299; 21 February 1903, pp. 211–12.

opined, so long as beer retained alcohol, its single 'real damaging ingredient'.[51] And while a handful of Liberal MPs favoured pure beer legislation on consumer-protection grounds, the party leadership saw it as an irrelevant distraction from the main goal of restraining the large brewers' increasing domination of the pub trade. The 1905–14 Liberal governments duly concentrated on licensing and made no attempt to restrict the right of brewers to choose their own wholesome ingredients.[52]

The Liberal government also faced a tricky legal problem over whisky. This was prompted by the successful prosecution of several retailers by Islington Borough Council in 1905 under the SFDA for selling blended whisky that was not of the 'nature, substance and quality' desired by the purchaser. Whisky, in other words, was defined by the prosecution as the spirit distilled from malted barley alone, rather than a mixture of spirit distilled from malted barley and other unmalted cereals. The case led to a period of lengthy legal debate and uncertainty about the definition of whisky. This intersected with efforts by grain producers, closely resembling the Pure Beer Campaign and equally unsuccessful, to compel Scottish grain whisky distillers to use a minimum percentage of home produce. Since the 1880s the distillers, like the brewers, had been using substantial amounts of imported grains, primarily American maize. In July 1906 John Burns, President of the LGB, received a delegation comprising representatives of the numerous parties involved in this debate, requesting a Royal Commission on the subject. This was granted and reported in 1908. To the satisfaction of unmalted grain distillers and blenders, the Royal Commission found that the term whisky could be applied to a spirit of malted barley or a mixture of malted and unmalted barley and other cereals. And to the dismay of barley producers, 'Scotch' was found to be this type of spirit that had been distilled in Scotland – so the source of its constituent grains was immaterial.[53]

Bureaucratic discretion: the Foods Section and the 1907 Public Health Act

While the Pure Beer Campaign intersected, as in the case of whisky, with other unsuccessful attempts to arrest domestic agricultural decline through new government regulations, one important change to the general food regulatory framework was instigated by the arsenic crisis. While eliminating the prospect of beer materials legislation, Kelvin's Royal Commission inspired the establishment of a dedicated Foods Section within the Local Government Board's Medical Department. In his Final Report Kelvin suggested that the state should employ a panel of experts, with proper laboratory assistance, to undertake research on the types of ingredients and substances that were liable to contamination from arsenic and other poisons, and advise local authorities accordingly. Such work and advice was particularly vital, Kelvin argued, because the food industry was rapidly changing,

---

[51] Parliamentary Debates, Fourth Series, Vol. 39, 117, 25 March 1896.
[52] Gourvish and Wilson, *British Brewing Industry*, pp. 288–95.
[53] Ronald Weir, *The History of the Distillers Company, 1877–1939* (Oxford, 1995), pp. 122–35.

with an increasing number of prepared products sold in inadequately labelled bottles, packets and cans, often under 'fancy' names.[54]

Kelvin's suggestion of a dedicated panel of experts reflected an earlier recommendation, from the 1894–6 Parliamentary Select Committee on Adulteration, that a central scientific expert bureau be established to examine food adulteration and contamination. The idea had also been supported by the 1901 Departmental Committee on Food Colourings and Preservatives. More generally, a considerable public debate was developing over health and nutrition, prompted by the poor state of volunteers for military service.[55] Political pressure was also being exerted by MPs with an established interest in food regulation. Hudson Kearley, the multiple food retailer who had sat on the 1894–6 Select Committee and worked closely with the Society of Public Analysts in pursuit of new regulatory mechanisms, was a particularly vocal critic of existing arrangements. In June 1904, when the LGB's annual financial allocation was being debated in Parliament, Kearley argued that the department should either take its food responsibilities more seriously or transfer them to a more active regulatory body.[56] Such political pressure presumably had an indirect bearing on the subsequent establishment in 1905 of a Foods Section within the LGB's Medical Department, charged with monitoring food purity and adulteration through all 'suitable inquiries and investigations'.[57] Fittingly, given its substantial origins in the arsenic crisis, the new section was headed by George Buchanan, who had investigated the crisis in Manchester in 1900 and served as the Royal Commission's secretary.[58]

Until the birth of the Foods Section, and illustrating the general validity of Hudson's Kearley's Parliamentary criticism, the LGB had not been a forceful advocate of new food legislation. Although it had played a minor role in exhorting local authorities to enforce the SFDA more thoroughly, the primary impulse for the 1875–99 regulations came from local medical officials, public analysts, business representatives and farmers. The latter eventually looked to the Board of Agriculture for regulatory initiatives that they had failed to obtain from the LGB. The localised administration of the Sale of Food and Drugs Act, particularly the absence of uniform geographical coverage, is certainly consistent with Harris' emphasis on the haphazard nature of the growth of centralised state intervention.[59]

[54] Final Report of the Royal Commission to Inquire into Arsenical Poisoning, pp. 44–6.

[55] David Smith and Malcolm Nicolson, 'Nutrition, Education, Ignorance and Income: A twentieth century debate', Harmke Kamminga and Andrew Cunningham (eds), *The Science and Culture of Nutrition* (Amsterdam, 1995), pp. 288–318.

[56] Parliamentary Debates, Fourth Series, Vol. 135, 669–77, 2 June 1904.

[57] Local Government Board, Annual Report. Supplement Containing the Report of the Medical Officer of Health, 1905–6, Cd. 3656, p. xiv.

[58] These various activities made Buchanan extremely busy, but not particularly wealthy. Having worked unremittingly to complete his report on the arsenic outbreak in January 1901, losing several weeks of leave in the process, the Treasury expected him to take a pay cut in order to assume the Royal Commission post. Only with Walter Long's intervention was his full income restored; Personal File of Sir George Seaton Buchanan, MH 107/24, PRO.

[59] Jose Harris, *Private Lives*, pp. 57–8, 180–219.

The likelihood of central government initiating new food regulations, minimised by the general dynamics of the British state, was further impeded by the structure and established priorities of the LGB. The department was responsible for the poor law, local government, housing, town planning and public health, but its origins on the bones of the Poor Law Board ensured that this first responsibility took precedence. From its establishment in 1871 the LGB's internal culture discouraged 'technical bureaucracy', according to Bellamy, and MacLeod depicted a poorly led department which was further constrained in the 1890s by Treasury financial controls.[60] The recent study by Eyler, moreover, indicates that experts lost influence over policy-making to officials who controlled access to Ministers.[61] The LGB's limited conception of its role in administering and developing the SFDA was articulated by Herbert Preston-Thomas, then principal clerk in charge of the Public Health Department, in his testimony before Commons' committees in 1886 and 1894. Preston-Thomas acknowledged the inactivity of many local authorities, blaming the presence of shopkeepers in council chambers. But he opposed any central government role beyond the collection of statistics on the grounds that the SFDA was a local responsibility and any coercion would be ineffective. Rather than further legislation, Preston-Thomas suggested that farmers' organisations should undertake their own sampling and initiate prosecutions.[62]

Despite the election of a progressive Liberal government, the LGB's priorities hardly changed during the 1905–14 period, with the failure to introduce much-needed public health and housing reforms generally ascribed to a combination of bureaucratic reaction and incompetence on the part of the Minister, John Burns.[63] It is difficult to assess the precise commitment of the Edwardian LGB to food regulation, because most of the relevant government papers are missing, jettisoned by officials or destroyed by Luftwaffe bombs, although from his extensive diaries it is clear that Burns himself took little interest in food.[64] In general terms, however, a

---

[60] Christine Bellamy, *Administering Central-Local Relations, 1871–1919: The Local Government Board in its fiscal and cultural context* (Manchester, 1985), pp. 14–16; R. Davidson and R. Lowe, 'Bureaucracy and Innovation in British Welfare Policy, 1870–1945', in W. J. Mommsen (ed.), *The Emergence of the Welfare State in Britain and Germany, 1850–1945* (London, 1981), pp. 107–30; Roy M. MacLeod, *Treasury Control and Social Administration: A study of establishment growth at the Local Government Board, 1871–1905* (London, 1968).

[61] John M. Eyler, *Sir Arthur Newsholme and State Medicine* (Cambridge, 1997), pp. 220–6, 382–3.

[62] Report from the Select Committee on the Butter Substitutes Bill, testimony of Sir Herbert Preston-Thomas, 1887 (208), pp. 6–9 and 1894 (253), pp. 1–32.

[63] William Kent, *John Burns: Labour's Lost Leader* (London, 1950), p. 357; Brown, 'John Burns at the Local Government Board'.

[64] 'Local Government Board, History and Functions', *Current Guide*, PRO; John Burns Diary, 7 February 1906, ADD. 46324, British Library Manuscript Collection. An early biographer described these diaries as 'mirrors in which Burns admired himself'. Those who have read them may sympathise with this biographer, who also wrote, 'Interesting as they were, the diaries brought a nauseation I could not convey to my readers without boredom'; Kent, *Burns*, p. xi. The painful atmosphere of the diary is captured in the entry for 26 January 1906, in which Burns records a useful day at the office: 'Many interviews. Letters. Papers. Much work got through. A fine day's work for the people in many small ways'; John Burns Diary, 1906, ADD. 46324.

reformist 'New' Liberal government might have been expected to enhance consumer protection through some degree of closer food regulation. Anthony Howe has certainly shown that the Liberals saw food as an important political issue, yet this concern was almost solely to do with free trade and the provision of cheap food, and fell well short of regulating quality and safety. So in opposition the Liberals opposed the Conservative government's short-lived 1902 bread tax, repealed in 1903, and the Liberal government sought to promote cheaper food by reducing duties on tea (1906), sugar (1908) and cocoa (1911). But the government's wider reform programme focused on areas of public infrastructure, welfare and education and, in Howe's view, precluded regulation of economic matters, including industrial production and relationships between capital and labour.[65] In this context it is significant that in March 1906 the new Prime Minister accepted the possibility that a Court of Reference could be a precondition for effective control of food adulteration, but he ruled out the prospect of immediate legislation to establish such a body.[66] If this had been set up along the lines suggested by Kelvin, it would have monitored the production as well as the sale of food.

The prospect of a more interventionist policy, driven by a transformed LGB, briefly flickered when Asquith succeeded Campbell-Bannerman as Prime Minister in the spring of 1908. Asquith offered Winston Churchill, then a staunch advocate of social reform, a position in Cabinet as President of the LGB. Although fearing that this would lead him into 'a soup kitchen with Mrs Beatrice Webb', Churchill accepted on the understanding that the LGB would become, in the words of Paul Addison, 'the powerhouse of social policy', with pensions, labour exchanges and unemployment insurance added to its departmental responsibilities. But at the last minute Churchill was switched to the Board of Trade. Already conducting labour policy, this was deemed a much more suitable vehicle for social reform, so Burns and the LGB were left undisturbed until around 1910.[67] At this point, according to Roy MacLeod, the LGB made several new appointments, including Horace Munro, whose presence indicated the stirrings of greater departmental activism.[68]

It was within this context of minimal central intervention that the new Foods Section operated from 1905. The elements of continuity are worth reiterating: for all its social-reformist reputation, the Liberal government had a very minor direct impact on the priorities of the LGB or the development of the food regulatory regime, which was shaped by career civil servants rather than politicians. The immediate origins of the new Section were in the arsenic crisis, a great public scandal followed by a major official inquiry. This will not surprise readers who are familiar with the standard historical view of the growth of centralised state intervention in social and economic affairs. The progression from the arsenic epidemic to Kelvin's Royal Commission and the foundation of the Section is indeed consistent with the George Kitson Clark and Oliver Macdonagh models of bureaucratic

[65] Anthony Howe, *Free Trade and Liberal England, 1846–1946* (Oxford, 1997), pp. 244–52.
[66] Parliamentary Debates, Fourth Series, Vol, 154, 97, 1906.
[67] Paul Addison, *Churchill On The Home Front, 1900–1955* (London, 1992), pp. 61–2.
[68] MacLeod, *Treasury Control and Social Administration*.

growth.[69] But the character and subsequent operation of the Section also resemble the model of regulatory behaviour described by some American economists as 'bureaucratic discretion'. This involves activity by government officials who, animated by a spirit of reformist activism, initiate and develop new regulations independent of external pressures. George Buchanan, head of the Foods Section, was certainly adept at lobbying within the LGB for greater attention to food matters. And he commanded a unit, staffed entirely by bureaucrats in the LGB's Medical Department, that was very different from the type of expert panel advocated by Kelvin's Royal Commission or witnesses at the 1894–6 Parliamentary Select Committee and the Preservatives Inquiry. Buchanan initially had only one part-time assistant, Arthur MacFadden, along with a small laboratory; by 1914 there were four food inspectors. Even so, it provided the LGB's first dedicated research on food quality and safety. Once in place the Section concentrated on producing a series of reports. At the same time these reports inadvertently provided a new focus for attempted capture of the regulatory process, as business 'expert' representatives sought to influence their contents. There was considerable scope for such capture, given that the reports were generally based on interviews with food processors and distributors as well as analysts and doctors, together with visits to factories and shops and reviews of scientific literature. Research was sometimes conducted within the Section or commissioned from the Government Laboratory or academic scientists. But Buchanan and his inspectorate often relied on analysts, manufacturers or retailers for samples and expertise. These consultations with external groups reflected the Section's own limited resources and a scientific approach based on collecting evidence where possible. All sides usually had an opportunity to present their views, but, since the food inspectors produced the final reports, the Foods Section retained discretionary control of the process of interpreting and presenting the information.

In the course of its first year the Section produced just two reports on the properties and qualities of individual products, the first on tinned meat essences and the second on tartaric acid and cream of tartar.[70] The first report was a direct response to lobbying by a British manufacturer who wished to prevent the re-importation of meat extract originally sold to the army during the Boer War.[71] Although the report identified no obvious health hazard, some discolouration and a conceivable risk to invalids were sufficient grounds for Buchanan and the local Medical Officer of Health at Southampton, where the goods had come ashore, to declare the consignment 'technically unsound' and a risk to invalids. The importers then agreed to destroy the consignment, thereby satisfying the British manufacturer. In the Section's second report, Dr MacFadden recommended new standards for lead and arsenic in tartaric acid, citric acid and cream of tartar. This report followed up

---

[69] George Kitson Clark, *The Making of Victorian England, Portrait of an Age: Victorian England* (London: 1953, reprinted 1977); Macdonagh, *Early Victorian Government, 1830–1870*.

[70] LGB (Medical Department) Report of Inspectors of Foods, 1906–1908 (London: HMSO, 1908).

[71] LGB (Medical Department), Report of Inspectors of Foods, 1, 'On changes in certain meat essences kept for several years in tins', by Dr Buchanan and Dr Schryver (London: HMSO, 1906).

issues highlighted in the arsenic in beer cases. Then a new food scare, principally over imported meat, suddenly increased the fledgling Section's workload and inflated its significance for civil servants and Ministers.

The crisis was generated by critical accounts of conditions in the vast stockyards and packing plants of Chicago. Suspecting that the existing legal framework did not allow either central or local government to regulate food imports adequately, Buchanan undertook a lengthy investigation on the subject and successfully pressed John Burns to authorise new legislation. This campaign arguably conforms with the Kitson Clark and Macdonagh characterisations of bureaucratic growth in the UK. It is also an example of 'bureaucratic discretion', resulting in the 1907 Public Health Act, which provided central government with new areas of potential responsibility, including the right to seize and destroy contaminated imports. This activism qualifies the standard picture of the LGB as inert and non-interventionist. The emergence of the 1907 Act and other aspects of the Foods Section's early work are considered in detail towards the end of the chapter. But it is important first to explore the American aspects of the crisis. These highlighted a range of regulatory issues which have already emerged in this study, notably the questions of 'public interest' and business capture, and had considerable immediate relevance in the UK in 1906 and 1907.

The controversy about Chicago and meat safety arose on both sides of the Atlantic with the publication of Upton Sinclair's novel, *The Jungle*, in February 1906. Famously, Upton Sinclair had not really been interested in food regulation. As a socialist, he wanted to highlight the iniquitous and sometimes barbarous nature of capitalism: brief passages on brutalised beasts, adulterated sausages and corrupt inspectors were intended as 'mere bits of local color' according to an early historian.[72] But amid the public controversy arising from these marginal details, skilfully manipulated by his publisher, the critique of capitalism was generally ignored. In Sinclair's own phrase, oft-quoted but still resonant, 'I aimed at the public's heart, and by accident I hit it in the stomach.' Nevertheless, containing 'revelations' about insanitary conditions in the vast stockyards, rendering plants and canneries of Chicago, and promoting concern about the general methods of food preservation, the novel initiated a series of Congressional hearings and two official inquiries, one by the US Department of Agriculture (USDA) and the other a special Presidential investigation. The USDA's inquiry led to the publication of a pamphlet in defence of the Chicago packers. In addition to rejecting Sinclair's allegations as unfounded, it addressed criticisms of the trade which had been published more than one year earlier in the British *Lancet*. Suspecting that the USDA had been compromised by the close relationship which some of its officials enjoyed with the packing industry, President Theodore Roosevelt appointed a special Presidential Inquiry. Conducted by Charles Neill, the Commissioner of Labor, and James Reynolds, a senior New York social worker, this led, through the

---

[72] Mark Sullivan, *Our Times: The United States 1900–1925. Vol. II: America finding herself* (New York and London, 1927), p. 476.

Congressional hearings, to new meat inspection regulations and the passage of the 1906 Pure Food Act.[73]

These American developments generated significant publicity in the United Kingdom, which was a substantial consumer of American meat, canned and non-canned, and other American canned products. The immediate loss of British consumer confidence in these products had a pronounced impact in America, where large companies stood to gain the most from improved general safety and quality.[74] As Gabriel Kolko and James Harvey Young have shown, Chicago packers supported the new inspection regulations in 1906 for two reasons. First, the system of inspection was to be financed by the Federal government rather than the packers themselves. Second, bearing the stamp of Federal authority, the regulations were designed to restore international consumer confidence in American produce. In other words, while regulation was needed to protect consumers from dangerous or adulterated products, it also provided producers with significant trading advantages.[75]

Mark Sullivan, perhaps the first historian to assess the economic and political consequences of *The Jungle*, rooted the book's celebrity in the unease with which many people regarded the rapidly changing character and structure of food provision in the United States. In the last quarter of the nineteenth century, railroads, industrial concentration and the development and application of new technologies, most notably canning and chemical preservation of food, had spread a 'cloak of impersonality' over food provision, undermining and even displacing the roles of the neighbourhood butcher, baker and dairy farmer. Popular suspicion of this trend already had a focus in Harvey Wiley, chief chemist at the Department of Agriculture from 1883, and other campaigners for pure food legislation, including consumer representatives.[76] The general process identified by Sullivan, the emergence of a society of consumers divorced from the production of food, was broadly similar in Britain, where only 8 per cent of the population were employed in agriculture by 1914.[77] As the following chapter on preservatives indicates, the character of food provision was also changing under the impact of new technology. While there was no significant canning industry in Britain before the 1920s, large quantities of glass-packaged chemically preserved food were being consumed from the late nineteenth century onwards.[78] Peas and other green vegetables mixed with copper sulphate were among the commonest items, and dairy and meat products preserved with boric acid and borax were also prevalent. In Britain, as in America, concerns were being raised by the end of the century about the public health implications of such foods, with medical experts anxious about the long-term

---

[73] James Harvey Young, *Pure Food. Securing the Federal Food and Drugs Act of 1906* (Princeton, 1989), p. 229.
[74] Libecap, 'The Rise of the Chicago Packers, pp. 242–62.
[75] Kolko, *The Triumph of Conservatism*, pp. 98–105; Young, *Pure Food*, p. 248.
[76] Sullivan, *Our Times. Vol. II*, pp. 483–524.
[77] Harris, *Private Lives*, pp. 42–3.
[78] Plummer, *New British Industries*, pp. 229–246.

cumulative effect of consuming chemical preservatives in small doses. These concerns were expressed at an official inquiry into the use of food colourings and preservatives, held by the Local Government Board between November 1899 and May 1900.[79]

There was an additional important point of similarity between America and the UK. The emergence of the Sale of Food and Drugs Act resembled the evolution of the American Pure Food Act: both were shaped by a combination of public and private interests. In the United States the practice of food analysis and the identification of food adulteration was undoubtedly in the 'public interest', bringing protection to food consumers everywhere. But the initial impetus for Federal reform came from farmers and farming States, where Departments of Agriculture, employing state chemists, had been established originally to protect dairy farmers by countering the sale of adulterated and imitation butter.[80] Harvey Wiley, the pure food campaign's central bureaucratic figure, began his public career as State chemist for Indiana.[81] To recapitulate an important earlier point, the passage of the 1906 meat inspection regulations reflected this combination of private and public interests. The public certainly favoured a more effective system of policing the stockyards and packing plants. But during the lengthy Congressional debate which followed President Roosevelt's official investigation, meat packers exerted a powerful and effective influence, and secured their aim of a Federally financed inspection scheme that would restore international consumer confidence in their produce.[82] In Britain, in public interest terms, food law was originally devised in the 1860s and 1870s to defend consumers against the sale of fraudulently or dangerously adulterated food. The key figures here were public-spirited doctors and scientists whose work in some ways anticipated the populism of American 'muck-rakers' like Upton Sinclair. Yet these formative decades also involved the type of regulatory activity which Gabriel Kolko identified as characterising Progressive-Era America. As indicated in chapter 3, general food law was shaped from the 1870s onwards by the arguments of food manufacturers, including two businessmen MPs, Jeremiah Colman, and George Peek. Through the 1875 SFDA these manufacturers secured a definition of adulteration which gave legal protection to compound products like mustard mixed with spices or cocoa blended with starch.[83]

While Sinclair's socialist polemics were largely ignored, another of *The Jungle*'s curiosities is that the 'revelations' which were publicised had appeared one year earlier as considered observations in the *Lancet*. This has been emphasised by James Harvey Young. The author of these 1905 observations, which elicited little public controversy on either side of the Atlantic, was Adolphe Smith, a highly

---

[79] Report of the Departmental Committee Appointed to Inquire into the Use of Preservatives and Colouring of Food, Cd. 833, 1902, p. xi.
[80] Kolko, *Triumph of Conservatism*, pp. 108–9.
[81] Sullivan, *Our Times. Vol. II*, pp. 517–19.
[82] Young, *Pure Food*, pp. 244–8.
[83] Report from the Select Committee on Adulteration of Food Act (1872). Proceedings and Minutes of Evidence, Parliamentary Papers, 1874 (262), pp. 54–63, 65–9, 111–16.

experienced English journalist and politically-committed social investigator. A founding member of the Social Democratic Federation in 1881, Smith was a relative of Henry Mayhew, and his best-known work, the commentary for John Thomson's pioneering exercise in documentary photography, *Street Life in London*, published in 1876–7, followed Mayhew's *London Labour and the London Poor* in highlighting the systematic nature of poverty in the Victorian Metropolis.[84] Smith became a leading European authority on slaughterhouses and was in Chicago as the *Lancet*'s sanitary correspondent when Sinclair arrived in December 1904.[85] The two were brought together through local socialist contacts and their common interest in Packingtown, and spent a day observing conditions in the stockyards and plants.[86]

Smith's reports on Chicago, which appeared in four consecutive issues of the *Lancet* in January 1905, are worth some consideration, because they brought evidence of dangerous conditions in Chicago into the public domain 13 months before the publication of *The Jungle* in February 1906.[87] His first report concentrated on the implications of the absence in Packingtown of dedicated abattoirs. Unlike Europe, where comparable slaughterhouse sites in big urban centres like Brussels and Berlin were municipally owned, Smith noted that Chicago did not even possess a privately owned abattoir; animals were killed in the same factories which processed them into canned products. Smith's second report emphasised that in these factories animals were treated as conventional inorganic raw materials. 'The sole object', he spelt out, 'seems to be to convert each animal into saleable product in the quickest and cheapest manner possible.' Anticipating, and presumably influencing, passages in *The Jungle*, Smith described a hog's rapid and brutal journey through the factory process, which exposed the meat to filth from floors and walls, and spit from handlers, some of whom appeared to be suffering from tuberculosis and other serious infectious diseases. Federal law stipulated that stockyard animals were supposed to be inspected before and after slaughter, but this was not always observed. According to Smith this reflected the 'sort of superstitious fear that exists in America of anything which might be considered as "interfering with business"'. Smith's third and fourth reports concentrated on the human aspects of Packingtown, exploring the prevalence and causes of infectious disease among the workforce, spelling out the immense need, given Chicago's international role in providing processed meat products, for much stronger regulation.

Smith's reports prompted a limited reaction in America, with the volume of meat condemned and destroyed in Chicago suddenly and dramatically increasing, but in Britain they were overlooked or regarded as simply unfounded.[88] Some

---

[84] Richard Ovendon, *John Thomson (1837–1921). Photographer* (Edinburgh, 1997), pp. 78–88.
[85] Young, *Pure Food*, pp. 222–3.
[86] *Lancet*, 28 January 1905, pp. 258–60.
[87] *Lancet*, 7 January 1905, pp. 49–52, 14 January 1905, pp. 120–3, 21 January 1905, pp. 183–5; 28 January 1905, pp. 258–60.
[88] *Ibid.*, 16 June 1906, pp. 1719–20; 29 Decmber 1906, pp. 1819–20.

critics, according to Smith, regarded his findings as 'too violent to be credited'; others, paradoxically, had seen them as too moderate to 'create sensation'.[89] Only with the controversy generated in America by the appearance of *The Jungle*, and published in the UK in May 1906, was public attention in Britain drawn to the safety of American meat products.[90] In Britain, as in America, the book's socialist analysis was generally ignored: journalists, politicians and business representatives concentrated on its 'revelatory' aspects and the consequent public debate in America about conditions in Chicago. This debate, it might be noted, excluded any significant reference to meat inspection and slaughtering conditions within the United Kingdom, where private slaughterhouses rather than public abattoirs were still the norm. Some progress was being made in this area, with Edinburgh and Glasgow beginning work on large-scale public abattoirs in the late 1900s, but elsewhere, notably in Liverpool and Sheffield, new municipal buildings were delayed by the war. The meat trade's continuing reliance on private slaughterhouses after the war was to be described in 1928 by G.H. Collinge, President of the National Federation of Meat Traders, as 'a matter of great regret'.[91]

In 1906 extensive press coverage of the Chicago crisis was initiated in *The Times* at the end of May, which relayed the initial findings and recommendations of Neill and Reynolds, President Roosevelt's investigators. Business was immediately affected in Britain. The point of entry for much American produce, including tinned meat, was Liverpool. At a meeting of the Liverpool Health Committee on 31 May, Councillor Hartley Wilson said that the news from Chicago and Washington had damaged sales of tinned meat, both American and non-American. The city's Medical Officer of Health, Dr Hope, was optimistic, noting that there was no evidence that the type of diseased meat discussed in *The Jungle* had passed through the port. *The Times* spoke to a member of 'an old-established Liverpool firm' who had visited an American packing house. The businessman had found conditions and 'the stench' terrible, so much so that he was unable to use the suit which he had been wearing for two weeks afterwards, and he favoured a more vigorous system of inspection for American meat imports. More generally, however, Liverpool importers seemed to feel that American packing houses, while conceivably cavalier with safety when preparing food for domestic consumption, were much more scrupulous with export material.[92]

Importers were the first business sector to be affected by the loss of consumer confidence in American produce. But as this loss of confidence extended to a wide

---

[89] *Ibid.*, 23 June 1906, p. 1788.

[90] Sinclair retrospectively attributed much of the book's celebrity, in America as well as Britain, to a review written by Winston Churchill, published in June in the first edition of a short-lived English newspaper, *PTO* (named after the Irish editor and publisher, T. P. O'Connor). But Churchill, it should be noted, was hardly a major international figure in 1906, only becoming a Cabinet Minister in 1908; Upton Sinclair, *The Autobiography of Upton Sinclair* (London, 1963), pp. 130–1.

[91] *The Retail Meat Trade: a practical treatise by specialists in the meat trade* (London, 1928), Vol. I, pp. 185–90.

[92] *The Times*, 1 June 1906.

range of canned and non-canned meat produce, the main impact of the crisis was felt by retailers. *The Grocer*, trade journal of the British Grocers' Federation, was appalled by developments, carrying an editorial entitled 'An 'Orrible Tale' on 2 June. Of *The Jungle* it was frankly dismissive. 'There has now come forward a novelist who compels people to take him seriously by making them sick.' *The Grocer* characterised the unnamed 'novelist' as a sensationalist, whose malevolent claims were entirely groundless. After all, 'these great packing establishments' employed 'carefully devised means for ensuring the safety of the consumer of their products. The counter-reply is that all these safeguards are useless because the Government inspectors, posted at every point where needed, are corrupt scoundrels in league with others still worse. All we can say is that we simply don't believe it.' Sinclair was not entirely to blame for lost sales, however; for taking the novel's allegations seriously, and precipitating the noisy and exaggerated public debate, President Roosevelt was also culpable. Invoking the 'good old British spirit of fair-play', the journal's readers were encouraged to listen to the packers' side of the story before reaching any conclusions: 'Let the criminal be heard before being shot.'[93]

A more decided view on the situation was presented in the *Lancet*. The journal's editor noted with great satisfaction that the substance of its 1905 findings had been 'reinforced' by *The Jungle*, and that the preliminary Neill-Reynolds report read like a summary of Smith's second despatch.[94] Interest in the controversy extended to Parliament. Just as Sinclair was never to figure by name in the Congressional debates, appearing only as 'a man who wrote a book', in the House of Commons Hugh Cecil Lea, newspaper proprietor and Liberal MP for East St. Pancras (in north central London), referred obtusely to 'a recently published book'.[95] With the House about to vote on Army Estimates, and having recently seen for himself the 'absolutely revolting' packing houses in Chicago, Lea said that the book was not exaggerated, adding that conditions in Omaha, St. Louis, were similar. He asked the Secretary of State for War, Richard Haldane, to give an undertaking that army canteens would not be supplied with American canned food until confidence in their 'purity and excellence' had been restored. Although replying that such a blanket ban would be unhelpful, given that bad tinned meat might come from sources other than America, Haldane promised that the army would obtain only the best and purest produce, from whatever source. A more positive government response followed one day later, on 8 June, when John Burns, impelled by the crisis for once to focus on food, said that Sir Edward Grey, the Foreign Secretary, had been asked to assess the reliability of the American system of inspection. The stockyards were duly examined by the British Consul in Chicago, who submitted a report which reached the LGB, via the Foreign Office, on 18 June. Despite persistent pressure from MPs, however, lasting until October, the contents of this report were never released.[96]

[93] *The Grocer*, 2 June 1906, p. 1555.
[94] *Lancet*, 9 June 1906, p. 1626.
[95] Young, *Pure Food*, p. 251.
[96] Parliamentary Debates, Fourth Series, Vol. 158, 544–6, 7 June 1906; 617, 8 June 1906; Vol. 159, 21–2, 19 June 1906; Vol. 163, 1102, 31 October 1906.

During the first week of June there were other signs of lost confidence in American produce. Poor Law Guardians at Birkenhead and Newton Abbot removed American tinned meat from workhouses, where they had been widely served. More seriously, having reflected on the matter, the Liverpool Health Committee advised the public against consuming canned products from Chicago, at least until there was evidence that the conditions alleged by Sinclair had been disproved or rectified. Dr Hope reasserted that there was no danger from the Chicago produce passing through Liverpool, but agreed that the Committee had to err on the side of caution, because President Roosevelt had lent 'his immense weight and authority to the exposure of the abominable conditions existing in Chicago'.[97] With pressure on retailers intensifying, *The Grocer* rejoined the debate on 9 June, providing an all-encompassing conspiracy theory for the crisis. First, it cursed the timing of the controversy. Coinciding with the early summer 'picnic' season, when sales of tinned meat usually rose, its impact on an important branch of the retail business was especially severe. Second, it questioned the apparently hidden motives of the individuals behind the allegations: 'is some party of capitalists bent on driving down meat shares? Or again, are the Vegetarians assisting the outcry?' Third, it re-emphasised the role of the President. His arguably 'necessary reform' was bringing 'a vast amount of mischief to thousands of innocent British traders'.[98]

Moved by the material losses of its members, the British Grocers' Federation contacted President Roosevelt directly. Advising that his actions had 'paralysed' sales of all American produce, the Federation warned that British grocers would boycott all American stock unless he provided an assurance that they were safe. With the meat inspection regulations finally passing through Congress in the last week of June, President Roosevelt could offer just such an assurance, which he did via the US Ambassador in London on 7 July. His telegrammed message from Oyster Bay to the Ambassador read, 'You are at liberty to inform the Grocers' Federation that under New Law we can and will guarantee the fitness in all respects of Canned Meat bearing the Government Stamp. If any trouble comes therewith protest can be made at once, not merely to sellers of goods, but to United States Government itself.' In conference in Sheffield on 12 July the Federation considered this response. Some delegates remained angry. J. F. Steel from Bolton, for example, said that in promoting the new regulations Roosevelt had 'damned the whole trade', made the public 'highly nervous' and affected home and colonial as well as American import trade. On the whole, however, the Federation announced its satisfaction.[99] A large poster was prepared for display on members' premises, reproducing the President's words in large-face type above a declaration from the Federation's Secretary, Arthur J. Giles: 'The Public will thus see that the Millions of Packages of Canned Foods consumed annually in the United

---

[97] *The Times*, 6–8 June 1906.
[98] *The Grocer*, 9 June 1906, p. 1619.
[99] *The Times*, 12 July 1906.

Kingdom are prepared under Government Supervision and therefore are reliable for Human Consumption'.[100]

Additional conflicting verdicts on the President's actions, supplied by American commentators, were carried in *The Times*. On 26 June it published a lengthy article by an anonymous American correspondent who welcomed the investigation and the meat inspection regulations. Following lurid tales of business malpractice in life assurance and railway management as well as in meat-packing, these actions had helped to restore the good name of American business and the United States itself. Literally balancing this view, taking up the opposite half of the page, was an 'Open Letter to President Roosevelt and the American Nation', placed originally in the American press on 8 June by the Franco-American Food Company of Jersey City. The essence of this protest was that neither Roosevelt's investigation or the new regulations had referred to the packers, presumably including the Franco-American Food Company, 'whose methods are above aboard and whose goods are of such high quality as to be a credit to the American nation'.[101]

These contrasting optimistic views, on the positive character of the Federal reforms and the essentially progressive nature of the American packing trade, were challenged by Adolphe Smith, writing again in the *Lancet* in July and August. Responding to the US Department of Agriculture's published defence of the packers, Smith questioned the integrity of the American meat inspectorate. Patiently addressing the USDA pamphlet's criticisms of his original articles and *The Jungle* point by point, he asked why Federal officials were willing to 'appear before the public as if they held a brief on behalf of the Chicago packers?'[102] This, of course, echoed President Roosevelt's own suspicions about the relationship between the department and the industry. It will be remembered that the Neill-Reynolds investigation was only appointed because Roosevelt doubted the independence of USDA officials. Smith was anxious about the implications of 'the Popular Press' joining the crusade against the packers. Gabriel Kolko has commented on the ultimately conservative consequences of 'muck-raking': sensation-seeking journalists were concerned only with stirring up the fears and prejudices of their readers, and had no interest in altering wider configurations of economic and political power.[103] In similar vein, Smith warned that, while promoting public interest in reform, the popular press lacked the technical expertise to ensure that effective reform was actually carried out. In other words, popular news journalists would be incapable of assessing whether the meat inspection regulations brought real or merely cosmetic change.[104] The character of these regulations was considered by the *Lancet*'s editor, reviewing events at the end of 1906. Uncertain whether they were to apply to meat for overseas as well as domestic consumption, he urged public health authorities to remain vigilant examiners of American imports, and

[100] Copy of the Poster, dated 2 August 1906, MH 113/48, Public Record Office, Kew (PRO).
[101] *The Times*, 26 June 1906.
[102] *Lancet*, 14 July 1906, pp. 109–16.
[103] Kolko, *Triumph of Conservatism*, pp. 111–12.
[104] *Lancet*, 4 August 1906, pp. 323–4.

focused renewed attention on the role of the Federal inspectorate. Responsible for policing exports, this body consisted of just 411 officers. According to Sinclair's calculations, working 300 days each year, each of these officers would have to inspect 105 animals per hour. 'It is on such a guarantee as this', the journal noted, 'that for many years the British public has been consuming Chicago meat. No wonder if in these circumstances and when the facts became known there was a great falling off in the importations from Chicago.' The journal concluded by describing the 1906 pure food legislation and the new meat inspection regulations as superficial improvements: nothing less than the demolition of Packingtown and the erection in its place of proper abattoirs would render Chicago meat safe for consumption.[105]

This renewed call for regulatory vigilance can be read as the *Lancet*'s contribution to a debate about Britain's food laws. An alternative 'public interest' perspective had been expressed in August in the *British Food Journal*, organ of the British Analytical Control. This claimed that the scandal had alerted consumers to the general problem of adulteration and the dangers of alleged government activity. British Analytical Control undoubtedly saw the crisis as an opportunity finally to generate wider business support for its system of voluntary standards, emphasising that 'hurried advertising by manufacturers' would not be enough to regain public confidence in meat products. Such would only be forthcoming through 'independent' action – via the British Analytical Control, in other words.[106] This was to prove a false hope, however, and in Britain – as in America – the main regulatory consequence of the scare was pressure for new government legislation. Particular attention was given to the apparent need to improve the inspection of imported meat and meat products. This had long been viewed as an issue of concern, given the expansion of imports in the closing decades of the nineteenth century, bolstered by technological and transportation innovations like canning and refrigerated cargo holds. A Select Committee on Marking Foreign Meat had been established in 1893 to examine various aspects of the trade, most notably the practice – allegedly widespread – of 'misrepresenting' imported frozen meat as home-killed. The Committee noted that the main problem in this area was the covert substitution of American frozen beef for English and Scottish, although there was also an extensive trade in frozen mutton passed off as fresh.[107] While this earlier inquiry had concentrated largely on commercial questions, with domestic supply depressed by the growth of international competition, the official regulatory focus on 1906 fell more closely on public health and safety. Besides promising an inspection of the American stockyards and the effectiveness of their regulation, in Parliament on 8 June Burns had also said that he was looking at the powers held by British local authorities over the inspection of imports. He added later that if these

---

[105] *Ibid.*, 29 December 1906, p. 1820.
[106] *British Food Journal*, August 1906, p. 141.
[107] *Report from the Select Committee on Marking of Foreign Meat*, 25 August 1893, Parliamentary Papers, 1893–94, 214, pp. iii–xviii.

proved to be inadequate he was prepared to strengthen them through legislation.[108] This reflected George Buchanan's developing activities in the LGB's Foods Section. Buchanan exploited the unexpected American developments with great skill, eventually securing increased legislative powers for the LGB in the shape of the 1907 Public Health Act. Reporting to Burns on a regular basis throughout the crisis, both personally and by memo, he linked the packing-house conditions described in the Neill-Reynolds report and *The Jungle* with the recommendations of the earlier preservatives and arsenic-poisoning enquiries.[109] Collectively, he asserted, these findings and descriptions highlighted the need for centralised action to counter the sale of contaminated food. Buchanan strengthened the case for more robust regulation in two other ways. First, he could point to three new reports by the Foods Section which proposed controls to reduce health risks.[110] Second, he conducted interviews with the Medical Officers of Health who were responsible for food inspection in the Port of London. These officials told him that existing local powers were entirely inadequate, increasing the need, he insisted, for centralised direction of new regulations.[111] Such contacts between medical officals at the local and national levels signalled a major change from the LGB's previous style of detached recording of local adulteration statistics.

Having obtained Burns' ear, Buchanan then drafted what became the 1907 Public Health (Regulations as to Food) Act. This offered the prospect of an unprecedented degree of central government intervention in the regulation of food provision. Its primary object was to enable local authorities to conduct closer inspection and regulation of imports, with the power to seize and destroy contaminated produce. But where local authorities were unwilling or unable to act, central government, in the form of the LGB, was entitled to step in and assume like powers. In seeking enhanced powers for his department, Buchanan seems to have been pushing an open door, for the Liberal government apparently regarded the crisis of confidence in American produce as a significant political priority. Only three months earlier, it should be emphasised, Henry Campbell-Bannerman, the Prime Minister, had indicated that there was insufficient time to legislate for a Court of Reference. Now he sought talks with Burns on his department's intended response on 8 June, and the rest of the Cabinet pronounced its support for the proposed regulations on 10 July.[112] The Grocers' Federation opposed them, continuing to assert – in Buchanan's words – that 'there was nothing in the so-called "Chicago scare".'[113]

---

[108] Parliamentary Debates, Fourth Series, Vol. 158, 704–5, 8 June 1906, 1371–2, 18 June 1906.

[109] John Burns, Diary, 5 and 7 June 1906, ADD. 46324, The British Library Manuscript Collections.

[110] LGB (Medical Department), Report of Inspectors of Foods, 3, 'On certain imported meat foods of questionable wholesomeness', by Dr Buchanan (1906); 4, 'On inquiries with regard to the wholesomeness of tripe of home and foreign origin', by Dr MacFadden (1906); 6, 'On preservatives in meat foods packed in cans or glass', by Dr MacFadden (1906).

[111] Buchanan to Burns, 10 June 1906; Buchanan note of discussion with London Medical Officers of Health, 11 June 1906; MH 113/48, PRO.

[112] John Burns, Diary, 8 June and 10 July 1906.

[113] Buchanan to Burns, 26 October 1906, MH 113/48, PRO.

Opposition to the Act was also expressed within Parliament, largely because of the wide extension of central government powers which it proposed.[114] Dr George Cooper, Liberal MP for Southwark and chair of the Parliamentary Public Health Committee, described it as 'the most anti-democratic measure that had been introduced in the House of Commons in modern times'. Cooper's unsuccessful attempt to have the Bill's Second Reading postponed in August 1907 was supported by another Liberal MP, Henry Watt, a Glaswegian businessman and lawyer, who characterised its provisions as 'drastic'. Burns responded firmly, defending the Bill as 'simple, useful, necessary' and 'too long delayed'. To justify the proposed powers he referred to the large expansion in consumption of tinned imported meat since 1872, amounting to an increase of 14lb to 56lb per head per annum, and emphasised the American origins of 50 per cent of this produce, the great bulk of which came from 'a particular city'. Recalling the Chicago scare of 1906 in this manner, Burns indicated that proposed regulations would enable port sanitary authorities to deal with unwholesome imports and obtain information on the conditions under which items were manufactured, especially the sausages, brawn and other items which were 'consumed mainly in the poorer districts'. At the same time he asserted that responsible and honest traders in hygienic food would not be harassed or inconvenienced, and noted that any regulations issued under the Act would be placed before Parliament for 40 days before coming into operation. This concession to his critics, along with the government's substantial majority in the House of Commons, ensured that the new legislation enjoyed a comfortable Parliamentary passage.[115]

During the Bill's Second Reading Burns spoke at length about the case of the Liebig's tinned meat extract re-imported from South Africa which had been the subject of the Foods Section's first report. Without the 1907 Bill, Burns argued, the situation had only been resolved because the importer agreed to 'forego his profit' and have the goods destroyed. This was not quite the entire story, however, for the importer had only agreed to destroy the produce because George Buchanan, at the manufacturer's request, had inspected the produce at Southampton with a local Medical Officer of Health and declared it unsound.[116] For the manufacturer who had initiated the case, this result removed from the market a rival product, one of its own, without the cost of buying up the stock. With such an outcome the episode indicates that there were clear limits to the Foods Section's powers as a regulatory agency. In this respect the Foods Section's early activities, assisting rather than regulating the activities of food manufacturers, resembled the process which Gabriel Kolko observed to be at work during the emergence of the 1906 reforms in the USA. These benefited rather than hindered the big packing businesses, because the Federally financed inspection scheme restored consumer confidence in meat

[114] Kenneth Brown, *John Burns* (London, 1977), pp. 131.

[115] Parliamentary Debates, Fourth Series, Vol. 179, 1442–55, 2 August 1907; Vol. 180, 1723–45, 15 August 1907.

[116] LGB (Medical Department), Report of Inspectors of Foods, 1, 'On changes in certain meat essences kept for several years in tins', by Dr Buchanan and Dr Schryver (1906).

products at little cost to the industry. The successful lobbying by the Liebig's extract manufacturer also balances the picture of the 1907 Public Health as an example of undiluted bureaucratic discretion. Clearly there was an element of business interest in strengthening central government interventionist powers, which Burns explicitly recognised when justifying the need for new legislation. It might be significant that the vocal supporters of the 1907 Act in Parliament included Thomas Idris, chair of the mineral waters manufacturing company, who in welcoming the attempt to remove unwholesome imports from the market referred to his 40 years in the food and drinks industry.[117]

The Jungle's impact on the food industry and state regulation of business was not as great in Britain as in America. There was no substantial canning industry in Britain, and hence no significant industrial response to the crisis. And there was already in place a framework of regulation, designed to protect consumers against the sale of dangerously or fraudulently adulterated food. But by the early 1900s the 1875 SFDA was three decades old, and the preservatives and arsenic-contamination inquiries provided some evidence that the food industry, which was making increasing use of chemical and other artificial substitutes, had outgrown its original legal framework. *The Jungle* intersected with these concerns, and gave the newly established LGB Foods Section its first important job, and a considerable body of work thereafter. While the new Section clearly never matched the empire building of Harvey Wiley's chemical work within the US Department of Agriculture, George Buchanan, the Foods Inspector, obtained greater powers of inspection for the Local Government Board as a result of the crisis, which led to the 1907 Public Health legislation. Much of his early research was prompted by *The Jungle*. One of Buchanan's main concerns after 1906 remained that the US system of inspection, despite the introduction of the meat inspection regulations, failed to provide British consumers with sufficient protection. This reflected Adolphe Smith's misgivings about the USDA's connections with the packers, and the *Lancet*'s general concern that both the Pure Food Act and the meat inspection regulations had brought superficial rather than genuine change.

The Foods Section produced a series of reports before the First World War. In the third of these, 'On certain imported meat foods of questionable wholesomeness', Buchanan characterised the US Federal inspection system as reasonable in theory, but questionable in practice because of the scale of industrial operations and the small number of officials. The weakness of this system resulted, he believed, in the importation to Britain of much frozen scrap meat, notably tripe, kidneys and tongue, that was definitely a risk to health.[118] In terms of the impact of developments on business, in the absence of a significant canning industry in Britain the traders worst affected by the temporary consumer boycott of canned products in 1906 were retailers. The response of the Grocers' Federation to lost

---

[117] Parliamentary Debates, Fourth Series, Vol. 180, 125, 15 August 1907.
[118] LGB (Medical Department), Report of Inspectors of Foods, 3, 'On certain imported meat foods of questionable wholesomeness', by Dr Buchanan (1906).

sales, urging President Roosevelt to provide fresh assurances about the quality and safety of American goods, is a useful illustration of the value of comparative history. The Grocers' threatened boycott of all American canned goods surely added weight to the President's argument that new regulations, designed to increase international confidence in the Chicago packing trade, were unambiguously in the interests of business.

5

Assessing food additives: regulating chemical preservatives, 1888–1938

'I do not see why a grocer should drug me.' Thus Otto Hehner, a leading figure in the Society of Public Analysts (SPA) from the 1880s to the 1920s, encapsulated his profession's suspicion about chemical preservatives in food and drink when appearing before an official inquiry in 1900.[1] It would take another quarter of a century and a second investigation of preservatives, in which Hehner again featured, before the Ministry of Health introduced general regulations to control their use. The 1925 Preservatives Regulations were the product of a lengthy debate that illuminates the attitudes of business, analysts, the medical profession and government officials toward the food laws. The enactment of the 1925 Regulations also exerted a profound influence on the wider debate over food standards in the 1930s.

There was a long tradition of using dehydration, salting, pickling, bottling or smoking to extend the shelf life of the most easily perishable foods and to cope with gluts.[2] But from the 1870s there was a search for new and improved methods of food preservation that would cope with the increasing volume and variety of foods being transported over longer distances. The commercial objective was not simply to supply greater quantities of food, but to deliver food in a condition to obtain the premium prices associated with fresh produce. Freezing or chilling techniques came into wider use for meat and dairy products; canning and bottling advanced with newly designed containers and more mechanised processes. These new techniques presented technical challenges and often required investments in specialised production and storage facilities. Moreover there was consumer resistance, since canning had gained a poor reputation due to flawed methods of production in the 1850s and the new frozen meat was regarded suspiciously in the 1870s and 1880s. Such concerns about quality depressed the price of canned and frozen foods and led manufacturers and traders to employ chemical preservatives. For the food trades, chemical preservatives offered an inexpensive and convenient

---

[1] Report of the Departmental Committee Appointed to Inquire into the Use of Preservatives and Colouring of Food (London, 1902), Cd 833, 1902, p. 194 (hereafter Committee on Food Preservatives).

[2] C. Anne Wilson, *Waste Not, Want Not: Food preservation from early times to the present day* (Edinburgh, 1991); J.C. Drummond and A. Wilbraham, *The Englishman's Food: A history of five centuries of English diet* (London, 1939), pp. 374–87.

method of keeping foods fresh. They conformed most easily with established systems of food production and marketing, requiring less investment in specialist production or storage facilities than either canning or refrigeration. The chemicals had little effect on the appearance of foods and, with cookery writers identifying salted food as less nutritious from the 1850s, manufacturers and retailers regarded chemical preservatives as the best way to satisfy a developing consumer preference for milder-tasting butter or meat products.[3] A report by the Government Laboratory in 1900 indicated that 39 per cent of foods contained chemical preservatives or 'antiseptics'.[4] The most widely used preservative was boric acid which appeared in perishable foods such as milk, cream, butter and margarine, bacon, ham and pork pies as well as canned and bottled meats. Salicylic acid, derived from willow-bark, was employed in jams, wine, and cordials and drinks, particularly non-alcoholic, or temperance, and it was often added to fruit pulp to cope with summer gluts. A less-common preservative was formalin, a solution of formaldehyde, which was found in milk and meat products. The chemicals had medicinal applications: boron compounds and salicylic acid were used as antiseptics for treating wounds; formaldehyde was a disinfectant commonly employed for preserving medical specimens.[5]

The 1875 SFDA permitted food additives that were intended to keep food fit for human consumption, providing the compounds were not harmful, ineffective or merely added to increase bulk. And the medicinal applications of the chemicals used as preservatives might have been expected to legitimise their application to foods. Yet concerns about the 'antiseptics' soon appeared in the medical press. The *Lancet* questioned the health implications of salicylic acid in 1877, borax in 1879, and benzoates in 1886; several items attacked the practice of adding boric acid to milk as a danger, especially to children.[6] By 1888 preservatives were being criticised by public analysts and two years later both Otto Hehner and Charles Cassal, two leading analysts, advocated a complete ban.[7] The *Lancet* reported on their recommendations and staked out its own territory by calling for medical research on the effects of boric acid and salicylic acid.[8] In 1890–1 an LGB report noted that boric acid could be harmful in large quantities.[9] Given such suspicions, public analysts had the option of certifying preservatives to be a form of adulteration, but for a successful prosecution they would have to convince a magistrate that a specific chemical actually presented a danger to health. When Cassal, in his role as public

---

[3] Lynette Hunter, 'Nineteenth and Twentieth Century Trends in Food Preserving: Frugality, nutrition or luxury', in *Waste Not, Want Not*, pp. 142–8.
[4] Report of the Departmental Committee Appointed to Inquire into the Use of Preservatives, p. xi.
[5] Rio Tinto Zinc, *The Borax Story* (1953).
[6] *Lancet*, 6 January 1900, pp. 48–50 and 20 January 1900, p. 181.
[7] Bernard Dyer and Mitchell Ainsworth, *The Society of Public Analysts: Some reminiscences of its first fifty years and a review of its activities* (Cambridge, 1932), pp. 116–17.
[8] *Lancet*, 10 January 1891, pp. 96–7.
[9] *Ibid.*, 2 January 1897, pp. 56–60; Dyer and Ainsworth, *Society of Public Analysts*, pp. 116–17.

analyst for the Kensington vestry, declared a sample of butter adulterated due to the presence of boric acid, the local authority sought guidance from the LGB.[10] Alfred Adrian, an assistant secretary, replied that the LGB had no authority on the matter and that any public analyst could declare the level of preservatives in a sample to be 'excessive'. Kensington then consulted three eminent doctors who failed to agree on whether there was any health risk so Cassal proceeded on the basis that some boric acid was acceptable if declared on the label. This local ruling carried little weight in the absence of authoritative medical opinion against boric acid, especially when the chemical was present only in small quantities.

The next opportunity to publicise the analysts' criticisms came with the Commons' inquiry into the general operation of the SFDA in 1894. A petition from the Health Committee of the Corporation of Glasgow characterised preservatives as a new and increasing form of adulteration.[11] For the SPA, Cassal and Hehner criticised the use of the various chemical preservatives as fundamentally unsound and unnecessary. Hehner typified one recurring line of attack when he argued that since the chemicals were designed to inhibit the actions of bacteria, they must 'produce disorders of digestion'.[12] When recalled for closer questioning, Hehner retreated to the view that preservatives were unnecessary because they could be replaced entirely by refrigeration. In contrast government officials who appeared before the Commons committee were uninterested in the subject. The deputy-principal of the Inland Revenue's laboratory refused to express any opinion on the effects of preservatives on the grounds that it was a medical not a chemical question.[13] The only food trade witness to devote much time to preservatives was Frederick Lloyd, consulting chemist to the British Dairy Farmers' Association.[14] Lloyd favoured banning preservatives in milk on the assumption that eating chemicals was inadvisable; for cream, though fearful of the commercial effects of controls, he thought it a suitable issue for any future Court of Reference, the SPA's idea for a central panel on food matters. When it came to butter Lloyd enthusiastically advocated a complete ban on preservatives on the grounds that imported butter, then taking a growing share of the market, was 'loaded' with chemicals and a danger to public health. In its final report the Commons committee noted the absence of clear evidence that preservatives were harmful, but that several countries had introduced controls on their use. It recommended further investigations by 'recognised scientific authorities' to provide a definitive judgement.

The *Lancet* took up the challenge by first marking out the medical profession's territory and authority.[15] An editorial dismissively noted that the Commons committee of 'traders and politicians' lacked the scientific expertise required for

---

[10] Committee on Food Preservatives, pp. 131, 400–02.
[11] *Report on Food Products Adulteration*, 1896 (288), pp. 167–9.
[12] *Ibid.*, pp. 3, 60–1, 72–3.
[13] Report on Food Products Adulteration, 1894 (253), pp. 43, 72.
[14] Report on Food Products Adulteration, 1896 (288), pp. 31, 46–7.
[15] *Lancet*, 16 October 1897, pp. 56–60.

effective judgement. Equally the *Lancet* regarded the opinions of public analysts as worthless on health matters unless they possessed a medical qualification; the journal consulted the medical profession on whether preservatives were hazardous or required any form of regulation. Since preservatives were often used in milk, the subject intersected with the extensive research and debate in medical and public health circles from the 1880s about the relationships between milk and tuberculosis and epidemic diarrhoea.[16] But, despite the *Lancet's* self-confident tone, the ten published responses from leading doctors in the field of digestion agreed only on the lack of definitive evidence about preservatives. Two of the ten doctors favoured a complete prohibition on preservatives. German Sims Woodhead described preservatives as adulterants, arguing that the burden of proof should be on the seller. Dr Halliburton, a physiologist, distinguished between 'foreign' antiseptics, such as boric acid, that were suspect as not being found in foods naturally and others, like salicylic acid, that were. Others, though suspicious about the chemicals, were either uncertain about their effects, especially in the long-term, or unwilling to support regulation. Dr Pavy, a pioneer in chemical pathology, considered preservatives were unfair to fresh food producers, but he rejected any legal limit because it would imply that there was no risk below that point, thereby abrogating the seller's responsibility. Dr Lauder Brunton, one of the doctors previously consulted by Kensington vestry, described regulations as 'injurious and meddlesome' because decomposing food was a greater threat and he was confident that producers would naturally use the lowest possible levels of preservatives. Given the general uncertainty, the most common position was support for labelling to inform consumers about the presence of chemicals so they could choose to avoid them. Further 'public interest' pressure came from Alfred Hill, Birmingham's public analyst and Medical Officer of Health.[17] Hill's dual role unified the two strands of professional concern and satisfied the *Lancet's* criteria of professional legitimacy on medical matters. After conducting his own local sampling of preservatives in food, Hill persuaded the Society of Medical Officers of Health in 1899 to pass a resolution against preservatives.

The pressure from analysts, doctors and some local authorities created sufficient uncertainty about preservatives for the LGB to establish a Departmental Committee in 1899 to investigate preservatives and colourings in foods. The chairman, Sir Herbert Maxwell MP, was a government whip and author with a keen interest in natural sciences and connections to Scottish agricultural societies. The other members of the Committee were Professor Thorpe, head of the Government Laboratory and vice-president of the Royal Society, Professor Tunnicliffe, who had published papers on preservatives, and Dr Bulstrode. Between November 1899 and May 1900 the Committee took evidence from 78 witnesses, representing a broad range of

---

[16] Deborah Dwork, *War is Good for Babies and Other Young Children: A history of the infant and child welfare movement in England, 1898–1918* (London, 1987), chapters 1–3.

[17] J.F. Liverseege, *Adulteration and Analysis of Food and Drugs* (London, 1932), p. 94.

interest groups and opinion, though most testimony centred on milk, cream and butter. The emphasis on medical and scientific opinion was apparent from the presence among the witnesses of 30 doctors and Medical Officers of Health and 13 analysts, whereas doctors had been largely absent from the 1894–6 hearings into the workings of the SFDA.

The food industry's limited response to the criticisms of preservatives during the 1890s had allowed the pressure to build and indeed contributed to the appointment of the Preservatives Committee. The main business interests threatened by any regulation were chemical companies, but the majority were small firms with little incentive to engage in lobbying since sales of food preservatives were only a small portion of their business. There was one large enterprise, Borax Consolidated Ltd, an Anglo-American firm established in 1896 to combine the main US boron producer with a chemical company that was its leading British distributor.[18] Borax Consolidated was engaged in a defence of its products against American critics during the early 1900s. It was not asked to testify before the Departmental Committee, but circulated a pamphlet to doctors presenting scientific and medical evidence in support of boron food preservatives.[19] In the British hearings the case for preservatives was made primarily by food distributors and their trade associations with few manufacturers appearing, though a number of doctors and analysts testified on behalf of food processors. For the president of the Liverpool Provision Trade Association the matter was straightforward: 'Speaking from the commercial standpoint, we are not advocates of borax, we simply give the public and trade what they wish, and it is immaterial to us in what it is packed so long as the people take it.'[20] More often producers and distributors argued that preservatives were required to meet changing consumer tastes: people would no longer accept the more heavily salted butters and meats that had been popular 30 years earlier. A London provision broker reported that urban consumers of meat 'neither like salt nor fat; formerly they did not mind a little salt – a good deal in fact'.[21] Preservatives permitted milder flavours. In addition, trade witnesses supplied a 'public interest' defence of preservatives by stressing their value in keeping foods safe for longer. The Dairy Trade Protection Society's representative, an analyst, proclaimed boron as safer than, and preferable to, 'multiplied micro-organisms' in decomposing food which, while less than a ringing endorsement, offered a positive vision.[22] A cider maker urged that 'honest' producers should be trusted to employ a little salicylic acid which would benefit consumers and was preferable to poor quality cider.[23] Trade representatives made much of the value of the antiseptic qualities, associations with healing and medical properties of the new chemicals to counter the portrayals of them as new, sinister or unnatural.

---

[18] The firm passed wholly into British ownership by 1914; Rio Tinto Zinc, *Borax Story*, p. 15.
[19] Committee on Food Preservatives, pp. 172–5.
[20] *Ibid.*, p. 29
[21] *Ibid.*, p. 20.
[22] *Ibid.*, p. 137.
[23] *Ibid.*, p. 255.

With the 1890s agitation over preservatives really coming from analysts and doctors, there had been no sign of lobbying from the producers and suppliers of preservative-free products who stood to be the main beneficiaries of any regulation of 'antiseptics'. However, these commercial interests took advantage of the 1899–1900 hearings to advocate some control of their competitors. Thomas Blackwell testified that his firm's fruits, jams, vegetables and potted meats contained no preservatives, though some export lines had artificial colourings. He was willing to see labelling of the presence of preservatives, but did not press for a total ban.[24] A cider-manufacturing MP declared his product free of salicylic acid and then pointed to advertising which implied that various preservatives were used in imported ciders and some mineral waters.[25] Business opinions were most divided in the milk trade. Larger producers with cold storage facilities were less reliant on chemical preservatives: a Danish adviser to the Manchester Pure Milk Supply Company stated that chemicals were unnecessary. The managing director of the Aylesbury Dairy Company reported that adverse press comment had led his firm to abandon chemicals entirely.[26] He called for a total ban on the grounds that any legal limits would be unenforceable and argued that only preservative-free milk was pure. There was agricultural support from the Central Chamber of Agriculture whose representatives described preservatives as a potential danger to babies and invalids. This testimony reflected a belief among leading dairy farmers that preservatives depressed fresh milk prices by enabling retailers to dispose of supplies over a longer period. But farming opinion, and practice, was divided with a strong body of opinion regarding the chemicals as essential to supply distant markets.

The leading 'public interest' critics who had initiated the campaign against preservatives all testified before the Committee. Cassal and Hehner appeared in their roles as public analysts and Alfred Hill represented the Incorporated Society of Medical Officers of Health. Given the terms of the SFDA, they concentrated on trying to show that chemicals were injurious to health. As in earlier debates over water purity, the various expert opinions were an amalgam of science, philosophical assumptions and policy preferences, though few individuals agreed entirely or subscribed to the full range of objections.[27] One approach was to claim that chemical preservatives were fundamentally or inherently suspect even if there was no clear proof of harm. Professor McFadyen, principal of the Royal Veterinary College, asserted that, unlike salt, chemical preservatives were unnatural and 'foreign to the body' and liable to interfere with digestive processes.[28] Several physiologists argued that, since preservatives destroyed living organisms, there was a presumption of damage to humans, and Cassal made similar claims from the public

[24] *Ibid.*, pp. 30–7, 170–1.
[25] *Ibid.*, pp. 227–9.
[26] *Ibid.*, pp. 194–201.
[27] C. Hamlin, *A Science of Impurity: water analysis in nineteenth century Britain* (Bristol, 1990).
[28] Committee on Food Preservatives, pp. 59–61, 131–6, 222.

analysts' perspective. Another approach related preservatives to the broader health debates about milk. Thomas Stevenson, a doctor and public analyst who was president of the Institute of Chemistry, argued that boric acid inhibited the digestion of milk. From his work at Guy's Hospital Stevenson considered that infants and invalids were particularly at risk due to their less-robust digestive systems and above-average consumption of milk.[29] His hospital used only preservative-free milk and he advocated prohibiting chemicals in milk, but allowing them in other products. Alfred Hill suggested that preservatives might aggravate epidemics of infantile diarrhoea, though this link to a key medical debate was made cautiously with Hill noting a range of other contributory social factors.[30] Often doctors emphasised the greater risks to the poor who were less able to afford better quality milk. A rather different set of medical objections centred on chemical preservatives as drugs that the public should not consume unwittingly. Hehner outlined his objections to being drugged by grocers. Some doctors condemned unrestricted employment of preservatives for their unknown consequences and suggested that boric acid taken in food or milk might interact with prescribed medication, leading to overdosing or else counteracting a course of treatment. There was a general emphasis on the infringement on doctors' professional authority and relationship with patients. A further line of argument alleged that preservatives were actually associated with poor standards of food quality and hygiene so that the chemicals concealed rather than prevented tainted or decomposing food. From this perspective the proper objective was aseptic conditions in the manufacture and sale of foods rather than antiseptics designed to counteract or conceal potential risks. Professor McFadyen suggested that banning preservatives would promote improved cleanliness in milk production. According to Cassal, small retailers who relied on chemicals to keep milk fresh rather than investing in cold stores ought not to be in the milk trade.[31]

Professional medical organisations generally supported regulation. Two of the *Lancet*'s panel of 1897 appeared before the 1899 committee.[32] Halliburton represented the Royal College of Surgeons. His own research was cited by others as indicating that even 0.05 per cent of borax inhibited the action of digestive ferments, though Halliburton himself emphasised the lack of evidence. He favoured prohibiting formaldehyde, formalin and salicylic acid, but regarded boric acid as probably safe. Brunton of the Royal College of Physicians had opposed regulation in 1897 and still regarded preservatives as essential to keep foods, but now proposed strict limits on the quantities used. Shortly after the hearings ended the State Medicine section of the BMA's annual meeting supported banning preservatives from milk, butter, beer and wine and restricting their use in all other

[29] *Ibid.*, p. 167.
[30] *Ibid.*, p. 80.
[31] *Ibid.*, p. 131.
[32] *Ibid.*, pp. 105–8 and 260–2.

foods.³³ The Society of Medical Officers of Health insisted that all preservatives were unnecessary and a potential hazard to infants and invalids. Those who objected to preservatives offered various regulatory remedies ranging from a complete prohibition, as the public analysts favoured, to specified limits. The medical profession generally emphasised the importance of preservative-free foods being available to permit consumer choice, and there was support for compulsory labelling for the same reason, though some doctors noted that alternative, higher-grade produce was often too expensive for poorer families.³⁴

In the early 1900s similar pro-regulation views of farmers, the dairy trade and analysts were highly effective in promoting legislation in the contemporary debates about margarine, butter and milk standards. In the case of preservatives, though, other established dairy companies and their analysts defended milk containing boric acid by arguing that it was superior to sterilised, pasteurised or skimmed milks in nutritional value, taste and purity. The pro-regulation case was challenged by some medical experts. Dr Robert Bell of the University of Glasgow mounted a particularly vigorous defence of boric acid, although his own professional expertise was coupled with a commercial interest as a director of the Glasgow Dairy Company.³⁵ Bell cited the extensive use of borax in treating urinary infections and covering wounds after surgery as proof of its benign qualities. A consulting surgeon from Westminster Hospital considered that the amounts of salicylic acid in drinks or jams posed no danger, and if large quantities were consumed the food or drink itself would produce ill effects rather than the chemical. Professor John Attfield, of the Pharmaceutical Society and editor of the *British Pharmacopoeia*, talked about the manufacturers' commercial interest in their customers' health and the probability that daily consumption made people well aware of any hazards. Some of the medical professionals observed that the addition of selected chemicals made foods safer. Bell, for instance, argued that milk with preservatives posed less of a health risk than sour milk and preservatives promoted better diets and health by allowing a lower level of salt in foods. In a similar fashion, sections of the milk industry argued that boric acid in milk was superior in its composition, nutritional value and taste to sterilised, pasteurised or skimmed milks. These alternative products were presented as less natural or less pure which demonstrated that the debate over chemical preservatives was, in part, about wider systems of food production, distribution and taste.

The Committee faced an array of competing definitions of how 'public interest' might be interpreted and differing opinions about the preferred form of any regulations. The fundamental divide was between those doctors and analysts who demanded controls, even a total ban, and the majority of businesses who argued that there was no justification for any restrictions. Both sides marshalled scientific expertise. The Committee undertook its own investigations into the extent of

---

[33] *British Medical Journal*, 18 August 1900, pp. 424–5.
[34] Committee on Food Preservatives, pp. 256–7.
[35] *Ibid.*, p. 98.

preservative use by using the Government Laboratory to analyse samples sent in by 28 local authorities and 28 firms, primarily wholesalers. It also commissioned experiments on pigs, supervised by Professor Tunnicliffe. Its hearings revealed a variety of scientific research evidence based on feeding experiments with animals, testing the effects of preservatives on digestive ferments in laboratories or analysing preserved milk or foods. There was a good deal of such research and numerous publications, but little consensus about its relevance to human digestion or health, particularly the long-term implications of small doses. Indeed the available research provided little guidance to the effectiveness of the various preservatives in delaying the decomposition of foods. As a result the rival opinions were often based on a priori assumptions that preservatives were antiseptics and so inherently beneficial or, alternatively, that preservatives were suspect as unnatural or that any effects on bacteria implied a risk to human health. At the other extreme, anecdotal evidence was to the fore. Producers and distributors boasted of the quantities of preservatives that they and their families had consumed with no ill effects. Medical Officers of Health cited spectacular cases of illness attributed to preservatives. Dr Robinson, for example, described a case in Dover where five nuns became ill after eating milk and blancmange to which both the dairy and their own cook had added boric acid. When the remaining blancmange was fed to nine chickens, five of the birds died and Dr Robinson concluded that boric acid was a poison.[36] More idiosyncratically, Professor Attfield brought his personal experience with dyspepsia to bear by describing his habit over ten years of keeping boric acid on the dinner table to sprinkle on less-digestible foods, such as green vegetables. Use of this unusual condiment left the Professor confident that regular and sizeable doses of boric acid posed no danger to digestion. This confidence was based on his practice of using a tube to empty his stomach four or five hours after eating, in order to remove food presumed to be indigestible, allowing him to conclude that boric acid had no effect on his stomach contents.[37]

In the face of the conflicts and uncertainties, the Committee's final report in 1902 recommended prohibiting any use of formaldehyde, restricting the use of salicylic acid and permitting only boric acid and borax to be added in dairy products. Milk was taken to be a special case due to its liability to contamination, the potential for people to consume large quantities and the presumed special vulnerability of infants and invalids. Thus the report recommended banning all preservatives in milk as well as baby and invalid foods. In reaching its conclusions, the Committee cited the testimony of analysts, doctors and physiologists about the harmful effects of some preservatives and the possibility of interference with prescribed medication, thus accepting the 'public interest' arguments of the opponents of preservatives and assigning significance to the idea of the chemicals as drugs. At the same time the Committee acknowledged the absence of definitive evidence about health

[36] *Ibid.*, pp. 113–15.
[37] Ibid., pp. 223–37 Cassal's *British Food Journal* criticised Attfield's authority and the reliance on a 'dyspeptic stomach' for guidance; *British Food Journal*, March 1900, pp. 66, 70.

implications and proposed that labels should identify all preservatives, thereby allowing consumer choice and incidentally facilitating further research. Finally, the report proposed permanent arrangements to monitor the use of preservatives and colourings and to identify any dangers to public health. In terms of the monitoring mechanism the report suggested that any Court of Reference should include a chemist, bacteriologist, pharmacologist, doctor, physiologist and public health officer. However, it also made the alternative proposal that the LGB be given powers to investigate preservatives and colourings without the provision of a new Court of Reference.

Overall the preservatives report represented a considerable victory for the analysts, doctors and producers of preservative-free foods who had criticised preservatives. The LGB, however, made no effort to introduce legislation. Yet, under the decentralised regulatory system based on common law, the report had an immediate impact, because analysts and some local authorities used its recommendations as grounds for prosecutions.[38] Indeed the scientific evidence, and general arguments, along with several of the expert witnesses who testified before the Preservatives Committee featured in local prosecutions concerning boric acid in cream.[39] Thus Cassal was public analyst in a case brought in Kensington and Professor Attfield and Dr Bond appeared as witnesses for the defence. During 1905 Battersea Borough Council successfully pursued a case in Dorset against a farmer whose milk contained boric acid; a Manchester council used the threat of prosecutions to promote the voluntary abandonment of preservatives.[40] The 'public interest' campaign pressed for legislative implementation of the 1902 report. Camberwell Borough Council's call for the LGB to establish a limit on boric acid reportedly attracted support from 74 other local authorities.[41] Doctors and analysts still looked for legislation to give added force and greater uniformity to the regulation of preservatives.[42] The LGB's inactivity over the report was highlighted regularly in the press, but to no effect until 1906 when other developments brought the issue to the fore.[43]

Preservatives attracted greater attention in the United States where considerable publicity surrounded Harvey Wiley's 'poison squad' experiments in which volunteers received diets containing first boric acid and later the other chemical preservatives. When the resulting Bureau of Chemistry's reports appeared from 1904, they declared preservatives harmful and advocated their prohibition except in special cases. An intense controversy ensued as preservative suppliers defended their

---

[38] *British Medical Journal*, 14 February 1901, pp. 1757–9; Drummond and Wilbraham, *The Englishman's Food*, pp. 385–7.
[39] *British Food Journal*, April 1900, p. 98, August 1900, pp. 220, 239, February 1903, p. 25.
[40] *British Medical Journal*, 16 September 1905, p. 676.
[41] *British Food Journal*, January 1905, p. 8.
[42] *British Medical Journal*, 18 August 1906, pp. 350–3.
[43] *British Food Journal*, January 1903, p. 2, noted an article in *The Times* critical of preservatives and linking poor quality food to the 'national degeneration'.

products.[44] Wiley's work and the US debate apparently had little immediate impact in Britain since the evidence and competing arguments simply reinforced the established positions of the supporters and opponents of chemical preservatives. However, the 1906 scare over American meat imports provided a new sense of urgency with the early work of the recently established Foods Section concentrating on meat products with particular reference to preservatives and imports. Between 1905 and 1908 the Foods Section conducted six studies relating to meat products, each report collating information on scientific findings, undertaking further research and assessing food production and distribution systems. In 1906 an investigation by Dr Buchanan on imported scrap meat and offal recommended prohibiting imports of tripe, tongue or kidneys containing preservatives.[45] A separate study by Dr MacFadden characterised the presence of boric acid in American tripe as a potential threat to invalids and perhaps a means of concealing decomposition.[46] In the latter case the subject was first raised by reports from Birmingham's Medical Officer of Health, provoking public health concerns, though British tripe makers then took the opportunity provided by MacFadden's investigation to criticise the quality of the American product.

A further report by Dr MacFadden examined preservatives in meat products packed in cans or glass containers.[47] Its conduct offers insights into the implications for regulation of the new Foods Section. The Section sent 1,733 cans and jars of meat products for examination by public analysts, an indication of its reliance on outside expertise; the results showed that 19 per cent of the samples contained chemical preservatives, primarily boron. One analyst found boric acid penetrated the surface of American hams and was still present after washing. MacFadden visited canning factories and held discussions with representatives of the import houses handling American canned meat: both British and American companies claimed to be reducing their use of boric acid. However, MacFadden believed that sealed containers would keep products without preservatives and his inspections convinced him that standards of hygiene in food works were poor. Thus his report concluded that preservatives were an old-fashioned method used to conceal low quality food or unsatisfactory factory conditions, reiterating the critique of the chemicals as part of a broad system of production and accepting the criticisms by doctors and analysts in the 1890s.

MacFadden recommended banning boron compounds and other chemical preservatives in imported and domestic meats in cans or glass containers and placing limits on the proportions allowed in sausages, pies and other meat prod-

---

[44] Oscar E. Anderson, *The Health of a Nation: Harvey W. Wiley and the fight for pure food* (Chicago, 1958), pp. 103, 149–52; James Harvey Young, 'The Science and Morals of Metabolism: Catsup and benzoate of soda', *Journal of the History of Medicine and Allied Sciences*, 23, 1968, pp. 86–104.

[45] LGB (Medical Department), Report of Inspectors of Foods, 3, 'On Certain Imported Meat Foods of Questionable Wholesomeness' (London, 1908).

[46] *Ibid.*, 4, 'On Inquiries with Regard to the Wholesomeness of Tripe of Home and Foreign Origin' (London, 1908).

[47] *Ibid.*, 6, 'On Preservatives in Meat foods packed in Cans or Glass' (London, 1908).

ucts. A further report suggested that formaldehyde concealed stale or decomposing meat and that the chemical remained present after cooking. As a whole the Foods Section's work convinced George Buchanan, its head, that new US legislation did not guarantee the full safety of imports, especially as the Meat Inspection Act of 1906 permitted preservatives in exported products. Buchanan, in turn, persuaded John Burns, President of the LGB, to introduce the 1907 Public Health (Regulations as to Food) Act that gave the LGB powers to seize and destroy contaminated food, thereby extending its authority substantially. Under these powers the Foreign Meat Regulations, finally introduced in 1909, prohibited the application of boron preservatives in imported sausages, tripe, tongue and other meat products. Overall, then, the LGB extended its role and responsibilities rather than establishing an independent agency of the type envisaged by the preservatives inquiry, and initially directed its attention to meat imports in response to a new food scare. Yet, despite the crisis and MacFadden's critique of conditions in some British meat factories, chemical preservatives remained in general use. In a Parliamentary answer in 1908, Burns agreed that a preservative standard was an important but complex issue requiring further study given its health and commercial implications.[48]

Alongside the concerns about meat, policy towards preservatives in milk developed separately, reflecting purely domestic issues. Debates about preservatives, largely reprising the arguments presented in the 1899–1900 hearings, featured in the Board of Agriculture's investigations of milk and butter standards between 1900 and 1906. The 1906 report on butter regulations recommended that the LGB establish preservatives standards under the terms of the 1899 SFDA and the President of the Board of Agriculture, Earl Carrington, inserted an amendment into the 1907 Butter and Margarine Bill aimed at limiting preservatives in butter and permitting the LGB to ban or limit preservatives in butter or margarine.[49] Users of preservatives still emphasised their value in protecting consumers, but farming organisations and some dairy companies allied with doctors and analysts in support of a complete ban. The Preservatives Committee's recommendation of a 0.25 per cent level of preservatives in cream was never given legislative force, but in the decentralised system through which the food laws operated, it emerged as a *de facto* standard which some courts applied. Following sustained pressure from local authorities, the LGB issued a circular in 1906 on detecting formalin and boric acid in milk. It included advice on preservatives levels that should be taken as prima facie evidence of adulteration as well as advocating sampling and labelling.[50] Then in 1906 in the case of *Cullen v McNair* the courts declared that 0.313 per cent of boric acid could harm children and invalids, though not adults. In response the Cream Trade Protection Society pressed the LGB to sanction a level of 0.5 per cent in order to establish a higher legal limit and to obtain uniformity. In line with its

---

[48] Parliamentary Debates, Fourth Series, Vol. 187, 1031–32, 27 April 1908.
[49] Parliamentary Debates, Fourth Series, Vol. 180, 224–34, 8 August 1907.
[50] *British Food Journal*, July 1906, pp. 125–6; *British Medical Journal*, 4 November 1905, p. 1243.

general policy, the Board initiated a report on preservatives in milk and cream by Dr J. M. Hamill of its Foods Section in 1909.[51]

Like the earlier meat reports, the study drew on external expertise, with the Foods Section commissioning Dr Harden of the Lister Institute to determine the shelf life of cream with varying proportions of preservatives. Harden decided there were no physical or chemical criteria to indicate when cream was unfit to eat so his experiments relied on the opinions of two cream tasters provided by the Cream Trade Protection Society, the advocates of higher levels of preservatives. It was a very direct form of regulatory capture based on expertise. Harden's tests concluded that cream did indeed keep fresh for longer if it contained a higher level of preservatives, around 0.4 per cent. Hamill's final report blended the arguments advanced by the cream trade with those of the critics of preservatives. On the one hand, he accepted that boric acid was essential for commercial purposes and that a ruling by the LGB on permitted levels would avoid uncertainty. On the basis of Harden's experiments, Hamill proposed a legal limit of 0.4 per cent during the summer months, while retaining the *de facto* standard of 0.25 per cent in winter. On the other hand, having identified health risks to children and invalids, Hamill advocated clear labelling of preserved cream which would deter producers from resorting to preservatives unnecessarily. After further representations the LGB introduced the Public Health (Milk and Cream) Regulations in 1912. Preservatives were banned in milk or cream with a fat content below 40 per cent; for richer creams preservatives remained legal providing labels indicated their presence and the proportion of boric acid. But Hamill's report had failed to persuade the LGB that there was definitive scientific evidence about the health effects of preservatives or what was a safe minimum level, and the proposed standards were omitted from the regulations which concentrated on labelling instead so that consumers were able to choose whether or not to eat preserved cream. In defending the new regulations John Burns argued that they addressed health concerns, suited 'honest' traders and interfered as little as possible with legitimate business. The Board of Agriculture, which already set butter and milk standards, refused to take any role over cream.[52]

Despite central government's low key response, Hamill's report and recommendations actually operated as a further possible *de facto* standard for the courts to apply along with the Preservatives Committee's report and the 1906 judgement. Under Cassal's prompting, Kensington vestry's response to the Hamill report was to apply its own criteria based on the 1901 Committee's report. It prosecuted sellers of any cream containing more than 0.25 per cent of boric acid.[53] When the 1912 regulations appeared, Kensington again asserted its autonomy by arguing that the 1901 Committee's report provided the most authoritative guide and that its local responsibilities under the 1899 SFDA took precedence over the

[51] LGB, Reports on Public Health and Medical Subjects (new series), Food Report No. 10, 'On the use of preservatives in cream' (1909).
[52] Burns in Parliamentary Debates, 1912, Vol. 36, 433–5, 27 March 1912; Vol. 51, 1633–4, 1943–6, 14 April 1913.
[53] *British Food Journal*, February 1910, pp. 26–7.

1912 regulations.⁵⁴ With Cassal still the local analyst and a supportive public health committee, Kensington's policy emphasised the potential for local activism inherent in the SFDA. It ensured that the preservatives issue continued to be contested in court following the prosecution of a Kensington grocer in 1913 for selling cream containing boric acid. The witnesses included Cassal, Halliburton and Dr Tunnicliffe, a member of the 1901 Committee, who declared that boric acid was not harmful. The cream seller was convicted, prompting renewed agitation by the Cream Trade Protection Society for a central ruling that would control the actions of local authorities. In the Commons in 1914, Burns' successor at the LGB, Herbert Samuel, indicated that the 74 convictions relating to preservatives in cream between 1909 and 1912 involved proportions ranging from 0.25 to 0.75 per cent.⁵⁵ Such inconsistencies were highlighted by Hume-Williams, MP for Bassetlaw, who had been the defence barrister in the 1913 Kensington case, though the differences presumably also fragmented trade opposition since most cream sellers were not subject to the oversight of such an assertive authority as Kensington. When pressed in the Commons, Samuel promised to establish a new committee of experts to investigate preservatives in cream, an admission that the Foods Section's report and the 1912 regulations had failed to settle the issue or to satisfy the cream trade. The outbreak of war delayed immediate action. By 1916 the LGB was advising local authorities not to prosecute marginal cases until there had been a new investigation. In 1917 the Food Controller, Lord Rhondda, fixed the maximum quantity of boric acid in cream at 4 per cent.⁵⁶ This implemented the higher level recommended by Hamill, but applied it across the whole year. Public health concerns were reflected in the requirement for labelling as 'preserved cream' with the presence of boric acid to be declared along with a statement that it was not suitable for infants and invalids. Rhondda sought to appeal to all parties by advising traders to use the minimum possible levels and urging councils to accept the new standard. Again a future investigation was promised. And once again Kensington reasserted its intention to continue to operate its own criteria, in spite of complaints from the local Chamber of Commerce.⁵⁷ In the event, in the context of supply shortages and rationing, the tightening of food controls resulted in an effective ban on all cream sales except for invalids and infants for the remainder of the war.

The debates over cream from 1900 to 1917 were initiated by analysts, doctors and local authorities on the grounds that preservatives were harmful and unnecessary. The common law established *de facto* standards which, in turn, prompted cream traders to turn to the LGB in a search for less-restrictive and uniform regulations. The Cream Trade Protection Society achieved a significant form of capture over the research underpinning Hamill's report, but the 1912 regulations reflected

---

⁵⁴ *Ibid.*, May 1913, pp. 88–90, June 1913, pp. 128–30, August 1913, pp. 142–53.

⁵⁵ Parliamentary Debates, Fifth Series, 1914, Vol. 61, 17–18, 14 April 1914; 1046–50, 1063–64, 22 April 1914.

⁵⁶ Ministry of Health Departmental Committee, Preservatives and Colouring Matter, Use of Boracic Acid, 1923, Minute, 24 February 1920, MH56/19, PRO.

⁵⁷ *British Food Journal*, May 1916, pp. 283–4, February 1917, pp. 19–20, June 1917, pp. 91–2.

the LGB's desire to compromise between public health concerns about boric acid and the rights of traders to operate with a minimum of constraints. The LGB's cautious approach failed to satisfy either the 'public interest' lobby or the cream trade and Kensington's stubbornness emphasised the inability of the decentralised regulatory regime to deliver the central direction. Although wartime crisis produced a more assertive central government, it too left the contest between traders and local authority and the questions of scientific judgement unresolved.

When the wartime regulations on cream lapsed, the question of preservatives resurfaced in 1919, but in a 'public interest' form rather than in a reprise of the pre-war business lobbying. In contrast to the previous calls for regulations, the cream producers appear to have been satisfied by the higher wartime levels and were not calling for new measures in 1919. Local authorities resumed their prosecutions and again called for a central ruling on the maximum permitted quantities of boric acid in cream and recalled the earlier commitments to an inquiry. Since the Food Controller's order had given credibility to yet another level of preservatives, councils faced additional uncertainty when deciding whether to bring a prosecution. Kensington's activism continued: in 1924 the Royal Borough's Medical Officer saw active enforcement as part of the area's status as a 'high class residential borough'.[58] He cited the availability of preservative-free foods and refrigeration facilities as evidence that preservatives were no longer necessary. Such views were challenged by the local Chamber of Commerce which accused the council of harassing and disadvantaging local shop-keepers. Although the traders were able to mobilise opposition within the Public Health Committee and in the council chamber, they failed to halt Kensington's campaign.[59]

The question of how to respond to the local authority pressure on preservatives provided an important early test of the new Ministry of Health's ambitions in relation to the food laws. The Ministry has been seen as an example of initially high ambition and promise that was undercut by the Treasury's financial grip and frequent Ministerial changes. In the case of food, however, the Ministry's founding fathers showed caution from the beginning. J. N. Beckett, a middle-ranking official responsible for supervising food questions, tentatively proposed an investigation in 1920 which would stake out the Ministry's territory and avert independent action by the Department of Agriculture. But Sir Arthur Robinson, Permanent Secretary, and Sir George Newman, Chief Medical Officer, opposed a departmental committee and Christopher Addison, the Minister, decided there was no reason to act unless there was further pressure. The officials duly tried to deter the local authorities by arguing that any investigation would have to cover all foods rather than cream alone. It was a curious logic given that the debate since 1912 had centred on cream and this bureaucratic tactic ultimately led precisely to a wider study, since the local councils persisted in their demands with support from the medical profession. By 1923 the Public Health Committee of the BMA was

[58] James Fenton, 'Preservatives and Colouring Matter in Food', *Public Health*, August 1924, pp. 284–6.
[59] *British Food Journal*, May 1922, pp. 41–2, August 1922, pp. 71–4.

advocating maximum levels for preservatives and an editorial in the *Lancet* advocated a new examination of the effects of preservatives, perhaps by the Medical Research Council.[60]

While some officials opposed any inquiry, other developments brought government and business into co-operation. Bakers used liquid eggs which contained boric acid as a preservative and in 1921 their trade body, the Bakery and Allied Traders' Association (BATA), entered discussions with local Medical Officers of Health and Dr MacFadden, one of the inspectors of foods who had reported on preservatives in meat before the war. The bakers were under pressure from local authorities over preservatives and wanted an agreement with the Ministry of Health that would establish an acceptable, and lower, level of boric acid, but avoid formal regulations under the 1907 Public Health Act. An agreement was established on permitted preservatives and preservatives' levels, with use of liquid eggs prohibited in sponge biscuits and plain sponges on the basis that invalids were most likely to consume such products.[61] When prosecutions were threatened, BATA notified local Medical Officers of Health about the national agreement. As with cream, the business association found the authority of central government could be limited or illusory. In 1924 BATA complained that 'Whitehall is often ignored by local authorities'.[62] For MacFadden, this voluntary agreement represented the way ahead in dealing with food regulation generally and preservatives in particular, as his responses to the pressure for a new investigation indicated.[63] He considered that the available medical evidence on preservatives had advanced little since 1899 and did not warrant a ban on public health grounds, though he favoured prohibiting their use in foods for infants and invalids and noted that doctors still distrusted the chemicals as 'physiologically foreign materials'. Arguing that a complete prohibition on their use would jeopardise the supply of cheap food, which was far more in the public interest than restrictions on preservatives, he criticised Kensington's persistent campaign for failing to 'embrace the public interest generally'. MacFadden opposed a new departmental committee, and offered instead a more assertive vision of the expertise and administrative capabilities of the Ministry of Health. Any regulations should be based on clear evidence of a risk to health and be devised by the new department itself after careful study of specific foods to determine the optimum level of preservatives under best-practice forms of production and distribution. When Beckett proposed a departmental committee on a par with the 1899 investigation, MacFadden argued that this would be an 'unfortunate departure from the lines of development upon which we have been moving for the past fifteen or twenty years', and instead pointed to the Foods Section's scientific skills and the BATA agreement as more effective approaches.

[60] *Lancet*, 21 April 1923, pp. 808–9.
[61] *British Food Journal*, March 1923, p. 21.
[62] Bakery and Allied Traders' Association Minutes, 10 September 1924, Food and Drink Federation Library, London.
[63] Ministry of Health, Departmental Committee, 1923, Note by Dr A. MacFadden, 21 December 1922, MH56/19, PRO.

Despite MacFadden's opposition and Newman's lack of enthusiasm, a new Minister, Neville Chamberlain, finally decided in 1923 that the councils' persistent pressure left no option but to redeem the previous promises of a study by establishing a new departmental committee.[64] In this respect a politician over-ruled the preferences of his officials.

The 1923 Preservatives Committee received an almost identical remit to its predecessor of 1899: to assess the extent to which preservatives and colourings were used, whether there was a risk to health and if their presence should be declared. The inquiry embraced all foods, not just cream, with the official justifications for its creation being the earlier debates over cream, new scientific information since 1899 and the existence of new powers under the 1907 Public Health Act. The Committee was chaired by Sir Horace Munro, a former secretary of the LGB, and its membership consisted of eight scientists and doctors including Professor Frederick Gowland Hopkins, a Cambridge Professor of Biochemistry who pioneered vitamin research and had long-standing connections with the analysts. Four of the other scientists and doctors were attached to government departments including Dr Hamill, who joined the LGB's Foods Section in 1908 and now worked in the Ministry of Health, and representatives of the Ministry of Agriculture, a Government Chemist and the Scottish Board of Health. Certainly scientific, medical and official views were likely to be to the fore and the war period had increased the role and status of doctors in general and had resulted in a higher profile for scientific advisers in the area of food policy. The Food Manufacturers' Federation (FMF) failed to gain a place for its research director on the Committee which it criticised as lacking industrial experience. The initial presence on the Committee of Otto Hehner, who had advocated prohibiting preservatives since 1888, implied official willingness to see limits on preservatives. In the event Hehner resigned after a letter, which he apparently intended to be anonymous, appeared in *The Times* in September 1923.[65] This proclaimed the dangers from cumulative intakes of chemicals and poisons in foods, and ended with a rallying cry for action rather than 'reports by Committees or Royal Commissions for burial in Blue-Books'. Hehner was replaced by the current president of the SPA, Ellis-Richard, who had conducted research for MacFadden's 1906 report on preservatives in meat; this too signalled that the analysts occupied a far more central role in government policy-making than before the war. After the furore over Hehner, Munro proposed holding public hearings, but both Ministry of Health officials and the food industry preferred closed sessions in order to obtain frank testimony without prompting adverse press comment. A Ministry of Health official noted that food manufacturers would not attend open sessions, 'not because they are ashamed of their point of view, but on the ground that the Press are certain to garble their version and to pick out only

---

[64] Minute 24 February 1924, Preservatives and Colouring Matter, Departmental Committee, MH56/19, PRO.

[65] Otto Hehner, 'Chemicals in Food. Increasing Use of Preservatives: An analyst's view', *The Times*, 30 October 1923.

disquieting items for scare purposes ...'.[66] The recent discovery of arsenic in a batch of Rowntree's cocoa and a *Daily Express* campaign about food hygiene, highlighting the case for wrapping foods, perhaps contributed to the industry's caution. This decision ultimately restricted the availability of information about the evidence taken and, by controlling the supply of information, reduced the prospects of an effective challenge to the Committee's report, to the manufacturers' eventual chagrin.

As at the turn of the century, representatives of the food industry, medicine, and analysts testified, though there was a greater preponderance of witnesses from trade and professional associations and less concentration on milk. Doctors and analysts restated their case for regulation based on suspicions about the health implications of preservatives, though fewer medical witnesses appeared than in 1899 and their testimony was far less exotic. Representing the BMA and the Society of Medical Officers of Health, William Howarth described the situation as one of 'dangerous apathy'. Echoing the *Lancet*'s assertion of the primacy of medical authority, Howarth proposed a ban on all preservatives except those approved by a Medical Officer of Health. At the same time he acknowledged that medical opinions about preservatives varied and research findings were inconclusive. Controls on preservatives were supported too by the People's League of Health.[67] The 1899 Preservatives Committee had relied on the different witnesses to comment on research work, but the new Committee appointed Dr Edward Creed, director of the Pathological Department at Kings College Hospital, to evaluate the scientific evidence. Creed surveyed published research, conducted his own experiments and concluded that there was no definite evidence of harmful effects from preservatives, effectively vindicating MacFadden's opinion that there was little new medical information. When questioned by Dr Hamill, Creed accepted that boric acid might be a risk to infants and invalids. Hamill responded by suggesting that this made a complete ban essential since those at risk might conceivably eat any food containing the chemical. But, with Creed unwilling to go so far, definitive proof remained as elusive as it had been during the previous inquiry.[68]

The business testimony featured greater representation of manufacturers than in 1899. When the Committee was established, the FMF and Council of the Manufacturing Confectioners' Alliance initiated their own survey of the extent of preservative use among their members.[69] No record of the precise responses has

[66] Minute 25 October 1923, p. 2, MH56/19, PRO.

[67] We are grateful to David Smith and Margaret Barnett for sharing information about the People's League of Health (PLH) based on their own research. For PLH resolutions to the Ministry of Health see files in MH58/153, PRO.

[68] The relatively recent discovery of vitamins stressed beneficial effects of specific chemicals, perhaps increasing concerns about other hazardous additives. Contemporary doubts were evident in a book on diets which emphasised the limited information about the composition of processed foods and associated them with 'diseases of civilisation' such as indigestion, ulcers and cancer. See R.H.A Plimmer and Violet G. Plimmer, *Food and Health* (London, 1925), pp. 2–6.

[69] Food Manufacturers Federation Executive Minutes, 28 February, 31 May, 23 July and 9 October 1923

survived, but the general picture was apparently one of wide variations in levels of use and conflicting opinions about their merits and importance. These differences weakened the force of any business defence. In the case of salicylic acid, used widely in jams and fruit, the FMF attempted to pre-empt the Committee's findings by devising its own schedule of permitted levels and seeking approval from the Ministry of Health, but officials refused to co-operate. Although the FMF's preliminary survey revealed diverse attitudes among its members, a uniform business response was planned by a Co-ordinating Committee drawn from the FMF, the London Chamber of Commerce, the Grocers' Federation, and the Association of British Chemical Manufacturers. The latter's role contrasted with the industry's absence from the 1899 hearings and, like the FMF, reflected its wartime organisation. In Stigler's terms, there were no dominant interest groups favouring preservatives laws; instead the principal interests opposed changes which they recognised as a potential benefit to competitors or a threat to their established practices. Indeed *The Grocer* offered the hope that the Committee would counter 'silly prejudices' against preservatives.[70] Many of the firms that stood to benefit from controls were small producers and traders selling fresh local produce. Lacking an effective voice in the trade associations and other business organisations, their views were not heard by the preservatives inquiry.

In essence the business defence of preservatives reiterated arguments put to the 1899 Committee, namely that preservatives were in the public interest because they inhibited deterioration of produce and satisfied the consumer preference for less salty foods. A producer of boric acid described the chemical as 'antiseptic and very necessary'. On behalf of the FMF, George Shippam, the fish and meat paste producer, claimed that there was no evidence of ill effects from preservatives and suggested that in their absence tainted food would be more common.[71] A deputation from the meat trade argued that preservatives safeguarded poorer consumers who lived in the least hygienic conditions and purchased food in small quantities.[72] Leading meat producers complained that a ban on preservatives would benefit small local butchers supplying fresh produce at the expense of the larger firms catering to a national market. When the Committee raised the possibility of changing retail practices, the meat industry's representatives portrayed preservatives as an integral and valuable part of the system of production and distribution. The FMF regarded compulsory labelling as either unnecessary because there was no risk, or as threatening if it supplied information that led consumers to buy other products. It believed that the public would be unduly swayed by press reporting and were unable to understand the significance of information about the percentages of a chemical in a food. According to the Brewers' Society, the temperance lobby would seize on any references to preservatives, and the works chemist for Idris and Co., a mineral water producer, also claimed labelling would frighten the

[70] *The Grocer*, 19 July, 1924, p. 65.
[71] Preservatives file, Testimony of G. R. Shippam, pp. 1–3, MH56/18, PRO.
[72] Preservatives file, Testimony to committee, pp. 59–75, MH56/18, PRO.

public.⁷³ The reverse argument was advanced too, that information on labels would be ineffective because the poor bought small amounts rather than standard packages and so would not see labels. While the predominant mood among business was to oppose any controls, the FMF proposed that if there was any regulation, it should be implemented through an *ad hoc* committee of manufacturers and Ministry of Health officials with changes being made gradually so as not to damage trade or employment. This offered a vision of regulatory capture and a degree of confidence in relations with the Ministry of Health, as well as seeking to limit the threat to existing businesses from any regulations or a central advisory committee.

In 1924 the Committee issued a preliminary report which recommended a ban on using formaldehyde for preserving chilled beef. Then its final report proposed prohibiting salicylic acid and boric acid as well as placing restrictions on the permissible levels of sulphur dioxide and benzoic acid. Even more than in 1899 the report was a striking success for the analysts and doctors who had opposed preservatives, especially as the Committee justified its recommendations in their 'public interest' terms, namely that preservatives concealed or perpetuated poor quality produce and unhygenic manufacturing and distribution methods. The chemical and food manufacturers and traders had been far more centrally organised than in 1899, but again the business arguments were rejected decisively. The report emphasised the number of products made without preservatives; in this respect changing trade practices and the divided reaction of manufacturers in the FMF's survey had reduced the force of the business defence of preservatives. The report acknowledged the commercial implications of its proposals, conceding that there should be consultation. However, its priorities were evident in the claim that 'subject to the primary requirements of public health, every effort had been made to meet the demands of the traders' interests'. During the drafting of the final report one official called for the 'closest possible discussion between traders and scientific experts'.⁷⁴ Within the Ministry of Health there were contrasting views of the report. J.N. Beckett regarded the recommendations as idealistic, given the lack of decisive evidence on preservatives, and feared the report would lack credibility within the industry, while usefully forming the basis for negotiation. Sir George Newman, Chief Medical Officer, praised the Committee's expertise, though he expressed doubts about the claims of health risks given general improvements in mortality rates. Newman also believed some preservatives would always be required, given the long-term reliance on imported foods. The Ministry's eventual approach was to consult widely over the details of the regulations, but not to make concessions on the basic principles. This strategy was aided by the willingness of officials in the Ministry of Agriculture and Fisheries to accept the new regulations.⁷⁵

The SPA welcomed the report as 'admirably precise and unequivocal', and the *Lancet* and BMA were equally enthusiastic. Local authorities in Kensington and

---

⁷³ Preservatives file, MH56/18, PRO.

⁷⁴ Frank H. Coller, *A State Trading Adventure* (Oxford, 1925), pp. 308–9.

⁷⁵ Milk Advisory Committee, Public Health (Preservatives in Foods) Regulation, 1925, Minute sheet, 20 February–3 March 1925, MAF 36/216, PRO.

Southwark praised the report with the former indicating its intention to resume an active policy of enforcement.[76] Not everyone was completely satisfied. The Co-operative movement remained dismissive of regulation; an editorial in its journal claimed that 'If other manufacturers would keep in line with the CWS there would be no need for public health regulations re preservatives in foods for however chary we may be of the commodities of certain private traders, we can at least rely on those of the CWS'.[77] But co-operators supported the preservatives regulations, though they called for better housing and higher incomes rather than regarding the food laws as a priority.[78] Professor Mellanby expressed his hope that a future committee would prohibit all preservatives.[79] From the opposite side Professor Tunnicliffe, a member of the 1899 Committee, and Sir William Pope, a Cambridge Professor of chemistry, wrote to *The Times* in defence of boron and salicylic acid and preservatives. Despite acknowledging the expertise of the 1923 Committee, Pope claimed that no scientific evidence supported their conclusions. He also suggested boron compounds might be safer than benzoic acid which would be permitted.[80] Amid a flurry of letters, Gowland Hopkins defended the Committee's recommendations, reiterating the case against boric acid as a 'foreign' substance compared to sulphuric dioxide.[81] In essence the issues remained how far any risk could be determined and whether the acknowledged uncertainties made prohibition unnecessary or an essential protection. A leader in *The Times* supported banning suspect preservatives in case of risk though only where commercially practical.[82] But the *Lancet* acknowledged the lack of authoritative medical evidence, claiming merely that 'some obscure disturbances of health may be due to unknown preservatives'. Surprisingly, given its earlier stress on acting only on the basis of medical authority, the *Lancet* emphasised the public health value, administrative convenience and greater certainty for traders as the prime merits of the draft report.[83] The *British Medical Journal* concluded that the changes would not increase food prices and were in the public interest.[84] Its editorial welcomed the regulations, which were considered overdue, praised Chamberlain, the Minister of Health, for courage and fairness in consulting the trade, and anticipated a stimulus to the development of cold storage and refrigeration in distribution and to cleanliness and pasteurisation.[85]

The food industry's response took three different lines. First, there was uncertainty about the report's implications. Manufacturers feared that Medical Officers of Health and public analysts might apply the recommendations before there was

[76] *The Grocer*, 20 December 1924 p. 66 and 17 December 1924, p. 71.
[77] *Co-operative News*, 15 January 1927, p. 13.
[78] *Co-operative News*, 1 January 1927, p. 2; 8 January 1927, p. 12; 15 January 1927, p. 13.
[79] *British Medical Journal*, 10 July 1926, pp. 83–4.
[80] *The Times*, 22 January 1925; pp. 13–14 and 17 February 1925, p. 15.
[81] *Ibid.*, 7 February 1925 p. 7
[82] *Ibid.*, 12 February 1925 p. 13.
[83] *Lancet*, 1 November 1924, pp. 918–19.
[84] *British Medical Journal*, 1924, vol 2, p. 821.
[85] *Ibid.*, 22 August 1925, p. 349.

any legislation, a distinct possibility given Kensington's public statements and the previous operation of *de facto* standards based on official reports. The FMF's research director toured its provincial branches explaining the report and advising on the use of sulphur dioxide and benzoic acid. Since these chemicals would remain legal, it seems likely that many firms would become less concerned once they were able to establish how to adjust their methods to accommodate them or to dispense with preservatives. Several leading firms sought a competitive advantage from the publicity: Nestlé, for instance, publicised the fact that its products contained no preservatives, as did Heinz and United Dairies.[86]

A second set of responses criticised the report in the hope of preventing its implementation. The principal business objections were summarised in a memo by D.N. Veale, Chamberlain's private secretary, in 1926.[87] Some producers and traders questioned the Committee's competence, demanded publication of the evidence and called for further scientific investigation. Boron manufacturers offered to participate in new studies.[88] At the firm's AGM, the Borax chairman, the Earl of Chichester, stressed that food preservatives were only a small part of firm's overall business. While stating that the firm had no desire to sell hazardous products, he denied that borax was harmful, arguing it had made cheap foods more widely available and that an impartial study would show its merits outweighed any 'theoretical disadvantage'. The Earl blamed the agitation on 'faddists', 'well-meaning people mislead by incorrect or insufficient information', or rival trade interests seeking to gain from controls on preservatives.[89] Among manufacturers and traders who met at the London Chamber of Commerce to discuss their opposition were Harrods, Armour and Co., Lipton's, Sainsbury's, Van Den Bergh, the Bakery and Allied Traders' Association (BATA), the Brewers' Society, the Butter Importers' Association and the English Butter Factory Association (EBFA). F.W. Beck, a solicitor representing the butter industry and the Federation of Grocers, complained that, 'The trade has groaned long enough under regulations which were necessarily made in wartime.' The BATA was particularly vocal since the regulations negated its private agreement with the Ministry of Health, frustrating a modest experiment in corporatism. The BATA wrote to the Prime Minister and all members of the Cabinet, describing the new policy as 'wanton, gratuitous, unnecessary, and unjustified interference of precisely the kind from which a Conservative Government may properly be asked to protect us'.[90] A deputation, led by the London Chamber of Commerce, asked Chamberlain to establish an expert committee, including 'practical rather than scientific men, to advise before any final decisions were made'; this critique of the earlier committee did not, however, appeal to the minister.[91] Since the text of the Preservatives Committee's full

---

[86] *The Times*, 20 February 1925, p. 11 and June 14, 1926, p. 10.
[87] Veale memo, MH56/13, PRO.
[88] *Lancet*, 19 August 1925, referred to an 'active press campaign' by the pro-boron lobby.
[89] Report of Borax AGM, in *The Economist* 20 February 1926 p. 374.
[90] *The Grocer*, 1 August 1925, p. 91.
[91] *Ibid.*, 24 January 1925, p. 61.

hearings and evidence was unpublished, opponents had to rely on general arguments. They pointed to declining death rates and advances in health as proof of the absence of any ill effects. The secretary of the Federation of Grocers' Associations of the UK observed that the British must be a 'hardy race' since mortality rates had improved so much over the period of preservative consumption. Such arguments prompted the *British Medical Journal* to comment in relation to boric acid that, 'As long as trade interests are concerned in defending its use as a preservative there is no likelihood of the evidence against it ever being universally admitted as satisfactory. Hence we need expect no finality in the dispute as to the pharmacological action of boracic acid when used as a food preservative.'[92] *The Grocer* presented a mixed view. It stressed the retailers' preference for clear standards to prevent 'harassing prosecutions', but asserted the practical value of preservatives as opposed to 'theoretical' criticisms of their use.[93] The journal proposed co-operation with manufacturers to defend essential preservative use. Another approach was to argue that any regulations would reduce food supplies and increase food prices, especially as there was insufficient cold store capacity. These claims were linked to contemporary concerns by portraying the preservatives regulations as a threat to national security in the event of war or strikes.

In the face of this array of objections, Veale's memo summarised the Ministry's lines of defence in anticipation of a Parliamentary debate on the new regulations.[94] He asserted that it was no longer customary to publish evidence to committees. Veale claimed, without any obvious evidence, that the incidence of appendicitis, ulcers and stomach complaints had increased over the past 40 years and speculated that this might be due to preservatives. In one response to a trade lobby, Chamberlain emphasised the possible cumulative risks from preservatives as the reason for legislation.[95] Finally, Veale noted that the Royal Commission on Food Prices in 1925 had indicated the existence of considerable surplus cold storage capacity. This, he emphasised, undermined the assumption that preservatives were required to guarantee maintenance of food stocks in the face of all imaginable emergencies, including hyper-inflation, threats to the realm and – in the aftermath of the recent General Strike – industrial unrest. It also obviated the need for individual householders to install cold stores. The Ministry of Health's defence received useful support from the Food Council, an official consumer organization established following the Royal Commission. The Food Council accepted that cold storage capacity was available and preservatives were undesirable.[96] Veale's memo signalled a notable determination to introduce new controls against concerted business opposition in order to address the perceived threat to public health.

In the face of the Ministry of Health's resistance, the third strand of business reaction was to try to shape the final form of the regulations. The FMF led the

[92] *British Medical Journal*, 7 March 1925, pp. 468–9.
[93] *The Grocer*, 13 December 1924, p. 67.
[94] In fact, the promised debate was never held. Veale memo, MH56/13, PRO.
[95] *The Grocer*, 31 January 1925, pp. 89–90.
[96] *The Times*, 1 May 1926, p. 11.

campaign, making extensive use of its research director, Dr Macara, and the results from work in its laboratory. Its eventual verdict was that the final preservatives regulations were 'much less worse than was feared'.[97] In the main this reflected the continued availability of some chemical preservatives, but the Federation claimed to have achieved 30 concessions. The most important gains, in the eyes of the FMF's executive, were restricting inspection and sampling to raw materials and finished products and that an earlier proposal for inspection of manufacturing processes was abandoned. Another major concession, though one anticipated in the Committee's report, was a delay in the implementation of the regulations for those foods that had relied most heavily on boric acid. Both manufacturers and retailers had pressed for some delay to allow the sale of current stocks. The general regulations came into operation in January 1927, but there was a delay of one year for butter, cream, liquid eggs, bacon and ham. An advisory note from the Ministry of Health recommended initial leniency over any prosecutions where old stock still remained. Other amendments that the FMF highlighted were permitting preservatives in ingredients and raw materials providing finished products met the legal limits and restricting labelling to indicate the presence of preservatives to finished products. Nonetheless the final regulations marked a radical change and even the delays in implementation to allow clearing of stocks fell far short of the demands by the BATA others for no regulations.

If the final regulations represented damage limitation rather than capture, manufacturers and retailers saw potential benefits once the measures were in place. The FMF promoted new legislation in 1927 that made the terms of the preservatives regulations and the earlier Condensed Milk Regulations binding under the Sale of Food and Drugs laws.[98] The 1928 SFDA incorporated this provision. For business the measure was intended to prevent local authorities applying alternative and more rigorous standards through an SFDA-based prosecution. The idea featured in the Committee's report and public analysts accepted it, but the Ministry of Health had regarded it as too complex for the original preservatives regulations.[99] Thus, although business interests had not sought the preservatives regulations, they finally moved to use them to obtain a greater degree of legal certainty, removing the threat of a patchwork of local conditions.

Debates over the preservative regulations continued during the late 1920s. There was speculation that press coverage of food poisonings was an orchestrated business attack on the preservatives regulations. However, the FMF at least regarded any adverse publicity about food as undesirable because it threatened sales and consumer confidence generally.[100] The most sustained opposition came from the Scottish creameries and the National Association of Creamery Proprietors and Wholesale Dairymen (NACPWD) which claimed to represent over 80

[97] Food Manufacturers' Federation, *Bulletin*, 156, August 1925, pp. 75–9 and 157, September 1925, pp. 91–3.
[98] *Ibid.*, 174, pp. 25–7.
[99] Fenton, 'Preservatives and Colouring Matter in Food', pp. 284–6.
[100] Food Manufacturers' Federation, Executive Minutes, 27 September 1928.

per cent of the wholesale cream trade. These critics condemned any restrictions on preservatives in cream and butter variously as unnecessary or utopian and likely to increase food prices.[101] They offered their own public interest defence that preservatives were an asset to health rather than a cause for concern. In 1925 the NACPWD alleged that the changes handed the 'key of the Nation's food larder to the Cold Store monopoly', a reference to the merger that had created Union Cold Storage in 1923. Two years later the NACPWD complained that all householders would be forced to buy refrigerators, an eventuality that Veale's internal Ministry of Health memo explicitly ruled out. The NACPWD's central objective was to retain boric acid as a legal preservative and its lobbying was targeted on the Milk Advisory Committee of the Ministry of Agriculture and Fisheries which discussed preservatives in butter and cream regularly between 1925 and 1928.[102] Ministry of Agriculture officials supported the preservatives regulations because they were acceptable to United Dairies, the leading milk distributor, and to dairy farmers, they might lead to better quality produce, and they were to be applied to a luxury item that could bear any increase in cost. From the Ministry of Health, Beckett and MacFadden sought to maintain the MAF officials' co-operative attitude by emphasising the positive merits of the regulations. The smaller creameries represented by NACPWD were able to persuade the MAF Milk Advisory Committee to recommend rescinding the ban on boric acid in cream, but officials from MAF and the Ministry of Health agreed to ignore the proposal and, in the Commons, Chamberlain rejected calls for the advice to be published.[103] In 1930 a trade deputation, including the National Association of Creamery Proprietors, claimed that sales had fallen and demanded repeal of the regulations. Rural creameries in south-west Scotland and the Scottish Wholesale Co-operative Society were well represented and the deputation included the octogenarian Sir Herbert Maxwell, Lord Lieutenant of Wigtownshire.[104] Maxwell argued that his 1899 committee had considered the amounts of boric acid consumed in cream so small as to be harmless. But this lobbying was ineffective because the Ministry of Health and the Scottish Office considered that the food industry had adjusted to the 1925 regulations and any concessions would encourage other lobbying. Their position was buttressed by a decline in the official adulteration figures for cream after 1927, though the improved quality was accompanied by an increase in sales of artificial creams.[105]

The question of preservatives surfaced again in 1933 when Ministry of Health officials attended a meeting of the Food Products Committee of the Empire Marketing Board (EMB).[106] The EMB committee consisted of food manufacturers,

[101] Preservatives and Cream, 1925–9, MAF 101/320, PRO.
[102] For the debate see Milk Advisory Committee, Public Health (Preservatives in Food) Regulations, 1925, Preservatives in Butter and Cream, MAF 36/216, PRO.
[103] Parliamentary Debates, Fifth series, Vol. 210, 348–9, 2049–50, 1927.
[104] Preservatives in Cream; Ministry of Health files, 1930, MAF 101/321, PRO.
[105] *Food Manufacture*, January 1930, p. 1; Drummond and Wilbraham, *The Englishman's Food*, p. 387.
[106] Correspondence with the Empire Marketing Board, Food Products Committee, 1933, MH56/14, PRO.

retailers and wholesalers. Its vice-chairman, Thomas Clement, reiterated the Scottish creameries' grievances, but J.N. Beckett summarised the official case against boric acid. The EMB committee advocated greater uniformity of preservatives regulations in the interests of expanding imperial trade. While the Ministry of Health regarded such standardisation as desirable, its formal response emphasised the need to maintain the British regulations on preservatives, conceded little to commercial interests and stressed the priority of public health.

Meanwhile business opposition to the regulations was diminishing as manufacturing and distribution practices were gradually changing. From 1927 a new trade journal, *Food Manufacture*, supported the regulations as a contribution to more hygienic practice and higher grade ingredients as the best means of avoiding spoiled goods. It was confident that new scientific developments would overcome the absence of preservatives. An editorial about the regulations pronounced that: 'What at first appeared to be an imposition is in practice proving to be a potent factor working for an appreciable reduction in working costs, improved process engineering, and better products, both intermediate and final'.[107] Advertisers of food manufacturing equipment and packaging emphasised their products' merits in ensuring the purity and quality of foods without preservatives. Under the auspices of the FMF, there were meetings between representatives of government laboratories, public analysts and manufacturers who emphasised their shared interest in establishing safe preservatives.[108] A recently established, state funded body, the DSIR's Food Investigation Board was already researching new methods of preservation and storage and the Ministry of Health devised tests for the presence of sulphur dioxide and benzoic acid.[109] In such ways the various interest groups established greater consensus on the use of the permitted chemical preservatives compared to the previously antagonistic relationship. This involved elements of capture, through co-operation and work on technical standards and tests, by the analysts and business and a closer relationship with officials. Such developments indicated how the implementation of regulations operated as a stage in the regulatory process. It came close to MacFadden's ideas of co-operation as in the earlier BATA arrangements for boric acid in liquid eggs. The FMF's jam section also extended its earlier attempts to standardise trade practices by establishing a system of jam standards with the agreement of the SPA.

Moreover, the industry's defeat over the preservatives inquiry and report led the FMF to seek a higher political profile. In 1927 the guests at the FMF's annual lunch included Neville Chamberlain, J.N. Beckett and two of the scientists from the Ministry's Food Section. The FMF president, Sir Stanley Machin, expressed the desire of manufacturers to co-operate with the Ministry which he praised for its consideration of business concerns. However, he also called for a respite from further legislation. In reply, Chamberlain emphasised that his Ministry's primary duty was to

---

[107] *Food Manufacture*, December 1927, pp. 199–200.
[108] *Ibid.*, October 1928, pp. 473–4.
[109] Dyer and Ainsworth, *Society of Public Analysts*, p. 67.

protect public health. On a more positive note, he suggested that the preservatives episode highlighted the importance of having a Federation to advance industry's views and struck a conciliatory note, saying that he had been a 'manufacturer longer than he had been a politician'.[110] Two years earlier Chamberlain had offered the Provision Trade Section of the London Chamber of Commerce a similar reassurance based on his claims to a longer pedigree as a 'trader rather than a politician'.[111] Manufacturers were not content to rely on such expressions of sympathy. During the early 1930s, FMF was co-operating with the MCA in a Joint Advertisers' Council in an effort to reduce unfavourable references to foods in the press.[112] At the same time the FMF encouraged the establishment of a Parliamentary Food Group of MPs which had 40 members by 1936.

The protracted journey to the preservatives regulations is revealing in several ways. The pressure for controls originated with a 'public interest' campaign by analysts and doctors, emphasising health risks posed by preservatives, especially to vulnerable infants and invalids. In the 1890s medical opinion was divided about the effects of preservatives, though the main professional bodies advocated controls with labelling as a way to promote consumer choice. No business group called for regulations, but once the 1899 inquiry was established some firms took the opportunity to call for controls, though often this did not extend beyond advocating compulsory labelling. Resistance to regulations came more from food traders than chemical companies or food processors; the defenders of preservatives offered their own 'public interest' case based on the supply of cheap and safer food. The 1899 Committee's report largely accepted the case against preservatives, but was implemented in a curiously fragmented fashion. Though lacking any legislative basis, some of the Committee's recommendations were applied swiftly as *de facto* standards by local authorities and the courts. This, in turn, led to demands by cream producers for legislation to provide a higher and uniform permitted level of preservatives. In the case of meat products, food scares and some lobbying by domestic firms led to the extension of the LGB's research capabilities with the formation of the Foods Section and its regulatory powers. George Buchanan displayed some bureaucratic enterprise and ambition and the LGB moved beyond its inert approach of the 1890s, though in a cautious fashion. The contest between local authorities, notably Kensington, and the cream trade revealed the tensions within the decentralised and common law system of regulation which prompted both sides to seek central government direction in support of their objectives. In the absence of definitive scientific evidence, the LGB endeavoured to achieve a degree of compromise that satisfied neither side, and even under the crisis conditions of wartime, central government's authority was challenged by Kensington's independent approach.

The preservatives debate of the 1920s bore some similarities to that of the 1890s

---

[110] Food Manufacturers' Federation, *Bulletin*, xiv, no 1, 77, 1 June, 1927, pp. 69–74.
[111] *British Food Journal*, December 1925, pp. 111–12.
[112] Food Manufacturers' Federation Executive Minutes, 16 December 1931.

and early 1900s. Local authorities and the professional organisations of analysts and doctors revived the demands for regulations, aided by wartime promises of an investigation. Ministers and senior officials in the Ministry of Health preferred to postpone any action. MacFadden's bureaucratic self-confidence, embodied in the co-operation with the bakers' trade association, was not shared by his senior colleagues. The passage of the preservatives regulations indicates that business was neither automatically privileged nor easily able to capture the regulatory process. All sides were more organised and active in presenting their case and, in theory, business was particularly strengthened following the wartime development of new peak organisations. Yet the committee found in favour of the opponents of preservatives and the Ministry of Health proceeded to implement the recommendations despite considerable opposition from the business interests that were most affected. Indeed the cream trade, the most committed business lobby, and the BATA, which had established its own agreement with the Ministry of Health, were both disadvantaged by, and among the most hostile to, the new preservatives regulations. The explanation lies in a greater unity of views among doctors and scientists by the 1920s, whose status and advisory role in government had been strengthened during the First World War. Business associations campaigned for preservatives, but actual trade practices illustrated the viability of alternative methods of storing foods, thereby undercutting the food trades' 'public interest' defence of preservatives as essential to cheap and safe food. Businesses making and selling preservative-free foods exerted influence through the example of their practice rather than by direct lobbying. When it was clear that regulations would be introduced the FMF and other associations managed a degree of capture, and then adjusted to the new conditions with opposition continuing only among the cream trade which, ironically, had demanded regulations before the First World War. The FMF's efforts to establish closer contacts with politicians and officials were a significant part of its reaction to the Preservatives' regulations. More generally manufacturers were far more effective in their opposition to general food standards, the next major food regulation issue in the interwar period. In this case, which forms the substance of the next chapter, the industry abandoned complete opposition for the more nuanced argument that any regulations be limited to a small range of foods, thereby accepting elements of division across the food trade. The idea of limited measures also offered a sense of compromise and pragmatism rather than the earlier expectation that no regulation was desirable or likely. Even more significantly, the Ministry of Health accepted the FMF's view that industry deserved a rest from new measures and one legacy of the preservatives regulations was inactivity on other fronts.

6

Standards and central government, 1899–1938

The preservatives regulations emerged on the basis of concerns about public safety and their introduction raised the public analysts' hopes for the introduction of wider standards and definitions. They believed that official standards would encourage a greater number of prosecutions, simplify the process of obtaining convictions, and hence reduce adulteration. The 'public interest' argument for standards was balanced by business opinion. Some manufacturers favoured standards, which they hoped would establish the quality and primacy of their product over a particular rival. More generally, however, producers opposed compulsion, emphasising their commitment to high quality and the value to the consumer of voluntary and private standards as alternatives to state direction. There were a few examples of co-operation over standards between food manufacturers and both the SPA and the British Analytical Control. Central government resisted demands for general standards until 1938, when the Food and Drugs Act allowed the Minister of Health to make regulations 'prohibiting or restricting the addition of any substance to, and regulating generally the composition of, any food'. These powers subsequently provided the basis for the wartime Ministry of Food's programme of food standards. This chapter examines the journey to the 1938 Act, focusing on competing business arguments and the limited establishment of official standards, the adoption by producers of some voluntary standards, and the important discretionary role of state officials. Developments surrounding the establishment and operation of a Departmental Inquiry on Food Standards between 1929 and 1934 were a vivid indication that the Ministry of Health was only interested in regulation from a public health perspective. This was important, given that the 1875 SFDA had been based on the notion that consumers were being 'cheated rather than poisoned'.[1] In choosing not to defend consumers against the sale of food that was merely fraudulent, the Ministry of Health took a more selective approach, focusing on one aspect of the law. This reflected the belief, shared by John Burnett, that on the whole 'poisoning' was in retreat by the early decades of the twentieth

---

[1] Report from the Select Committee on Adulteration of Food Act (1872). Proceedings and Minutes of Evidence, Parliamentary Papers, 1874 (262), VI, 243.

century. The Ministry's assumptions about food safety and its limited regulatory responsibilities were unshaken by evidence which had emerged during and immediately after the First World War about unhygienic conditions in food processing. The existence of this evidence balances the notion that the SFDA had been fully successful in eradicating potentially dangerous food from the market. The chapter proceeds on a thematic rather than chronological basis, opening with a study of standards that were adopted for a few specific products, followed by a discussion of general standards and definitions. This distinction is worth bringing out, for individual product standards were easier to establish than more general ones, largely on the basis that the former were demanded primarily by unified or essentially unchallenged business interests. A general system of specification standards was less straightforward, often involving competing business views as well as potentially conflicting public and private interests.

Standards for specific products

As Kindleberger emphasised, standards can be set, and maintained, through private or collective initiatives so that the state is only one potential provider of a standard.[2] A firm's use of branded products and advertising would be an example of a private, or individual standard, established with the aim of stimulating repeat purchases by consumers. Where a group of producers or traders operate a common set of arrangements, the standard constitutes a collective good, intended to promote the reputation of their commodities or, perhaps, a generic product. In the case of a state standard, Kindleberger emphasised the potential for 'capture' by producers or for 'public interest' concerns to be the primary influence. As well as their institutional character, standards differ in their precise objective. From the SFDA of 1875, the food laws operated as a system of 'target' standards in that retailers were liable for any harmful or fraudulent features of a product.[3] The precise 'target' varied for each product and, in theory, in each individual case, though a degree of consistency developed through common law, the application of *de facto* standards derived from public inquiries, and the use of authoritative guides, notably the *British Pharmacopoeia* for drugs. Nonetheless, enforcement of the SFDA ultimately proceeded on a case-by-case basis, and, as the findings of one magistrate or court were not necessarily binding on another, it was often very difficult for local authorities to approach particular prosecutions with confidence. Given this uncertainty, and the high costs of mounting what could be lengthy prosecutions, many cases were simply dropped. Analysts advocated 'specification' standards, based on detailed descriptions of the composition of each commodity, so that, for instance, all custard powder would consist of the same ingredients in the same proportions. The publication of food analyses in journals, such as the *Lancet* and *The Analyst*,

[2] Charles P. Kindleberger, 'Standards as Public, Collective and Private Goods', *Kyklos*, 36 (3), 1983, pp. 377–96.

[3] On 'target' and other standards see Anthony I. Ogus, *Regulation: Legal form and economic theory* (1994), pp. 150–1.

and texts on food analysis were one means of establishing common criteria among analysts. From the analysts' perspective, specification standards would be more influential if they were enshrined in legislation or through official regulations. First, in 'public interest' terms, they would provide consumers with absolute certainty about the nature and safety of any commodity. Second, the analysts' professional standing stood to be increased if standards were defined in terms of a food's chemical composition because any deviations would be easier to identify. Third, greater certainty about the outcome of prosecutions would reduce the likelihood of an analyst's judgement being overturned by the Government Laboratory or criticised by local councillors following a failed prosecution. Some analysts were suspicious about legal standards which they anticipated would be set at the level of the lowest common denominator rather than ensuing superior quality. Another response was the establishment in 1899 of the British Analytical Control (BAC) by a few analysts. Manufacturers could subject their products to regular testing by the BAC to ensure that quality was maintained and in return use the association with the BAC in their advertising.[4] The scheme operated into the 1930s, but apparently attracted little interest from the food industry.

As the discussion in chapter 3 showed, manufacturers were ambivalent about standards. To the extent that the SFDA influenced industrial practice, food processors applied certain *de facto* standards and the proliferation of brand-name products represented a type of private standard, to the extent that a brand implied greater consistency in the character of a commodity. The willingness of Colman and Cadbury to assist retailers charged with adulteration, providing the branded goods had not been unpacked before sale, was testimony to the importance that certain manufacturers attached to their reputations. Brewers similarly emphasised product quality and the Quaker industrialists in the food trades also valued their reputations. As Sally Horrocks has shown, from an early date big producers did much to improve food quality and standards by engaging the assistance of professional chemists.[5] Backed by such expertise, in 1905 the manager of Rowntree's, T. H. Appleton, was able to challenge the view held by a London Medical Officer of Health that a sample of Rowntree's eucalyptus pastilles were 'chemically impure'. 'We have in our works', wrote Appleton, 'a well-equipped laboratory, and a specialised staff of Assistants for both Chemical and Bacteriological work': such well-resourced experts, he insisted, could not have allowed an impure product to enter the market. Significantly, perhaps, the London official did not test his view in the courts.[6] Another big confectioner which believed in the importance of internal product monitoring was James Keiller. In the 1890s Keiller employed Leonard K. Boseley, a member of the SPA, providing him with laboratory space at its Silver-

[4] *British Food Journal and Analytical Review* (*BFJ*), January 1899 and September 1900, pp. 267–74.

[5] Sally M. Horrocks, 'Quality control and research: the role of scientists in the British food industry, 1870–1939'; John Burnett and Derek Oddy, *The Origins and Development of Food Policies in Europe* (Leicester, 1994), pp. 130–45.

[6] T. H. Appleton to Butler Hogan (MOH for Tottenham), 6 May 1905, R/DH/SR 19, Rowntree Mackintosh Archive, Borthwick Institute.

town plant in east London, where he also examined samples from the company's other main factory in Dundee. At Keiller's the responsibility for quality testing was occasionally shared by company directors, who adopted a less scientific approach. At a Board meeting in February 1923 dishes of marmalade from each of the company's three factories were 'placed upon the table'. While the Dundee sample was described as 'excellent', the Silvertown version was merely 'quite good' and the third, from Paisley, was condemned as 'unsatisfactory'. Determined to maintain a uniformly high standard, and disregarding the inevitable fall in profits, the directors decided to supply only from Dundee until the other two factories had secured the required improvements.[7]

Given this degree of internal quality control, food manufacturers generally insisted on their right to operate with the minimum of regulatory restrictions. If private standards were acceptable to promote sales or to disadvantage substitute products, legal standards that specified the composition of all foods were a different matter. Although the idea of a Court of Reference was supported in the 1890s by the London Chamber of Commerce and the Grocers' Federation, in the main business was opposed to a central regulating body and to food standards themselves.[8] Both were regarded as liable to give too much weight to scientific opinion and too little to commercial imperatives. Manufacturers balanced this opposition to official definitions by promoting their strong material interest in high voluntary standards.

Retailers were ambivalent, tending to favour standards for some products, but preferring simply to transfer the responsibility for quality from the seller to the manufacturer. The significance of reputation as a source of standards rather than regulation was important in relation to the burgeoning Co-operative movement. Co-operative stores emphasised the provision of cheap and wholesome foods, especially the staple items like bread, flour and tea, that were so susceptible to adulteration. In addition, the Women's Co-operative Guild (WCG), established in 1884, proclaimed the potential consumer influence of the 'woman with the basket' in shaping attitudes towards production, marketing and politics.[9] Despite their ideals and organisational capacities, the Co-operative movement and the WCG paid only limited attention to adulteration law and their most central influence over national food policies came during the First World War in relation to prices and rationing. This reflected a fundamental suspicion of regulation as a strategy. In 1900 the *Co-operative News* described adulteration as an international problem

---

[7] James Keiller and Son Ltd., Analyst Reports, GD/K/22, Box 2; Directors' Meeting, 27 February 1923, Minute Book No. 3, Dundee City Archive.

[8] Evidence, Food Products Adulteration Committee, Parliamentary Papers (363), 1895, pp. 158–9; 1896, 256–9.

[9] Gillian Scott, *Feminism and the Politics of Working Women: The Women's Co-operative Guild, 1880s to the second world war* (London, 1998); Catherine Webb, *The Woman with the Basket: The History of the Women's Co-operative Guild, 1883–1927* (Manchester, 1927); Jean Gaffin and David Thoms, *Caring and Sharing: The Century History of the Women's Co-operative Guild* (Manchester, 1983); Martin Pugh, *Women and the Women's Movement in Britain 1914–59* (London, 1992).

that had not been checked by competition or inspectorates.[10] For the co-operators, the real remedy for fraudulent trading practices was an extension of co-operative enterprise rather than seeking to control or reform the economic system that had generated the problem of adulteration. Thus, in 1903 an editorial critical of adulteration proclaimed that under co-operation 'distributor and the consumer become one with united interests'.[11] Similarly co-operation was seen as a better means than regulation of ensuring pure milk since 'honest trading through fear of the law' would not alter underlying motivations or economic pressures.[12] In line with this approach, the WCG lobbied local Co-op stores to stock co-operative goods and there were union label campaigns promoting goods manufactured by unionised workers. The WCG's active engagement with national politics highlighted issues such as the franchise, maternal health, wages and the divorce laws rather than adulteration.[13]

The conflicting attitudes were evident in the debates surrounding the introduction of the first specified standards, the 1901 Sale of Milk and 1902 Sale of Butter Regulations which were discussed in chapter three. Issued under the 1899 Sale of Food and Drugs Act by the Board of Agriculture, both of these regulations emerged from a combination of public and private interests. The Milk Regulations, fixing a minimum standard of 3 per cent fat solids and 8.5 per cent of nonfat solids, gave legislative force to *de facto* standards already applied by analysts, the Government Laboratory and the courts and which were acceptable to farmers' organisations and leading dairy companies.[14] This combination of support overcame dairy trade opposition which advocated lower or variable standards. Farmers had a stronger hand in the 1902 Butter Regulations, drafted by a Departmental Committee which drew on technical advice from trade analysts and business representatives in England and Ireland in order to set an upper limit of 16 per cent water content.[15] Following further business pressure, from grocers as well as farmers, the butter regulations were consolidated in the Butter and Margarine Act of 1907, in which the upper 16 per cent limit of water was attached to margarine as well as to butter.[16] So the first specification standards emerged through the Board of Agriculture with the aim of assisting dairy farmers whose arguments were buttressed by the public analysts.

The LGB retained primary responsibility for the SFDA, but lacked both the

[10] *Co-operative News*, 19 May 1900, p. 509.
[11] *Co-operative News*, 6 March 1901, p. 229; 28 September 1907, p. 1203.
[12] *Co-operative News*, 9 February 1907, pp. 162–3.
[13] Scott, *Feminism and the Politics of Working Women*, pp. 68–70.
[14] Sale of Milk Regulations, 1901, Statutory Rules and Orders, 1901, No. 657; *The Analyst*, 27, March 1902, p. 83; House of Commons, Report on Food Products Adulteration, Parliamentary Papers, 1894 (253), pp. 28, 169.
[15] Sale of Butter Regulations, 1902, Statutory Rules and Orders, 1902, No. 355; Final Report of the Departmental Committee Appointed by the Board of Agriculture, Minutes of Evidence, 1904, Cd. 1750, pp. 333–40; 434–41; Plunkett to Hanbury (President, Board of Agriculture), 15 April 1902, MAF 36/54, Public Record Office (PRO).
[16] The Butter and Margarine Act, Public General Acts 1907, Section Four.

Board of Agriculture's informal assertiveness and its formal powers to set standards. The SPA's original suggestion of a national agency to advise government on definitions for a wide range of foods had been made in the 1890s, and the idea was supported by the 1894 House of Commons Select Committee on Food Products Adulteration and the 1903 Royal Commission on Arsenical Poisoning.[17] The Local Government Board's only practical response to these recommendations was the establishment of a separate Foods Section in 1905, which was intended to undertake research and advise local and central government. The new Section mounted a series of investigations of foods that recommended regulations for specific products, but acted on a case-by-case basis rather than providing a source of general standards.[18] The Foods Section's services were utilised in response to a high-profile campaign in 1911 in favour of legislation to designate wholemeal bread as 'standard' bread.[19] Weatherall's study of this episode identifies its roots in the activities of the Bread and Food Reform League, a group advocating wholemeal bread as more nutritious than the popular white bread, which gained support for an investigation of bread by the LGB from the Royal Institute of Public Health. Public analysts criticised the use of calcium sulphate as a bleaching agent in flours and baking powder. Weatherall highlights the significance of this 'public interest' pressure based explicitly on nutrition as the key health concern and its use of medical and scientific opinion, including support from Gowland Hopkins, the pioneer of vitamin research. In addition the *Daily Mail* backed the campaign, ensuring substantial publicity. Bakers and millers provided effective resistance, however, associating white bread with purity and brown bread with adulteration and poverty. In response the Foods Section undertook three reports on the use of chemical 'bleaching' agents and 'improvers' in white flours and baking powder. The reports drew on evidence from millers, bakers and analysts and lent tentative support to the claims that bleaching agents represented a risk to health and might be nutritionally harmful.[20] However, the continuing popularity of white bread ensured that the 'standard' bread campaign of 1911 petered out, though bread remained a central element in the controversy about 'clean' food, centring on packaging and handling of products.

A longer running debate centred on the merits of condensed milk. From the 1860s a number of producers, including Anglo-Swiss Condensed Milk and Nestlé,

---

[17] Final Report of the Royal Commission to Inquire into Arsenical Poisoning from the Consumption of Beer and other Articles of Food and Drink, November 1903, Cd. 1848, pp. 44–6.

[18] LGB, Annual Report. Supplement Containing the Report of the Medical Officer, 1905–06, Cd. 3656.

[19] Mark Weatherall, 'Bread and Newspapers: The making of "A Revolution in the Science of Food"' in Harmke Kamminga and Andrew Cunningham (eds), *The Science and Culture of Nutrition, 1840–1940* (Amsterdam, 1995), pp. 179–212.

[20] House of Commons, Report to the LGB on Public Health and Medical Subjects (new series 49), Part I, On the bleaching of flour and the addition of so called 'Improvers' to Flour by Dr J.M. Hamill; Part II, On the Chemical Changes produced in Flour by Bleaching by Dr G.W. Monier-Williams (Food Report 12), 1911, Cd. 5613. Report to the LGB by Dr J.M. Hamill on the presence of calcium sulphate in Baking Powder and Self-raising flour, 1911, Cd. 5614.

promoted their product in terms of its quality and nutritional value, targeting advertisments at mothers with young children. Medical endorsements were deployed as part of the marketing strategy in an industry that was prone to surpluses and overcapacity.[21] By 1875 some doctors were questioning the nutritional value of cheaper skimmed milks and criticising its high sugar content, a feature intended to extend the shelf-life of the condensed milk. Condensed milk was used extensively for feeding infants in working-class households, which buttressed the 'public interest' case for regulation since children were regarded as a particularly vulnerable group deserving protection.[22] The advent of new machinery for skimmed milk added to the concern that the fat content was too low.[23] London doctors and public analysts petitioned the Local Government Board in 1894 in support of labelling condensed skimmed milk to distinguish it from the full-cream product.[24] In response Dutch and German firms organised a Condensed Milk Defence Association. For such firms Britain was a key market given the scale of demand and spread of protectionism elsewhere. The leading producers were investing in British factories by the 1890s to expand their presence in the market. The 'public interest' pressure was partially successful, with the 1899 Act requiring that imported skimmed or separated products be labelled as 'machine skimmed' or simply 'skimmed milk'. In the 1900s the medical lobby maintained its campaign on condensed milk, leading to a study of the subject by the LGB Foods Section in 1911. This found that the practice of feeding infants with machine skimmed condensed milk had not been ended by the 1899 labelling requirements. As the Board's Medical Officer believed that babies fed on skimmed condensed milk were more prone to rickets, the Foods Section report recommended labelling all skimmed condensed produce as unfit for infants, along with a ban on all preservatives except sugar, and compulsory labels indicating the milk fat content, manufacturer's name and the date of canning. This was the first suggestion of standards for condensed milk, but draft proposals were abandoned with the outbreak of war. An orchestrated campaign for their introduction awaited the impact of the First World War, when American imports expanded to fill the gap created by the non-availability of European supplies. Nestlé, the leading Swiss producer, further expanded its multinational investments in response to milk shortages and re-established its US presence, having sold its American holdings in 1899 to Borden. The result was an increasingly competitive international industry. When the war ended, imports of skimmed milk continued to expand.[25] The Condensed Milk Defence Association

---

[21] Jean Heer, *World Events, 1866–1966: The first hundred years of Nestlé* (Switzerland, Rivaz, 1966), pp. 40–3, 67, 73–5.

[22] Anthony S. Wohl, *Endangered Lives: Public health in Victorian Britain* (London, 1983), pp. 22–4.

[23] Drummond and Wilbraham, *The Englishman's Food*, pp. 356–9, 449–51.

[24] Report on Food Products Adulteration, Parliamentary Papers, 1894, (253), pp. 28, 169 and Departmental Committee to inquire into the desirability of regulations under the Sale of Food and Drugs Act, 1899, for Milk and Cream, Minutes of Evidence, Cd. 484, p. 3.

[25] Ministry of Agriculture and Fisheries, Departmental Committee on Distribution and Prices of Agricultural Produce, Interim Report on Milk and Milk Products, 1923, Cmd 1854, p. 77.

now adopted a pro-regulatory strategy, perceiving the introduction of minimum fat standards as a means of undermining their American rivals. The Association's Dutch founding firms now had British factories and had recruited Nestlé and other British-based producers. Business pressure on the Ministry of Health led to the establishment of an inter-departmental committee in 1920 to consider whether standards should be introduced for condensed and evaporated milk under the broad discretionary powers of the 1907 Public Health Act.[26]

The business case for standards was presented to the committee by representatives of Nestlé, St Ivel and United Dairies: each asserted that the British market was 'flooded' with low-fat American condensed milk, especially the machine skimmed variety. With sales declining during 1920, the industry encountered significant overcapacity and resulting financial difficulties, notably at Nestlé. Such conditions increased the attractions of regulations that would disadvantage US imports.[27] Nestlé's representative wanted to limit application of the term 'condensed milk' to produce derived from full cream milk with minimum fat and non-fat solids requirements which he believed American produce was incapable of meeting on a consistent basis. Other goods would be described as 'unsweetened milk' or 'machine-skimmed milk', with the latter to be labelled as unsuitable for infants. As the Committee gathered evidence, Nestlé publicised the alleged need for legal standards by running a series of advertisements. Claiming that standardisation was in the interests of consumers and retailers (the adverts were placed in the trade journal of the Grocers' Federation), Nestlé guaranteed that its condensed milk would meet any standard adopted in Britain. The firm's promotional material included data from analyses conducted by Otto Hehner, the leading Public Analyst, which showed lower proportions of water and higher percentages of fat and milk solids in Nestlé sweetened milks than several American milks. The Nestlé adverts also drew attention to the existing American standard of a minimum of 8 per cent fat per gallon, which was characterised as being too low.[28]

Hehner made a more direct contribution to the debate by providing the Inter-Departmental Committee with evidence on behalf of the SPA. Reflecting the SPA's general position on food standards, Hehner supported condensed milk standards on consumer protectionist grounds. Nestlé's use of his analysis appears to have been accurate, for Hehner identified a trend towards lower levels of fat and solids in condensed milk, particularly in American produce. He favoured a system of labelling that would distinguish this lower-concentrated produce from nutritionally superior higher-fat milks. Representatives of the American producers mounted no objection to informing consumers through standards and labelling, but argued that the existing US standard would provide British consumers with

---

[26] Inter-departmental Committee on Condensed Milk (1920 papers), MH 56/62, PRO. Chaired by an official from the Ministry of Health, the committee comprised representatives from the Ministries of Agriculture and Food, the Scottish Board of Health and the Board of Trade, along with the Minister of Health for Ireland and the Government Chemist.

[27] Jean Heer, *World Events, 1866–1966*, pp. 132–42.

[28] *The Grocer*, 1920, pp. 809, 856, 887.

sufficient protection. Armour, Libby and American Milk Products all conceded, however, that this argument was also based on business imperatives: given the small proportion of their output that was exported to Britain, manufacturing to a higher standard might be uneconomical.

Competing views on the subject were offered by different government departments. The Board of Trade fully supported the use of a standard to protect home manufacturers, despite considering that any proposed minimum fat content might lower the quality of domestic produce if manufacturers chose to adopt it as a maximum level. The Ministry of Agriculture, meanwhile, recommended a standard based on the highest possible fat content in order to improve dairying practices generally, and the Government Chemist's Department considered that labels indicating the degree of quality would allow consumers to make informed purchases without the introduction of official standards. The Ministry of Health's position was presented by Dr Arthur MacFadden, who was serving the new Ministry as a senior Medical Officer with special responsibilities for food inspection. In a direct line from the LGB's earlier nutritional concerns, MacFadden's main interest was that condensed milks could be reconstituted as 'good average quality milk', particularly for feeding babies, and he believed that this was where the primary 'public interest' resided. Standards in themselves were of minor significance, and in any event he was dubious about the motives of pro-regulation producers, some of whom had sought to evade standards which had been stipulated in military contracts for condensed milk during the war. The force of these concerns was such that the chair of the committee, J.N. Beckett, a departmental colleague of MacFadden, dissented from the final report on the grounds that any standard above US levels threatened the national supply of milk. This reflected the developing Ministry of Health position that new food regulations could only be justified where they directly advanced public health. Hence the department's support for the limits that were imposed on the use of chemical preservatives in the 1920s; hence also its opposition, in the later 1920s and early 1930s, to a general system of standards and definitions.

MacFadden's evidence carried some weight. On the basis of the Inter-Departmental Committee of Inquiry's recommendations, the Public Health (Condensed Milk) Regulations were introduced in 1923. These required producers to label cans with instructions on how to dilute the milk and the quantity of milk that would be obtained after reconstitution. More generally, however, the regulations worked to the clear disadvantage of American importers by establishing four grades of condensed milk, all based on contents of fat and milk solids which exceeded the American standard. In this manner the regulatory process had been captured unmistakably by the British-based producers. Nestlé used the new standards to promote its brands, though apparently any competitive advantage was modest as American Milk Products responded with advertisements for Carnation milk claiming that it was 'Guaranteed Full British Standard'.

Other industrialists sought to emulate the condensed milk producers in obtaining legislation that would undermine business competitors, but few succeeded. In a number of cases producers tried to secure exclusive rights to a trade name or even a generic name. From 1930 onwards the National Farmers' Union, collaborating with Cheshire County Council and the Society of Public Analysts, attempted vainly to restrict the use of the Cheshire cheese name to products made in the county. As with condensed milk, this campaign was intended largely to disadvantage importers, particularly in this instance from the Netherlands.[29] In the ice cream industry the commercial case for standards was promoted by the Ice Cream Association (ICA) through the pages of its journal, *Ice Cream Industry*, established in 1926. The ICA believed that the scale of the American market was the result of a system of standards which guaranteed consumer confidence in the product, and saw standards as the route to increased sales in Britain. In this the ICA was supported by dairymen's associations, the NFU and, in the 1930s, the newly established Milk Marketing Board.[30] There were 'public interest' arguments, including health benefits, for ice cream standards, advanced by Public Analysts and local authorities hoping to simplify prosecutions. In this respect, with business and 'public interest' views partially intersecting, the ice cream debate was similar to the condensed milk debate, but there were key differences in the form of domestic business opposition and an absence of government enthusiasm. Walls and Lyons, the two leading manufacturers, both resisted calls for standards in the mid 1920s, and as they refused to join the ICA the force of its campaign was minimised. A further complication was a debate over the relative merits of bacteriological standards or measures of fat content. The Ministries of Agriculture and Health discussed the matter in 1927 and concluded that neither possessed the authority to act, despite the power which had been exercised under the 1899 SFDA to determine standards for milk and butter. Pressed again by the ICA in the early 1930s, the Ministry of Health cited the existence of the on-going Departmental inquiry on general standards as preventing the possibility of immediate action on ice cream alone. In truth Health officials were opposed to ice cream standards, although they were reluctant to say so openly, fearing that this opposition would be interpreted as assisting Walls and Lyons at the expense of their smaller competitors.[31]

A similar sequence of events transpired, competing business interests intersecting with bureaucratic ambivalence, when vinegar brewers pursued a lengthy campaign to secure monopoly rights on the term 'malt vinegar'. Brewers who made vinegar through a process of fermentation competed against smaller producers who used acetic acid obtained through chemical processes, a cheaper and less capital-intensive approach. Malt brewers wanted the less-expensive rival products to be labelled as either 'imitation' or 'artificial' vinegar, and lobbied the Local Government Board on the issue as early as the 1890s. By 1901 the London and County Vinegar Brewers Association had been established with the primary objective of reducing price competition. Since the cheaper acetic acid vinegar threatened both

---

[29] *The Analyst*, 56, April 1931, p. 223.
[30] *Ice Cream Industry*, July 1926, p. 7; November 1926, pp. 7–8.
[31] Ice Cream Standards papers, 1924–45, MH 56/308, PRO.

price agreements and market share, the brewers' association continued to lobby for distinct legal definitions. The LGB's Foods Section subsequently made vinegar the subject of one of its first investigations in 1905. Hamill's report accepted that malt vinegar was a superior product and that, ideally, it should also contain malt if sold as such. But as there was no effective chemical test to distinguish the two forms, and doubting the need for regulations on public health grounds, the LGB resisted the call for standards.[32] The 14 member firms of the malt brewers' association, now renamed the United Vinegar Brewers, accounted for around half of total vinegar output and by 1920 their system of price regulation operated effectively enough to attract the attention of the Parliamentary Standing Committee on Trusts' investigations of profiteering. A sub-committee, including Hamill and Arthur Giles, secretary of the National Federation of Grocers' Associations, concluded that prices and profits had been stabilised by the brewers' price agreements.[33] It was estimated that production costs for acetic acid vinegars were only half those of brewed vinegars, but the price differential was far smaller. The sub-committee recommended that acetic acid vinegars be labelled to distinguish them from the brewed malt vinegars. However, Alfred Mond, then President of the Board of Trade, bluntly suggested that the matter be left to consumer choice.[34] Despite the evidence of stable profits, the malt brewers appear to have regarded standards as a means of strengthening their private agreements on prices and they sponsored their own Vinegar Bill in 1924.[35] This proposed legal definitions for 'malt' and 'imitation' vinegar, but made no progress in Parliament; a similar Bill foundered in 1927. Frustrated in the Parliamentary sphere, malt brewers used their advertising to proclaim the quality of their product. White-Cottell and Company's advertising directed a series of 'chats on vinegar' at retailers, emphasising their 100 per cent quality malt vinegar.[36] The trade association, renamed Malt Vinegar Brewers' Federation (MVBF), turned to the common law basis of the food laws and in 1935 reached an agreement with the SPA which recognised the distinct character of the malt article.[37] This was a form of regulatory capture, since the SPA's standards influenced individual Public Analysts, and thus increased the likelihood of prosecutions where acetic acid vinegar was sold as malt. Nonetheless the MVBF still lobbied for official standards, seeking support from the Ministry of Agriculture, while business rivals defended their interests through a new Association of Pure Vinegar Manufacturers. In the face of such clear conflict, the Ministry of Health again avoided expressing any views on the desirability, or likelihood, of any standards.

Co-operation with the SPA on voluntary standards was also embraced as a

[32] J. M. Hamill, 'On the Preparation and Sale of Vinegar in relation to the Administration of the Sale of Food and Drugs Acts', Local Government Board Foods Section, Report No. 5, 1906.
[33] House of Commons, Sub-Committee of the Standing Committee on Trusts, Report on Vinegar, 1921, Cd 1355.
[34] Parliamentary Debates, Fifth Series, Vol. 144, pp. 49–50.
[35] *British Food Journal*, July 1921, p. 63.
[36] *The Grocer*, 4 July 1925, p. 100.
[37] Ministry of Health file, 'Vinegar: definition and standards', 1933–9, MH 56/333, PRO.

commercial ploy by jam producers. In the mid-1920s the FMF's jam section attempted to control price cutting and reductions in weight and fruit content by establishing its own jar sizes and definitions of 'full fruit'. In 1930 the jam section enlisted the SPA's support for an agreement requiring members to grade their product as 'Lower' or 'Full Fruit Standard'.[38] Jam producers were able to refer suspect jams for analysis by the FMF's Research Department which would notify local authorities, presumably in the hope of proceedings under the SFDA. The scheme attracted scornful criticism in the pages of the *British Food Journal* and *New Statesman*, though as much on the grounds that the FMF standards did not promote the use of home-grown fruit as that they failed to promote high-quality produce.[39] This criticism was ironic in a sense, given that the jam standards were a step towards the co-operation between analysts and manufacturers that the *British Food Journal* had always advocated through its British Analytical Control scheme. Private standards as a means for regulating competition were considered by the FMF's Meat and Fish Section, which discussed the idea of defining 'paste' in 1927, but concluded that it would be sufficient to indicate the ingredients on labels, though the issue continued to be debated in the 1930s.[40]

The SPA's involvement with producers of cheese, jam and vinegar was a firm indication of improving relations between manufacturers and analysts. This was cultivated partly by *Food Manufacture*, the industry's progressive new trade journal, which allowed space in its pages for Public Analysts to state the case for tighter regulation in general, including the introduction of standards. Writing in December 1928, G. D. Elsdon, Lancashire County Analyst, recounted the usual Public Analyst arguments for standards, but he added an appeal to the self-interest of food manufacturers and retailers. In the long run, he argued, consumer confidence would increase as a result of improved quality and overall trade profits would therefore expand: 'the true interests of trader and consumer are identical'.[41] The SPA's President, J. T. Dunn, took great satisfaction from these various developments, citing them as evidence of his profession's changing relationship with industry. In the early days of the SFDA, he noted, 'the public analyst was looked on as more or less the natural enemy of the manufacturer', but manufacturers had come to value chemical analysis as a potentially huge commercial asset. He repeated Elsdon's argument that higher product standards would lead to increased sales and improved profits.[42]

The post-war decline in farm income stimulated a similar strand of interest in the marketing potential of quality standards in the form of state-support for agricultural produce. In 1924 the Linlithgow committee's report on food prices and

[38] *Food Manufacture*, May 1931; Food Manufacturers' Federation, *Bulletin*, 2 July 1934, 21 (262), pp. 171–4 and *Bulletin*, 1 January 1938, 25 (304), p. 2.
[39] *British Food Journal*, November 1930, p. 101–2, December 1930, pp. 113–14, January 1931, pp. 2–3, March 1931, pp. 21–4, June 1931, pp. 51–2.
[40] *Food Manufacture*, July 1939, pp. 229–31.
[41] *Ibid.*, December 1928.
[42] *The Analyst*, 56, 1931, p. 222.

marketing proclaimed the need for farmers to 'break with the inertia of custom' in favour of improved quality, grading and standardisation, describing the latter as 'a first principle of modern commerce'.[43] Four years later the Agricultural Produce (Grading and Marking) Act permitted MAFF to establish quality standards for home-grown produce: grades were to be defined under a National Mark scheme, with accompanying logo, and enforced by Ministry inspectors. An early scheme used grades such as 'All-English Malt Flour' based on levels of ash, moisture and fibre; the flour was accompanied by the slogan 'Empire Buying Begins at Home' and a label with a silhouette map of England and Wales containing the Union Flag emblem.[44] The grades were also described as complying with the 1928 SFDA. Although covering a narrow range of products, the National Mark scheme attracted considerable criticism. Food processors feared higher raw material costs. By 1930 the FMF declared its opposition: its jam section feared that a National Mark would impose higher standards than those presented in the joint scheme with the SPA.[45] For its part the Ministry of Health unenthusiastically acknowledged the protectionist impulse behind National Mark standards. In its role as health service provider, however, the Ministry engaged in a confused attempt to avoid paying the higher prices for National Mark malt extract and cod liver oil without leaving itself vulnerable to allegations of depriving insured people of the best-quality products. The use of grading was extended in the 1930s, stimulated by Agricultural Marketing Acts introduced by the Labour government in 1931 and the National government two years later. Marketing boards were established for milk, bacon, potatoes and hops; import quotas, subsidies and price controls were adopted and policy making began to see closer relationships between farmers, processors and civil servants.[46]

General standards: early debates and the 1913–20 Food Bills

As the piecemeal development of standards developed through the Board of Agriculture, the SPA retained its grand ambition for a system of specification standards for all foods. These hopes appeared close to fruition when the President of the LGB, John Burns, announced in March 1913 that he was preparing legislation 'dealing with the question of the purity of food'.[47] The subsequent Food and Drugs Bill of 1913 allowed the LGB to define foods.[48] The LGB presented the 1913 Bill as a means of protecting consumers against fraudulent and dangerous food, which was precisely the Analysts' 'public interest' argument for standards and the SPA regarded

---

[43] Ministry of Agriculture, Food and Fisheries, Departmental Committee on Distribution and Prices of Agricultural Produce, Final Report, 1924, Cmd 2008, pp. 13, 19, 41.

[44] Agricultural Produce(Grading and Marking) Act, 'Malt Extract etc., 1929–36', MH56/39.

[45] Food Manufacturers' Federation, Executive Minutes, 29 April 1932, p. 181.

[46] Charles Loch Mowat, *Britain between the Wars, 1918–40* (Oxford, 1955), pp. 437–40.

[47] 'Sale of Food Bill – Food Definitions', 1920, MH56/30, PRO. The memo was drafted by C. J. Bayley, a Ministry of Health Staff Clerk; Parliamentary Debates, Fifth Series, Vol. 50, 1648, 26 March 1913.

[48] Food and Drugs Bill, 1913, Clause 1(1), copy in MH 56/12, PRO.

the Bill as a welcome, if belated, measure. The SPA's sustained campaign had been reinforced by the activities of a series of elite reform associations centred in London which brought together concerns about food quality and health, particularly in relation to milk. The topic of food standards was one item on the agenda of a conference of food manufacturers and distributors organised by a National Pure Food Association (NPFA) in 1910.[49] The Association proposed to attract the 'best traders and manufacturers' and the companies represented included Brown & Polson, Chivers, a cider producer and several smaller dairy companies. From the surviving reports, it is clear that the various firms regarded standards as a means to gain a competitive advantage for their products. Arnold Brown proposed defining cornflour as a product solely made from maize with no other starch; Kilvert and Sons hoped to reduce imports of cheap lard and a cider maker criticised the use of chemical preservatives. Within a few months the NPFA had been reorganised as the National Society for the Prevention of Adulteration and Sophistication, numbering Addison, Conan Doyle, and Harvey Wiley among its membership and with an entertainments committee chaired by the Duchess of Portland. In the process manufacturers and traders were less in evidence and tensions among the food reformers were evident in the new society's proclaimed opposition to any 'special dietetic creed'.[50] Following a further change of title, to the Pure Food and Health Society of Great Britain (PFHS), in 1911, the reform organisation held lectures, conferences and lobbied for legislation on milk quality and general food standards. With Parliamentary connections such as Waldorf Astor and support from the *Daily Express*, the Pure Food and Health Society proposed its own Pure Food Bill in 1913 incorporating the idea of a Court of Reference.[51] It is likely that Burns' Bill of 1913 was introduced at least partly in response to this concerted metropolitan campaign, though too late in the Parliamentary Session to progress beyond a First Reading. By 1914 the PFHS was advocating the creation of a new Ministry of Public Health, separate from the LGB. The Society's effective publicity was apparent in the publication of a special issue published by *The Times* in June 1914.[52] The editorial offered support for the idea of a Court of Reference and food standards, largely in order to provide clear criteria for analysts to enforce. As with the 1910 NPFA, there were signs of a potential alliance between leading manufacturers and food reformers. The special edition featured articles about, and advertising for, leading firms including Colman's, Crosse & Blackwell, Huntley & Palmers, St Ivel and Glaxo. The articles on the food factories offered rather cautious imagery, stressing quality and reputation, but based on traditional or old-fashioned methods rather than fully fledged modernity. The editorial also emphasised the merits of the better-quality retailers, placing some of the blame for adulteration upon the pressures created by the consumers' excessive zeal for low prices. A new Food and

[49] *British Food Journal*, May 1910, p. 84.
[50] *Ibid.*, November 1910, pp. 201–3.
[51] *Ibid.*, May 1913, p. 170, September 1913, p. 170, November 1913, pp. 205–7, January 1914, pp. 1–2.
[52] *The Times*, food number, 8 June 1914; see also reactions to the issue in the 9 June edition of the paper.

Drugs Bill appeared in 1914 with the millionaire MP Sir Philip Sassoon abandoning the Pure Food and Health Society's planned Bill in support of Burns' new measure which proposed the establishment of a 15-member central advisory tribunal, the Food and Drugs Advisory Committee, with nominations divided equally among the LGB, the SPA and the food industry. Analysts were concerned that they would have insufficient influence on such a body.[53] The 'public interest' lobby achieved some success with the passage of the 1914 Milk and Dairies Act, but general food standards remained elusive.[54] Low in any case among the government's priorities, the 1914 Bill was abandoned on the outbreak of war without even being discussed in Parliament.[55]

The First World War, as Margaret Barnett has demonstrated, was a period of unparalleled government activism in food policy.[56] With curtailed access to the imports that had become established features of the British diet, a dedicated Ministry of Food was established to control and direct physical supplies. Fearing the impact on munitions production of industrial unrest arising from prolonged shortages, the government was eventually forced to extend these controls to include rationing of select items in 1918. Paradoxically, perhaps, while introducing new physical controls, the wartime government relaxed established controls on safety and quality, with the operation of the SFDA practically suspended between 1914 and 1919. According to the official Ministry of Health account there were two reasons for this. First, the practical administration of the legislation was greatly undermined as both local authorities and the LGB found themselves short of staff with personnel leaving to take up positions in the armed services. Second, in a period of great shortage, government policy understandably concentrated on questions of supply rather than quality.[57]

While this involved suspending the SFDA and its routine appraisal of food on the market, the concentration on supply involved some new forms of quality regulation. The Ministry of Food introduced price-fixing schemes for several foods, including sausages and jam, which entailed setting temporary standards and definitions for the regulated items. Wartime controls also extended to prescribing the composition and approved weight of bread and the stricter regulation of weights and measures applied to tea and other commodities. In 1919 the Consumers' Council, a working-class consultative body established in January 1918, called for these standards and the Ministry to be adopted on a permanent basis. In particular, the Consumers' Council favoured a continuation of wartime standards on quality and

[53] *The Analyst*, 39, March 1914, pp. 112–13 and 40, March 1915, pp. 80–1.

[54] The related issue of the accuracy of the weight of foods, especially packaged goods, featured in the report of a Select Committee on short weight in 1914. Its hearings highlighted criticisms of the existing legislation by local authorities and the Society of Inspectors of Weights and Measures, testimony by manufacturers and traders, and views from the Board of Trade, the responsible government department; see Select Committee, Report and Evidence, 1914 (359).

[55] Ministry of Health internal memo, 'Sale of Food Bill – Food Definitions', 1920, MH 56/30, PRO.

[56] L. Margaret Barnett, *British Food Policy in the First World War* (London, 1985).

[57] Ministry of Health, First Annual Report, 1919–1920, Cmd. 923, p. 55.

sale by net weight for jam plus quality standards for lard, margarine, jam, cocoa and other items. But the Consumers' Council possessed limited longer-term influence, having been established by the government as a wartime crisis measure. Food shortages were believed to be at the heart of a sudden escalation of industrial and social unrest in November and December 1917, which significantly disrupted the production of munitions. To avert wider rebellion and, in the words of a contemporary civil servant, to persuade people that the Food Controller 'meant well', in January 1918 the Consumers' Council was formed to access working-class opinions on rationing and related food matters.[58] The Council was headed by the moderate Labour leader, J. R. Clynes, and included representatives from the War Emergency Workers' National Committee, the Trades Union Congress, the Co-operative movement and the Women's National Industrial Organisation. Described by Peter Gurney as a 'kind of safety valve for the antagonism of working-class consumers', the Council retained significant influence only for the duration of the war.[59] So its attempt in 1919 to shape the post-war regulatory framework by calling for the permanent retention of the Food Ministry, characterised as the only government department capable of meeting food consumers' broad needs, was unsuccessful. The Consumers' Council, it should be noted, had little faith in the LGB's emerging successor, the Ministry of Health, which would only be concerned about food 'from the point of view of health ... [and] without consideration of the economic side of the matter, or of the methods of production'.[60]

The establishment of standards and retention of the Food Ministry were both resisted by food processors, whose dislike of the Consumers' Council was due, in part, to its advocacy of food standards. In 1919 the President of the Food Manufacturers' Federation described it as 'a continual source of irritation to traders and no little yearly expense, £2500 to £3000 or more, to the community'.[61] A joint call for the termination of the Consumers' Council came from the FMF, the Federation of British Industry, the London Chamber of Commerce and the Federation of Grocers' Associations.[62] Editorials in *The Grocer* attacked the Council's proposals for a permanent Ministry of Food as unreasonable and unnecessary given falling adulteration levels under the existing SFDA. Such sentiments typified a general mood throughout the food industry in favour of ending controls and returning to free markets.[63] The prospects for a permanent system of official standards were reduced further by the developing position of the new Ministry of Health, which succeeded the old Local Government Board on 1 January 1920. One of the LGB's final acts was

---

[58] Frank H. Coller, *A State Trading Adventure* (Oxford, 1925), pp. 126–32.
[59] Peter Gurney, *Co-operative Culture*, pp. 215–16.
[60] 'Report adopted by the Consumers' Council on the Future of the Food Ministry', May 1919, CC REF. 55, National Museum of Labour History, Manchester.
[61] Bulletin of the Confectionery and Preserved Food Manufacturers' Federation, 10 April 1919, pp. 39–41 and Report of the Executive Committee, 1919, p. 9; copy in Food and Drink Federation Library and Archives (FDFL), London.
[62] Food Manufacturers' Federation, *Bulletin*, 10 April 1919, 69, pp. 39–41.
[63] *The Grocer*, 3 January 1920, pp. 4–5 and 28 February 1920, p. 401.

to veto a draft Sale of Food Bill, circulated by the Ministry of Food in April 1919, which raised the prospect of naming specific articles for standardisation.[64] The Ministry of Health was equally obstructive. Just as the Consumers' Council had predicted, its senior officials decided in July 1919 that the new department 'would stand for health' and concentrate 'upon all the important National Health problems'.[65] It is worth reiterating that the LGB's Foods Section, a modest enough specialised bureaucratic division, was not retained by the new Ministry, which set Dr Arthur MacFadden the task of monitoring food quality with the assistance of a small number of general departmental officials. This reasoning and the lack of a significant number of specialised personnel determined the department's position on food regulation, with new measures only given serious consideration where they offered the prospect of securing improved standards of public health. In the same vein the Ministry adopted a narrower view of existing legislation, abandoning the dual basis of the 1875–99 Acts which were designed to protect consumers against commercial fraud as well as against health risks from contaminated food. The new Ministry's narrow view of its food responsibilities reflected its generally cautious inclination, which was to co-ordinate and administer existing regulatory authorities and mechanisms rather than initiate new policy. Like much of the Ministry's work, expense was also a consideration: closer regulation, especially of production, would burden manufacturers and retailers, and involve increased administrative expenditure for local authorities.[66]

These priorities explain the Ministry of Health's response to a second post-war Sale of Food Bill, produced by the Ministry of Food in the autumn of 1920. This reprised the core of the 1913 Bill, allowing the Food Ministry to make regulations 'defining an article of food in connection to its nature, substance, or quality'. It also envisaged authorising the inspection of all food-manufacturing premises, and the taking of samples at any stage in the manufacturing process.[67] Such powers were only available to inspectors of margarine and butter factories (under the 1907 Butter and Margarine Act). Although this provision had been recommended by the 1903 Royal Commission on arsenical poisoning, it was omitted from all previous Bills, including the 1913 and 1914 measures, and would have constituted a major alteration to the legal framework introduced in 1875.[68] A Sale of Food Order was introduced requiring bread and tea to be sold by weight and establishing criteria for the fruit content of jams and the labelling of certain meat products. These measures represented the legacy of the wartime food controls and the Consumers' Council's pressure for greater precision and uniformity. But the proposals for

---

[64] 'Account of developments to 1919 based on Sale of Food Bill – Food Definitions', 1920, MH56/30, PRO.

[65] 'Organisation of the Medical Staff of the Ministry of Health', 7 July 1919, Personal File of Sir George Newman, MH 107/26, PRO.

[66] A good example of the Ministry's thinking is presented in a Cabinet Paper which it produced on Milk and Dairies in 1922; CP 2004, 30 May 1922, copy in HH 64/48, SRO.

[67] Sale of Food Bill, 1920, Clauses 8 and 10; copy in MH56/30, PRO.

[68] First Report of the Royal Commission to Inquire into Arsenical Poisoning, July 1901, paras. 27, 30.

wider inspection powers were more controversial. Such a change was deemed necessary on the basis of evidence initially gathered by MacFadden's assistant at the LGB in 1913, J. Spencer Low, following an attempt by the Bradford local authorities to enact bye-laws requiring all food premises to register. This was disallowed by the House of Lords on the basis that such powers could only be the subject of general legislation. Low was detailed to investigate, and concluded that conditions in many small premises of food production were such that compulsory registration – based on meeting a number of minimum requirements – was desirable, throughout the country and not just in Bradford.

Although Low's report was buried by the outbreak of war in August 1914, international hostilities indirectly contributed further evidence that, in the absence of adequate regulation, food manufacturing conditions were unsatisfactory. To supervise establishments where food was being prepared for the services, the War Office enlisted LGB food inspectors. According to an LGB account of this scheme, these inspectors established that 'many of the larger factories, sometimes belonging to firms whose names are household words in this country, have been found to be working under conditions which as far as their effects on the products manufactured are concerned were most unhygienic, while the state of large numbers of smaller places of the kind has been little short of appalling'. This 1919 memorandum emphasised that only detection through frequent inspection and re-inspection, along with the threatened cancellation of lucrative service contracts, had forced errant firms to improve conditions. The obvious conclusion was that unhygienic production practices would only be checked in the future by mandatory licensing and regular examination of manufacturing premises.[69]

These reports about unsatisfactory conditions were behind the provisions of the 1920 Food Bill which authorised the inspection of all food premises. MacFadden, the Food Inspector, evidently sympathised with the Ministry of Food's aims. Along with J. N. Beckett, a junior colleague in the Ministry of Health, he attempted to supplement the Food Bill by preparing regulations requiring all producers of meat and fish products to register, and defining the physical conditions which would have to be met before registration was granted. But MacFadden and Beckett were unable to win wider departmental support either for the 1920 Bill or their regulations. The Ministry of Health's central objection to the Bill was articulated by L. G. Brock, the Assistant Secretary detailed to consider its desirability. 'Our primary object', he noted, 'must be to protect the public from being starved or poisoned and not merely to secure value for money.' In other words, despite the 1919 memorandum acknowledging wartime evidence to the contrary, the Ministry did not believe that the Bill was needed to protect public health and in these circumstances could not be obliged to support it. Brock added that in any case the Bill was unpopular with food manufacturers, who opposed its 'heroic measures' on factory

---

[69] Departmental memorandum, 'Food Contamination during Preparation', 20 February 1919, MH 56/33, PRO. The author of this memorandum, which includes the account of Spencer Low's 1914 investigation, is not identified.

inspections and sampling. By contrast retailers supported factory inspection as a means of raising standards in smaller factories.[70] With food processors opposed, however, when trade conditions worsened in the wake of the sudden collapse of the post-war boom, it was most unlikely that the Bill could attain Parliamentary approval. Brock did advise colleagues that the Bill offered one possible advantage: as the Ministry of Food would take on the task of setting standards, it would have lightened the Health Ministry's ever-expanding administrative load.[71] But Sir George Newman, Chief Medical Officer, demurred, adamant that his emergent department should concede none of its established powers.[72] In this he was supported by MacFadden, who observed that the increasing application of science to food manufacturing meant that the Ministry of Health might need to increase rather than reduce its powers under the Sale of Food and Drugs Acts.[73] An interdepartmental conference duly decided that the Food Ministry would only ever be allowed to issue standards with the 'concurrence' of the Ministry of Health.[74] But neither the Bill or MacFadden's draft regulations were accommodated in the 1920–1 Parliamentary session, with the government again citing the pressure on administrative business caused by an unforeseen external crisis – this time it was civil war in Ireland – as the insurmountable obstacle to progress.[75] Beckett noted two years later that the inability to secure the new measures also reflected problems of geography. As many newer food factories were located in rural county districts rather than large towns, their produce was not substantially consumed locally, so the responsible local authority would have 'no special inducement to undertake a special supervision'.[76]

In the early 1920s food remained a sensitive subject, some people with wartime experience in the Ministry of Food or Consumers' Council lobbied for greater planning or further consumer representation, drawing on support from the Labour and Co-operative movements. There was also a wartime legacy of concern about higher food prices. During the 1920s the various political debates revealed the existence of rather different policy networks. In 1921 the FMF still anticipated a Sale of Food Bill including regulations on sale by weight, misdescription and quality and attributed such concerns to the Consumers' Council, co-operatives and unions. The Federation's Bulletin sourly asserted that, 'Apparently the manufacturers' point of view does not count at this stage'.[77] In some respects such gloom proved unwarranted. After 1920 there was no further concerted attempt to secure registration of food-processing premises. And the prospect of any further departmental challenge to the Health Ministry's responsibilities under the SFDA was

---

[70] *The Grocer*, April 1920, pp. 860–1.
[71] Brock to MacFadden (Inspector of Foods, Ministry of Health), 25 October 1920, MH56/30, PRO.
[72] Correspondence between MacFadden and Newman, 8–9 November 1920.
[73] MacFadden to Newman, 23 November 1920, MH56/30, PRO.
[74] Minutes of Inter-Departmental Conference of 26 November 1920, MH56/30, PRO.
[75] *The Analyst*, 47, 1922, p. 110.
[76] Beckett to MacLachlan, 19 October 1922, MH 56/33, PRO.
[77] Food Manufacturers' Federation, *Bulletin*, 3 January 1921, p. 8.

finally removed in 1921, with the dissolution of the Ministry of Food. A contentious outstanding issue was food prices, with a Royal Commission being appointed in 1925 to investigate the subject. Its hearings featured testimony from manufacturers and retailers, but also from the Co-operative and labour movements which advocated the establishment of a Food Consumers' Council. Pugh noted that the Labour Party included good food as part of its health programmes in the 1920s and women's organisations also campaigned on food prices. The National Council of Women of Great Britain and Ireland testified before the Royal Commission and the influential Women's Co-operative Guild (WCG) was a significant pressure group as part of its advocacy of the rights of women as consumers.[78] The WCG was particularly vigilant about the brands, prices and quality of goods stocked in the Co-op stores. While prominent over prices, the Labour, Co-operative and women's organisations were not so involved in the debates over weights and measures and food standards. There was some further legislation; the Consumers' Council's pressure did result in the continuation of some of the wartime regulations of the weight of commodities. The Sale of Food Order of 1921 provided for the sale of bread and tea by net weight, a minimum fruit content for jams and the identification of imported bacon, ham and lard.[79] Although opinions were divided, there was trade support for these measures, notably from leading bakeries.[80] After a series of annual renewals, the issue of weights and measures was investigated by the Food Council in a report to the Board of Trade in 1926.[81] The Food Council concluded that existing legislation was cumbersome and ineffective, particularly in relation to pre-packaged goods, so that there was considerable diversity in, for example, the practice of selling by gross weight including packaging or by the net weight of the actual food or drink. Calls for more prescriptive legislation came from several local authorities and the Incorporated Society of Inspectors of Weights and Measures, a lobby very similar to the combination of councils and the professional organisations of analysts and doctors. But there was also support from retailers, notably the Co-operative Society, Scottish grocers and the Association of Multiple-Shop Proprietors. Many business associations accepted the merit of regulating on short weight, especially for pre-packaged goods. Such support came from the London Chamber of Commerce and from associations, such as the bakers, in trades where the earlier Sale by Weight orders had proved acceptable. Lipton's solicitor stated that the sale of tea by net weight had contributed to an increase in the firm's market share and profits. The main opposition was the National Federation of Grocers' Associations and the FMF who argued that fraud was uncommon, liability should lie with the employees who weighed foods with employers, and if legislation was to be introduced many items

---

[78] Martin Pugh, *Women and the Women's Movement in Britain, 1914–59* (London, 1992), pp. 105–6, 124, 132–3, 230–4, 236.
[79] *British Food Journal*, September 1921, pp. 82–4.
[80] Inter-Departmental Committee, Sale of Bread by Weight (1921), Cmd. 1400.
[81] Food Council on Question of Short Weight and Measure in Sale of Foodstuffs, vols 1–4, October–December 1925.

should be exempt. The FMF argued that chocolates, fruit and bottled goods were 'count' goods that were sold by item or number rather than by weight. For such products, consumers accepted price not weight as the most relevant information; the FMF representative claimed, 'Money is the standard. There never has been a weight standard.' The majority of FMF testimony centred on jam, a reflection of the intense competition in the sector. For jams, the FMF claimed that jars could not be made to precise volumes, though this was disputed by a representative of Hartley's. The debate led to new legislation in 1926 to tighten the regulation of weights and measures. In this respect the government was addressing aspects of fraudulent selling, and a 'public interest' alliance, with some trade support, plus backing from the Board of Trade, overcame resistance from manufacturers and some grocers. Such conditions were not present in the separate debates over food standards.

The Willis Inquiry and assumptions about production

With the removal of the government department which had been seeking enhanced methods of consumer protection, in the 1920s the public interest case for general food standards was advanced by the Public Analysts alone. The standards debates attracted less public attention than the question of food prices and did not engage the active involvement of the Labour, Co-operative or women's organisations. The Co-operative movement was based on promoting food quality, but regarded its own stores as the route to this, emphasising the importance of the Co-operative ideology, rather than seeking to regulate the food trades generally.[82] As a result councils and the Analysts remained the most prominent advocates of standards. Pointing to the changing nature of food manufacturing, with the growth of prepared and pre-packaged foods, the SPA argued that the Sale of Food and Drugs Acts had become out-dated. The original legislation had been a useful weapon to counter the use of poisonous adulterants, but it did not afford the consumer adequate protection against the more 'sophisticated' manufacturing practices of the 1920s. Under the SFDA the prosecution had to demonstrate that a fraudulent article was not of the 'nature, substance and quality demanded'. In the face of conflicting 'expert' evidence proffered by the defence, the absence of definite standards complicated the task of securing legal convictions and in the 1920s the SPA had to content itself with the piecemeal addition of the few standards, some via reputation and others via private agreement, described earlier. The SPA also welcomed the establishment of official guidelines on a limited number of preservatives in 1925, under the Public Health (Preservatives, etc. in Foods) Regulations. These were regarded as 'admirably precise and unequivocal', and apparently strengthened the Analysts' argument for a broader range of similarly unambiguous definitions.[83]

---

[82] Jean Gaffin and David Thoms, *Caring and Sharing: The centenary history of the Co-operative Women's Guild* (Manchester, 1983), pp. 55, 92–3, 101–3.

[83] *The Analyst*, 51, 1926, p. 125 and 52, 1927, p. 191.

But, in contrast to the weights and measures issue, standards received little support from the food trades or the relevant government department. Indeed food processors regarded the earlier attention paid to food prices and the new legislation, notably the Preservatives Regulations, as justification for no further interference in their affairs. In his address to the 1927 FMF lunch, Sir Stanley Machin, the Federation's president, proclaimed that 'No one can desire pure food, sound food, best quality food more strongly than the manufacturer himself for he depends for his existence on maintaining the confidence of the consumer'.[84] With the Minister of Health and three of his food officials in the audience, Machin accepted the government's responsibility for monitoring quality, but rejected any definitions of recipes on the basis that the consumer was the final arbiter. In reply, Neville Chamberlain portrayed his Ministry's role as protecting public health rather than 'prescribing' standards.

In May 1929, having failed to overcome the Ministry of Health's opposition to standards, the SPA asked the Committee of Civil Research (CCR), forerunner of the Economic Advisory Council which was established in 1930, to investigate the issue.[85] The Analysts proposed standards for 27 foods including vinegar, jam, chocolate, margarine, ice-cream, and meat and fish pastes. This initiative prompted an anxious discussion within the Ministry of Health. While departmental officials had supported the introduction of the preservatives regulations on health grounds, they did not feel that standards were justifiable on the same basis and were well aware of the food processors' opposition to any new legislation. Sir George Newman told Sir Arthur Robinson, Permanent Secretary, that the 'general temper of the trades concerned at the present time would not welcome an inquiry into further restrictions and definitions'. Neither was he convinced that standards and definitions were required from a public health viewpoint.[86] At the same time Health officials viewed the SPA's approach to the CCR as a potential threat to their authority on food and drugs questions. Newman was advised by one of his colleagues that the 'analysts have evidently grown weary of our reluctance to do anything ... and have cast around to find some other body from which more might be hoped.'[87] J. N. Beckett, who had led the Ministry's conduct of the preservatives inquiry, found an ingenious method of reconciling this opposition to standards with the need to regain the initiative from the CCR. Instead of basing the inquiry on the sole and direct issue of standards, Beckett suggested that it be set up as a more general survey of 'composition and description of food' under the SFDA. As the Ministry of Health already bore the general responsibility for the SFDA, the relative interests of other departments in such an inquiry would be slight.[88]

[84] Food Manufacturers' Federation, *Bulletin*, XIV, no 177, 1 June 1927, pp. 69–71.
[85] Peter Hennessy, *Whitehall* (London, 1990), p. 82; Edward Hinks (President, Society of Public Analysts) to A. F. Hemming (Assistant Secretary, Committee of Civil Research), 17 May 1929, MH56/1, PRO.
[86] Newman to Robinson, 11 December 1929, MH56/1, PRO.
[87] Hamill to Newman, 9 July 1929, MH56/1, PRO.
[88] Beckett to Robinson, 2 October 1929, MH56/1, PRO.

The Department of Health in Scotland, which had initially favoured an inquiry by the CCR, accepted this position in November: the inquiry would be undertaken by an ordinary Departmental Committee under the stewardship of both departments.[89] At this point, however, there was a significant delay in proceedings, arising from the Ministry of Health's essential reluctance to undertake the inquiry. Sir George Newman was especially cautious, convinced that business opposition to further state intervention, following the introduction of the preservatives regulations, would make it impossible to secure standards. A departmental memo prepared in January 1930 gives the flavour of Newman's thinking, noting that producers 'regarded themselves as having been already unduly harassed by the legislation and regulations of recent years'. Given the additional fact that adulteration figures had been falling steadily for around 50 years, the memo concluded that 'there was a case for postponing the question of further legislation'.[90]

Eventually, with the need to preserve the Ministry's undiluted food and drugs responsibilities over-riding the basic opposition to new regulations, a general inquiry of the type favoured by Beckett was established in May 1931. Sir Frederick Willis agreed to chair a Departmental Committee to assess whether changes to the law on 'the composition and description' of food were desirable.[91] Willis was a former Medical Officer at the LGB and Chairman of the Board of Control from 1920 to 1928, but he was also a member of the People's League of Health, a pressure group concerned with a wide range of social policy issues including food quality, diet and eugenics.[92] In this sense Willis was a bureaucratic figure with connections to a reform movement. Having met just once, on 24 June, the 15-member Committee was promptly suspended in September, as the Whitehall Heads of Divisions sought economies in state expenditure in the weeks following the formation of the National government. The Ministry accepted this postponement without complaint, and although the worst aspects of the financial crisis had apparently been averted by the spring of 1932, no attempt was made to revive the Willis Committee. A.B. Maclachlan, a departmental Medical Officer, noted on 9 March that the 'cumbersome body' did not need to be reconvened, and if it expired then at a later date a 'smaller and more manageable committee' could be established.[93] On 18 March Sir Arthur Robinson told the new Minister of Health, Edward Hilton Young, that the Food Committee 'can very suitably remain suspended – departmentally we were never keen on it'.[94] This frank admission strongly suggests that senior Ministry figures were content to use the political and financial crisis as a pretext for suppressing the investigation which had been thrust upon them by the SPA and the CCR.

[89] Fraser to Beckett, 6 November 1929, MH56/1, PRO.
[90] Unsigned memo, 10 January 1930, MH56/8, PRO.
[91] Report of the Departmental Committee on the Composition and Description of Food (Willis), April 1934, Cmd. 4564, p. 2.
[92] Greta Jones, *Social Hygiene in Twentieth Century Britain* (London, 1986), pp. 81–2.
[93] Maclachlan memo, 9 March 1932, MH56/1, PRO.
[94] Robinson to Hilton Young, 18 March 1932, MH56/1, PRO.

Having been formed as an expedient, in 1933 the Willis Committee was revived as an expedient, at the request of Walter Elliott, the Minister of Agriculture. Elliott's intervention was prompted by persistent calls in Parliament for cheese standards from a Cheshire MP, R. J. Russell. Russell's activities were an echo of the NFU's negotiations with the SPA in 1930, and he claimed that the case for standards enjoyed the 'unanimous support' of cheese producers in Cheshire and Somerset.[95] The Ministry of Agriculture was embarrassed by a campaign with this type of rural support: while opposing compulsory food standards it was anxious to avoid publicly opposing an influential section of the farming industry. Elliott duly asked Hilton Young to revive the Willis Committee. This would allow Elliott's department to cite the existence of a general inquiry on food standards as an explanation for failing to support particular standards for cheese.[96] The Ministry of Health agreed to Elliott's request, taking the opportunity to narrow the Committee's terms of reference from the general question of whether the SFDA required alteration to the particular question of whether definitions or standards were desirable.[97]

Re-appointed on 24 July, the Committee began gathering oral evidence on 20 September 1933 before submitting its report on 20 March 1934. The SPA used the hearings to restate its case for comprehensive standards based on the advice of a standing committee with wide investigative powers. This position was supported by analysts from the Society of the Chemical Industry, the Society of Medical Officers of Health and the representative bodies of the local authorities charged with enforcing the SFDA, namely the County Councils' Association and the Municipal Corporations' Association, along with the Co-operative Congress. All of these advanced a public interest case based on informing and protecting consumers, although there were differences of opinion about the character of any standing advisory committee.[98] Further support came from Professor J.C. Drummond on behalf of the People's League of Health which favoured a broad range of standards. He argued that misleading advertising and labelling undermined consumers' ability to choose and, thus, required legislation to maintain best practice and to raise quality.[99] The County Councils' Association similarly emphasised that standards would not harm reputable firms. The traditional emphasis on inexpensive foods was linked to the developing concern with nutrition as the Society of Medical Officers of Health was anxious that standards should not jeopardise the supply of cheap nutritious foods.[100] The most interesting new source of testimony was provided by representatives of the recently formed Food Group of the Society of

---

[95] Parliamentary Debates, Fifth Series, Vol. 274, 822–4, 14 February 1933.
[96] Elliott to Hilton Young, 3 May 1933, MH56/12, PRO.
[97] Report of the Departmenal Committee, Cmd. 4564, p. 3.
[98] Departmental Committee on Food Law; evidence from meetings held on 10 October 1933, 1 November 1993, 9 January 1934, 20 February 1934; MH56/2–4, PRO.
[99] *British Medical Journal*, 3 March 1934, pp. 386–7.
[100] For the parallel debates over nutritional standards see Paul Weindling, 'The Role of International Organisations in Setting Nutritional Standards in the 1920s and 1930s', in Kamminga and Cunningham(eds), *Science and Culture of Nutrition*, pp. 319–332.

the Chemical Industry. Established in 1932, the Society consisted of chemists employed in the food industry and its meetings included discussions with academics and public analysts.[101] The Food Group's first meeting included a discussion of possible bacteriological standards for milk and ice cream. It represented by far the strongest expression of opinion about food regulation by industrial analytical chemists, compared to the earlier testimony before official inquiries by individual company chemists.[102] The Food Group's principal witness before the Willis Committee was Dr Leslie H. Lampitt, who was chief chemist at Lyons and, as Horrocks has shown, considered food scientists to be the vital element in ensuring a supply of cheap and safe food.[103] In his evidence, Lampitt suggested that standards could be introduced without raising prices and might be applied to tea, coffee, jam, cream and cheese to protect consumers. Lampitt claimed that standards were not required for chocolates and cakes.[104] Even this qualified support for standards created consternation within the FMF because its combination of professional and industrial expertise provided greater legitimacy than testimony from Public Analysts or others whose views could be portrayed as impractical. Apparently some processors discussed the position with their works chemists so as to 'avoid a recurrence of the difficulty'.[105] Lampitt continued to speak publicly in favour of food standards, though in terms of the difficulties of establishing them beyond a narrow range of products and the dangers of undermining the industry's self-discipline over quality.[106]

This internal FMF debate reflected a wider division of business opinion. Several of the firms and associations who were already seeking regulation to give their products a commercial advantage, notably the Malt Vinegar Brewers' Federation and the Cheshire Cheese Federation, repeated their calls for selected definitions, although they opposed mandatory general standards.[107] The Food Manufacturers' Federation and the Manufacturing Confectioners' Alliance, along with the Margarine Manufacturers' Association, opposed any extension of the limited existing framework of standards and definitions. Indeed the FMF's Bulletin's initial response to the SPA's evidence emphasised the Analysts' self-interest in promoting standards in order to simplify their own work and to ensure convictions.[108] The

[101] *Food Manufacture*, 8(1), January 1933, p. 1.

[102] Evidence of opposing views among analysts can be found in discussions of food standards in the pages of *Food Manufacture* in 1933. The journal's editorials stressed clear labelling as a more appropriate way to inform and educate the public than the introduction of compulsory food standards. See *Food Manufacture*, January 1933, pp. 17–23, February, 1933, pp. 62–6, June 1933, p. 204–7.

[103] Sally Horrocks, 'The Business of Vitamins: Nutrition Science and the Food Industry in Inter-war Britain', in Kamminga and Cunningham (eds), *Science and Culture of Nutrition*, pp. 245–6.

[104] Departmental Committee on Food Law, Lampitt testimony, 9 January 1934, MH56/4, PRO; Food Manufacturers' Federation, *Bulletin*, 21, 257, February 1934, pp. 21–2.

[105] Food Manufacturers' Federation, *Bulletin*, 20 February 1934.

[106] *Ibid.*, 21, 265, p. 228.

[107] Departmental Committee on Food Law; evidence from meetings held on 11 and 31 October 1933; MH56/2, PRO.

[108] Food Manufacturers' Federation, *Bulletin*, November 1933, p. 243.

FMF distinguished between 'natural' products like butter and cheese for which the SFDA provided sufficient regulation and other commodities that required greater processing. On this occasion manufacturers were better organised than they had been during the preservatives hearings in 1923, submitting detailed written and oral testimony. Importantly, perhaps, they also adopted a more conciliatory tone. The FMF's President, G. P. Shippam, the meat and fish paste manufacturer, insisted that standards were both unnecessary and unenforceable: unnecessary because essentially the industry already delivered a high-quality product to the 'housewife', and unenforceable because most food was too complex for exact analysis. At the same time, however, Shippam conceded that some items, including jams and baby foods, might usefully be standardised on a voluntary basis; all were sectors where private discussions about trade practices were well established in the hope, often unrealised, of limiting competition. Shippam even accepted the idea of a central advisory committee, provided it was based on business expertise rather than the SPA. Such agreement was predicated on the development of an agreed system of analytical tests, by no means a straightforward proposition.

Other trade associations remained obdurate. The National Federation of Meat Traders claimed all legal standards were impractical given changing consumer tastes and incomes. The manufacturing case against standards was also made by Paul S. Cadbury of the Manufacturing Confectioners' Alliance (MCA), who claimed they would prevent producers from developing products to meet changing consumer taste, inflate prices and so restrict the overall confectionery market. In a memorandum to the committee, the MCA argued that the 1928 SFDA provided sufficient protection against harmful or fraudulent products as well as protecting manufacturers from 'food faddists'.[109] Paul Cadbury argued at length that unregulated market forces and branded goods were the best guarantee of quality. Asked whether minimum milk fat standards would enhance consumer confidence in milk chocolate, Cadbury replied, 'the best confidence is that you sell a good quality article and put money into advertising it, and it would be very foolish to do anything which would shake confidence in a proprietary article. I think that is far better than any standards.' The MCA depicted the Analysts' claims about fraud and deception as attacks on the intelligence of consumers and 'worse ungallant, because the purchasers are generally women'.[110] Unlike manufacturers of products like condensed milk and malt vinegar, Cadbury was opposed to standards that might, in theory, have given his own goods a competitive advantage over budget rivals. Alleging that standards would force cheaper items off the market, he added, 'I am not speaking with any personal interest in the lower quality articles, but I like to see children develop a taste for chocolate which I hope as they grow up and have more money will be to my personal advantage.'[111] This sense of a common interest in the condition of the industry

[109] Ibid., pp. 244–5.
[110] Ibid., pp. 244–6. The memorandum noted the MCA's resistance to continental chocolate firms' efforts to set international standards in 1911 and 1930.
[111] Departmental Committee on Food Law; evidence from meetings on 27–8 November 1933 and 9 January 1934, MH56/3–4, PRO.

perhaps reflected the established tradition of associationalism in the chocolate trade as well as its acceptance by the 1930s of the importance of marketing. Another explanation for the MCA's opposition was the prospect that standards created a basic level of quality which depressed prices and profit margins. The Federation of Grocers' Associations was more equivocal than the manufacturing organisations, suggesting that standards might raise prices as well as quality, so penalising the poor, but reasserted its traditional case that responsibility for any illegalities should be placed on producers rather than retailers.[112]

Willis also heard evidence from the Ministries of Health and Agriculture. Beckett summarised the highly ambivalent position of his department thus: 'We see there are certain abuses, or potential abuses, in the absence of standards and definitions, and we see there are certain difficulties about prescribing standards or definitions.' Indicating a preference for only a limited number of definitions, the Health Ministry was particularly anxious that compulsory jam standards, for example, would cut 'off from the market the inferior jams which are quite good, quite pure and harmless, good food and cheaper'. Such arguments reflected the belief of leading Ministry of Health officials that nutritional deficiencies were related more to ignorance than low incomes and that improvements were possible, through additional education and advice, without major extensions of state intervention.[113] The Agriculture Ministry advocated voluntary standards, in line with existing grading and marking schemes.[114] Willis' conduct of the hearings revealed little of his own views, though he consistently highlighted the idea of standards set by the Ministry of Health rather than by an expert standing committee.

The Willis report was completed on 20 March 1934 and prior to its publication the FMF anticipated recommendations for standards for baby and invalid foods only.[115] In the event Willis broadly endorsed the views of the manufacturers, finding that 'a large proportion' of food was of high quality and that 'many manufacturers take a pride in the production of good-quality articles and exercise great care in their manufacture'. The Committee also asserted, contrary to a view which had been expressed by the SPA, that 'the average housewife' was capable of exercising skill and discretion when making her purchases.[116] There was little sign of Willis applying the

---

[112] Departmental Committee on Food Law; evidence from meeting on 14 November 1933, MH56/3, PRO.

[113] Smith and Nicolson, 'Nutrition, education, ignorance and income, pp. 296–8.

[114] Departmental Committee on Food Law; evidence from meetings on 20 September and 14 November 1933; MH56/2–3, PRO.

[115] Food Manufacturers' Federation, Executive, Minutes, 20 February 1934.

[116] This argument provides an interesting sidelight on the contemporary arguments within and around the Ministry of Health's Government Advisory Committee on Nutrition set up in 1931. Its concerns with diet, calorie intakes and health included a controversy over whether poor health was due primarily to low incomes or to ignorance and poor purchasing decisions. The latter view, articulated by EP Cathcart, among others, was used to counter suggestions that higher wages were required; the committee's work remained largely mired in internal diagrements. See Greta Jones, *Social Hygiene*, (1986), pp. 127–33 and David F. Smith, 'Nutrition Science and the Two World Wars', in David F. Smith (ed.), *Nutrition in Britain: Science, scientists and politics in the twentieth century* (Amsterdam, 1997), pp. 149–54.

arguments of the People's League of Health, despite his membership of the organisation. In answering its main brief, the Committee was therefore cautious. Although recommending the desirability of changing the law to allow the establishment of standards and definitions, the Committee urged that these be adopted on a limited basis only: 'the case for the extension of standards and definitions to all articles is not made out'. The other main recommendation was also liable to please the Ministry of Health and manufacturers rather than the SPA, emphasising that the responsibility for definitions should reside with the Ministry of Health and the Scottish Health Department alone. On the basis that these departments possessed the necessary resources and expertise to determine any appropriate standards, the idea of establishing a new advisory body was definitely ruled out.[117]

Food producers reacted favourably to the Willis report. *Food Manufacture* described it as a 'very satisfactory document', welcoming in particular the rejection of a standing Advisory Committee, and noting with equal satisfaction that Willis and his colleagues were content 'as to the integrity of the British food manufacturer and the quality of his products'.[118] Having hoped in 1932 that the inquiry would lead to 'the removal of anomalies and objectionable features' from the existing legislation, the SPA's response was understandably less effusive. In March 1936 John Evans, the Society's President, told members that, 'Whatever may be our individual views regarding this Report, it is highly satisfactory to note that the main contention of the Society, namely, the necessity for extended statutory powers for establishing definitions and standards for articles of food, has been conceded.'[119] The leading medical journals took rather different views. The *BMJ* noted the report's 'moderate' tone and reasonable proposals; the *Lancet* criticised the rejection of any outside advisory body, arguing that 'informal conferences with manufacturers and other interests' would limit effective representation and the ability to 'stimulate' the Ministry of Health into action.[120]

The government departments which had commissioned the report, the Ministry of Health and the Scottish Health Department, viewed it with a mixture of satisfaction and complacency. John Vallance of the Scottish Department, who had served on the Committee, told Godfrey Collins, the Scottish Secretary of State, that the recommendation against a standing committee was 'on the right lines', and that the report in general would commend itself to Ministers.[121] Vallance and Beckett of the Health Ministry, who had also been on the Committee, drafted a memo outlining the manner in which the Willis Report's recommendations could be legislatively implemented. But Beckett's senior colleagues once again blocked any changes to the law in the short term, Maclachlan noting on 18 May that he saw 'no immediate prospect for legislation'.[122]

[117] Report of the Departmental Committee, Cmd. 4564, para. 16–18, 32–4.
[118] *Food Manufacture*, June 1934.
[119] *The Analyst*, 57, 1932, p. 216 and 61, 1936, p. 229.
[120] *British Medical Journal*, 12 May 1934, pp. 855–6; *Lancet*, 19 May 1934, p. 1076.
[121] Vallance to the Secretary of State, 5 June 194, HH 64/4, Scottish Record Office (SRO).
[122] Maclachlan to Beckett, 18 May 1934, MH56/12, PRO.

Health officials were content to leave the existing legal framework intact essentially because they, like Willis, took the testimony of the FMF and the MCA at face value. Like the members of the original Parliamentary Select Committee which had drawn up the 1875 SFDA, these officials believed food producers who said that there was nothing unsatisfactory or dangerous in manufacturing methods and ingredients. This important belief was simply untested. Although the wartime reports and the draft regulations of 1920 had raised doubts about the safety of manufacturing conditions, local authority efforts under the SFDA were still concentrated almost exclusively on the sale rather than the production of food. Shopkeepers rather than manufacturers were the target, and Health Ministry officials themselves made no effort to examine manufacturing conditions in the 1920s and 1930s. To some extent this assumption about the safety of production was justified, given the industry's growing deployment of scientific research and expertise. As Sally Horrocks in particular has indicated, some companies had been making extensive use of scientists by the interwar period. The record on quality and safety of giant manufacturers like Rowntree and Keiller who used such expertise was especially impressive.[123] In 1925, moreover, the Food Manufacturers' Federation established the British Food Manufacturers' Research Association. This worked alongside a separate research association, set up in 1919, for Cocoa, Chocolate, Sugar Confectionery and Jam producers, the two bodies sharing a Research Director and a laboratory in North London.[124] But the industry's use of science was limited. Although the Food Research Association was patronised by a number of meat and fish producers, despite the FMF's corporate sponsorship it was unable to secure much wider support, with smaller companies expressing very little interest in research and development. This failure was ascribed by the Research Association's Secretary to the fact that manufacturers, 'as a body', simply did not appreciate the relevance or potential value of scientific research.[125]

This imbalance between big companies that were committed to research and small companies that were not is extremely important. Despite the growth of industrial concentration, in the food trade as elsewhere, big firms like Rowntree and Keiller (which from 1920 was part of the larger Crosse and Blackwell combine) contributed only a minority share of the industry's output. As was indicated in chapter 2, the 1930 *Census of Production* showed that the 29 largest employers in the food, drink and tobacco trades, each comprising more than 1,500 individuals, were collectively responsible for approximately one-quarter of the industry's gross and net output. Hence the bulk of production – the remaining three-quarters – was conducted by the 5,000-plus smaller enterprises which employed between ten and 1,500 individuals and which, broadly speaking, were much less committed to scientific research than their larger rivals. In other words, the typical unit of production was a small unit employing between 11 and 24 people, of which there were

[123] Sally M. Horrocks, 'Quality control and research', pp. 130–45.
[124] British Food Manufacturers' Research Association, Memorandum and Articles of Association, 31 December 1925; copy in DSIR 16/71, PRO.
[125] Memorandum by R. M. Leonard, 7 November 1934, DSIR 16/149, PRO.

2,245 in 1930, or a slightly larger unit, employing between 25 and 49, of which there were 1,449.[126]

As there was no systematic regulation of these smaller units in the 1920s or 1930s, no evidence about the physical conditions of food production was centrally gathered, and hence the Ministry of Health's positive general view of manufacturing was not necessarily legitimate. This relaxed view – of conditions and the absence of information concerning these conditions – is worth re-emphasising, because as late as 1920 the Ministry had been presented with substantial evidence which supported an entirely different picture of food production. It is possible that officials later obtained evidence that all producers – small and large – had taken the war-time inspections as a salutary experience and irrevocably mended their unhygienic ways. And it is also possible that many smaller producers followed the unsophisticated 1927 advice of *Food Manufacture*, and picked a 'young, intelligent hand' from the shopfloor, financed his path through junior technical classes at the local night school and placed the said journal 'into his hand every month'.[127] Yet as late as 1934 the FMF's own Research Association was bemoaning the industry's basic disinterest in scientific research. This undermines the general validity of the Willis report and the Ministry of Health's assumption about food production, which were both drawn from an extremely narrow focus on the practices and evidence of a small number of giant manufacturing companies that may have been unrepresentative of the industry as a whole.

The Food and Drugs Act, 1938

The 1938 Food and Drugs Act emerged four years after the publication of the Willis report on standards. In July 1934 Edward Hilton Young, Minister of Health, told the House of Commons that while the Willis report was 'under consideration', no changes to the law were imminent. This remained the government's position for a further three years, Young replicating these words – more or less verbatim – in February 1935, and on several occasions in 1936 and 1937 his successor, Kingsley Wood, also refused to commit the government to implementing Willis's recommendations. Wood eventually communicated the reasoning behind the delay, informing Parliament in November 1937 that the appropriate legislative changes were being considered by the Local Government and Public Health Consolidation Committee.[128] Like the Willis Committee, this had been formally established by Arthur Greenwood, Minister of Health in the 1929–31 Labour government, to explore the possibility of consolidating in one item of legislation the various public health measures in England and Wales. The largest part of the work of this Committee, chaired by Lord Addington, had been completed with the passage of the

[126] HMSO, 4th Census of Production, 1930, Vol. 3, p. 10 (1931).
[127] *Food Manufacture*, December 1927, p. 201.
[128] Parliamentary Debates, Fifth Series, Vol. 292, 509–10, 12 July 1934; Vol. 298, 1286, 28 February 1935; Vol. 315, 1715–16, 30 July 1936; Vol. 324, 452, 27 May 1937; Vol. 326, 1476, 15 July 1937; Vol. 328, 1131–2, 4 November 1937.

1936 Public Health Act. But in November 1936 Kingsley Wood prolonged its life by extending its terms of reference 'to include the enactments relating to the adulteration of food and drugs'.[129]

This meant bringing together statutes and regulations on food issued under the Public Health as well as the Sale of Food and Drugs Acts, a move which had been considered by the Ministry of Health in the 1920s, prior to the issue of the 1928 Food and Drugs Act. But although regarded in 1928 as the 'the ultimate object', consolidation had then been considered impractical, largely because the public health and food and drugs measures were administered by different authorities.[130] By the mid 1930s the Ministry of Health had presumably altered its thinking to the extent of believing that consolidation was a realisable goal in administrative terms. At this point officials may also have felt that an early introduction of regulations for defining standards would have unfairly pre-empted the work of the Consolidation Committee. Given the Ministry's previous record, however, in setting yet another committee to investigate the future of the food and drugs laws, including standards, officials may simply have been seeking a device to extend the delay in implementing change.

Addington's findings on food and drugs were published in December 1937, the Consolidation Committee's third report overall. Public health, it noted, was only one of the objectives of existing food and drugs law, the other being to protect the consumer from 'fraud and deception'. The Draft Bill offered by the Committee – published as a separate Command Paper – was thus sensitive to precedent, attempting to consolidate the law in such a way that both objectives would be secured.[131] Hence it included the 1928 Sale of Food and Drugs Act, the 1915 and 1922 Milk Acts, the food sections of the 1875 Public Health Act and its 1890, 1907 and 1925 amendments, and the other sundry public health items on Markets and Fairs, slaughterhouses and knackers' yards. Beyond these consolidatory measures the Bill offered nothing that was original, although it did support the main conclusion of the Willis Report, that the Ministry of Health be permitted to provide standards and definitions of particular foods. Clause 8(1)(c) of the Bill allowed the Minister to issue regulations 'prohibiting or restricting the addition of any substance to, and regulating the composition of, any food'.

The Draft Bill duly became the Food and Drugs Act of 1938 with only one significant alteration. While the Bill was sensitive to both the public health and consumer protection objectives of all preceding food and drugs legislation, it completely ignored – or overlooked – the fact that the SFDA had been applied comprehensively to the United Kingdom as a whole, and not just to England and Wales. The Bill therefore excluded any reference to how its provisions might be applied in Scotland or Northern Ireland. In November 1937 the Scottish Health

---

[129] Local Government and Public Health Consolidation Committee. Third Interim Report (Addington), December 1937, Cmd. 5628.
[130] Unsigned Ministry memo, July 1928, MH56/27, PRO.
[131] Local Government and Public Health Consolidation Committee. Draft of a Food and Drugs Bill, December 1937, Cmd. 5629.

Department pointed out to the Ministry of Health that if Clause 8 was not applied throughout the United Kingdom, 'any of the articles prescribed which did not come up to standard in England could be dumped in Scotland'.[132] This omission was later reversed, with Section 8 becoming one of a handful of the Act's provisions that were adopted in Scotland. Yet even this limited extension left Scottish public analysts dissatisfied. In a letter to the Scottish Health Department, the Secretary of the Society of Public Analysts' Scottish Section, J. B. McKean, pointed out that the 1938 Act was the first item of Food and Drugs legislation that had not been entirely applied on a UK basis. McKean insisted that there were a number of the Act's missing provisions in Scotland, notably on labelling and water content in margarine, 'which would, with advantage, apply equally well in Scotland'; and he added that local authorities would be greatly inconvenienced in having to administer different parts of two separate Acts.[133]

With the clause allowing the Minister of Health to issue regulations for specific products, and almost ten years after the SPA had originally approached the Committee of Civil Research about hosting an inquiry into food standards, the principle had finally been established that the contents of any item of food could be unambiguously and statutorily defined. The SPA, which had spent five decades campaigning for such a provision, was therefore greatly heartened. Its President described the measure as 'a valuable piece of legislation and one which will commend itself to all those who desire to see that only pure and wholesome foods reach the public'.[134] Some manufacturers were also pleased. Following the passage of the legislation the Ministry of Health was contacted by the Malt Vinegar Brewers' Federation, seeking a standard on the lines of the 1924 Bill which had provided for distinct categories of malt and 'imitation' vinegar. A Health official observed that the Federation 'apparently supposes, like some other interested parties, that on 1 October next [1939, when the Act took effect] standards and definitions in accordance with their own views will descend like manna from Heaven'.[135] Given the Ministry's previous record, any change was likely to be at a slow pace. In the event conditions changed radically following the outbreak of war and the Ministry of Health's powers became the basis for a far more interventionist approach by the new Ministry of Food. An Inter-Departmental Committee was established in 1942 to advise the new Ministry on food quality standards; among its members were representatives of the Ministry of Health and the SPA. By 1945 there were 13 standards, including ones for mustard, vinegar, custard powder and self-raising flour.[136]

---

[132] Scottish Health Department memo to the Ministry of Health, 13 November 1937, HH 64/2, SRO.

[133] J. B. McKean to the Secretary of the Department of Health for Scotland, 27 December 1938, HH 64/3, SRO.

[134] *The Analyst*, 63, 1938, p. 238.

[135] Departmental minute, unsigned, 29 June 1939, MH 56/333, PRO.

[136] A.G. Ward, 'Advising on Food Standards in the United Kingdom', in MAFF, *Food Quality and Safety: A century of progresss* (1975), pp. 26–8, 38.

Conclusion: market competition or statutory regulation?

To a large extent the debate about standards represented the broader debate about food regulation in microcosm. Business and other interest groups adopted views on standards that were consistent with their broader regulatory positions. The Society of Public Analysts saw the absence of standards as the central weakness of the SFDA and, particularly after the First World War, exploited the material interest of specialist producers in specific definitions to extend gradually the number of official or generally accepted voluntary standards. The advocacy of standards by some producers, meanwhile, was a demonstration of the potential role of business capture in the regulatory process, most vividly in the case of the UK-based condensed milk manufacturers who obtained regulations which undermined their importing rivals. The condensed milk episode illustrated the manner in which debates about broad standards involved conflicting interpretations of the 'public interest'. While some 'expert' witnesses insisted that consumers would benefit from standards as producers strived to improve quality, others argued that consumer choice would be hindered, either because standards would force producers out of business and reduce the overall volume of supply, or because premium manufacturers would level quality down to meet the bare minimum standard required.

These latter anti-regulation 'public interest' arguments were used by manufacturers during the official standards inquiry in 1933 and 1934, the character and outcome of which was directly linked to the 1923 preservatives inquiry. While the preservatives regulations increased the SPA's confidence that standards could be attained, they also strengthened the determination of manufacturers to resist new legislation. The earlier debate also encouraged their peak-level organisations, the Food Manufacturers' Federation and the Manufacturing Confectioners' Alliance, to adopt a more flexible and self-confident position. Insisting throughout the Willis hearings that their methods and ingredients were completely safe, manufacturers successfully persuaded the state that closer regulation of production was unnecessary. During the Willis Inquiry Cadbury argued that branded goods and market competition were a better way of securing improved quality than statutory regulation. This market forces argument increased the distinction between the Willis Inquiry and the specific standards for condensed milk, jam or malt vinegar which were pursued by companies seeking competitive advantages over foreign or budget rivals. At the Willis Inquiry giant companies which manufactured a wider range of products appear to have been confident enough about the longer-term position of their goods to oppose standards that might have brought benefits in the short term by eliminating budget rivals from the market. Cadbury said that he wanted nothing to inhibit the growth of public taste for chocolate in general, trusting that through advertising and product development he would in the longer term capture a growing proportion of the market, and emphasising that this market would grow more quickly if subjected to a minimum degree of regulation.

The absence of bureaucratic initiative on standards was also rooted in the preservatives episode. In the aftermath of the occasionally fractious debate between business and the state over preservatives, Health officials were reluctant to burden manufacturers with further regulations in a period of great economic and financial difficulty. In addition, the case for standards did not meet the Ministry's unwritten rule for new food regulations in the 1920s and 1930s: unlike the preservatives regulations, for example, standards would not unambiguously improve public health. The architects of the original 1875 SFDA, it will be remembered, based the justification for limited regulation – concentrating on retailers and not producers – on the assumption that the public was being 'cheated rather than poisoned'. During the standards inquiry the Ministry's representative, J. N. Beckett, conceded that prosecutions were failing against traders who were strongly suspected of supplying fraudulent – although not definitely dangerous – items because of the absence of standards.[137] In refusing to support standards the Ministry effectively tolerated the fact that some 'cheating' of food consumers was inevitable, apparently content in the assumption that 'poisoning' was not a factor. But as the evidence from the 1914 and wartime Local Government Board investigations suggests, this assumption was untested. In 1932, Sir George Newman, the Chief Medical Officer, partly recognised this, briefly departing from his general position of sympathising with the needs and methods of food manufacturers. In his annual report he dwelt on the changing nature of food production, characterising the increasing 'scientific "treatment"' of food, including the addition of vitamins and chemical preservatives, as 'A New Problem in Food Adulteration'.[138] This placed Newman in broad sympathy with the SPA and its views about 'sophisticated' forms of food adulteration, and appeared to suggest that the Ministry was contemplating more stringent methods of regulating production. Yet the final outcome of the standards inquiry, and the limited provision for regulations on 'composition' to be issued under the eventual Food and Drugs Act of 1938, demonstrated the opposite. As the following chapter on milk confirms in a more positive fashion, the Ministry remained committed only to regulations which had a direct bearing on public health.

[137] Departmental Committee on Food Standards, First Meeting, 20 September 1933, MH 56/3, PRO.
[138] Ministry of Health, On the State of the Public Health. Annual Report of the Chief Medical Officer (1932), pp. 135–42.

7
Conflicts of interest: milk regulation, 1875–1938

Within the broad study of food regulation, cow's milk merits special attention for two main reasons. First, more than any other item of food, milk was the ideal vehicle for carrying and transmitting infectious diseases, both human and bovine. In 1857 Dr. Michael Taylor, Medical Officer of Health for Penrith, attributed an outbreak of typhoid to human-infected milk, and in 1867 traced an epidemic of scarlet fever to milk supplied by a single cowkeeper with a sick child. According to P. J. Atkins this precipitated a lengthy debate within the medical community about the infectious properties of milk, so that by the 1890s doctors and other medical professionals generally accepted that milk consumption could be hazardous.[1] In 1891 the annual meeting of the Society of Medical Officers of Health accepted that the potential hazards included the transmission through milk of bovine tuberculosis to humans.[2] Individual milk-borne infections drew much publicity, such as the severe septic throat epidemic which killed an estimated 65 people in Brighton in 1929, and the outbreak of paratyphoid which led to seven deaths in Essex in 1931.[3] The Essex outbreak prompted Arthur Greenwood, Minister of Health in the Labour government, to observe that until a pure supply was obtained the authorities – including himself – would be 'acquiescing day by day in the murder of honest citizens'.[4] With this Greenwood indirectly acknowledged the cumulative effect of individual fatalities caused by milk infected with bovine tuberculosis. In the late 1920s and early 1930s about 2,000 infants were killed in this manner each year in the United Kingdom.[5] Second, while milk could easily be contaminated, it was also the single most adulterated item of food or drink. The Local Government Board

---

[1] P. J. Atkins, 'White Poison? The social consequences of milk consumption, 1850–1930', *Social History of Medicine*, 5, 1992, pp. 216–18.

[2] Public Health. Report of the Annual Proceedings of the Society of Medical Officers of Health, Vol. IV, 1891, pp. 136–7.

[3] The estimate of the Brighton fatalities was provided by the London School of Hygiene, *The Times*, 15 May 1934; the Essex epidemic is described in the Ministry of Health, Annual Report, 1930–1, Cmd. 3937, p. 45.

[4] *The Times*, 2 March 1931.

[5] F. B. Smith, *The Retreat of Tuberculosis, 1850–1951* (London, 1988), pp. 185–6.

acknowledged this in 1905, fatalistically noting that 'the facility with which milk can be adulterated militates against any appreciable reduction in the percentages of adulteration'.[6] Frequently containing contaminated water, this adulterated milk was dangerous as well as fraudulent. Atkins attributes the poor quality of milk partly to lengthening lines of communication, as urban centres drew their supplies from increasingly distant sources, which exaggerated the opportunities for infection and deterioration. Growing demand from the 1880s was also significant. Almost out-stripping supply, this tempted some producers to stretch capacity through adulteration, sometimes with skimmed milk as well as water.[7]

The clear dangers of the liquid commodity and the problems of adulteration, which were difficult for consumers to identify and threatened infants, a group usually regarded as requiring special protection, ensured that from the 1890s milk assumed an important position in several different areas of public health debate. These have been analysed by Deborah Dwork, and include the short-lived milk depots movement, efforts by doctors and others to reduce and eventually eliminate tuberculosis, early campaigns for family allowances, attempts to 'educate' mothers and enhance child welfare, and discussions about the role of sanatoriums and cures.[8] Possibly as a consequence of the very diversity of these interests, the different groups or strands of pressure never really crystallised into a concerted and lasting 'public interest' campaign for strengthened local and central government regulation of milk and dairies. Certainly the debate about milk quality and safety was generally conducted without direct input from these various social reform groups, with milk consumers' interests being represented in debates about safety by the medical profession, urban local authorities and Local Government Board and Ministry of Health bureaucrats. This pattern of consumer representation, it might be noted, fits in with Ingeborg Paulus's observations about the post-1899 development of food regulation generally, where consumers were excluded from the dialogue between civil servants, medical experts and food producers which settled the shape and detail of new legislation.[9] This absence of a strong 'public interest' campaign allowed central and local government regulation to remain extremely weak, which was arguably the most important factor in permitting dangerously unhygienic conditions of production and distribution to persist long into the interwar period. Only with the growth of pasteurisation in the 1920s was the safety of milk consumption significantly increased. This chapter reinforces the analysis of state regulation of food and drink across the broad 1875–1938 period by examining the failure to eradicate the potential hazards of milk. Extending Atkins's critical appraisal of the pre-Second World War history of milk quality and safety, it focuses on the manner in which state regulation was shaped by the

[6] Local Government Board (LGB), Annual Report, 1904–05, Cd. 2661, p. clxxvi.
[7] P. J. Atkins, 'Sophistication Detected: Or, the adulteration of the milk supply, 1850–1914', *Social History*, 16 (3), 1991, pp. 317–39.
[8] Deborah Dwork, *War is Good for Babies and other young children* (London, 1987).
[9] Ingeborg Paulus, *The Search For Pure Food: A sociology of legislation in Britain* (London, 1974), pp. 39, 84.

agricultural lobby, acting through the Ministry of Agriculture. Responsible for 25 per cent of agricultural output by 1914, Britain's 200,000 dairy producers were the most important section of the farming community.[10] This economic strength was largely derived from the fact that, unlike other farmers, producers of fresh milk were generally removed from the threat of competitive imports. By the 1890s local and national associations of dairy farmers were further defending their members' interests by advocating restrictions on imported tinned and preserved produce.[11] The Sale of Food and Drugs Act of 1899 duly created a procedure for Customs to sample cheese, milk, condensed milk and cream at the point of entry. If suspect then Board of Agriculture officers would trace goods to the point of sale.[12] The comparative advantage over imports gave dairy farmers a strong negotiating position during debates about milk safety and quality. Faced with regulations which they disliked, they routinely threatened to jeopardise domestic supply by simply abandoning milk production and moving into other areas of agriculture. These farmers represent possibly the strongest example of political capture in the general 1875–1938 story, exploiting to good effect their strong relationship with the Conservative Party, which was especially important during the lengthy periods of Conservative government in the 1920s and 1930s.

The strength of the dairy producers' lobby, and the comparative weakness of any 'public interest' pressure, is illustrated by the particular case of pasteurisation. There were attempts by public health campaigners and medical professionals to lobby for its introduction on a statutory basis. These were supported by a considerable body of bacteriological research. Among the pioneers in this respect was George Newman, the Ministry of Health's first Chief Medical Officer. In 1903, when Medical Officer of Health for Finsbury, Newman and Harold Swithinbank devised a method of pasteurisation, keeping heating in closed pasteurisers for at least 20 minutes at no less than 140°F, which apparently destroyed tubercle bacilli without injuring the cream properties or general consistency of milk.[13] Pasteurisation, by this or slightly varying means, was gradually adopted by parts of the dairy trade on a voluntary basis, and Atkins rightly emphasises that it played an extremely important part in eliminating the transmission of bovine and human infectious diseases through milk. But its wider extension, and particularly the attempt to make it compulsory, was blunted by significant divisions within the public health lobby. Many medical professionals and social reformers opposed pasteurisation, believing that it deprived milk of important nutritional properties and deflected attention from the 'real' goal of milk policy, namely the production of pure milk in clean dairies. Only in the 1930s did a pro-pasteurisation consensus

---

[10] Mathias, *The First Industrial Nation*, pp. 316–18.

[11] E. H. Hunt and S. J. Pam, 'Prices and Structural Response in English Agriculture, 1873–1896', *Economic History Review*, 50 (3), Autumn 1997, pp. 477–505.

[12] Board of Agriculture and Fisheries, Annual Report of Proceedings under the Sale of Food and Drugs Acts (1904), 1904, Cd. 2187, pp. 4–5.

[13] Arthur Guy Enock, *This Milk Business: A study from 1895 to 1943* (London, 1943), pp. 108–9.

take shape among reformers, a development reflected in the acceptance by the Ministry of Health, where Newman was now helping to direct government policy, that the public health case for compulsory pasteurisation was unambiguous. There were, by comparison, no serious divisions within the producing community. Operating in conjunction with Ministry of Agriculture officials, dairy farmers resolutely and successfully opposed pasteurisation, largely on grounds of cost, although arguments about the nutritional implications of heat treatment were also deployed to good effect. Only with the changing political and social imperatives of the Second World War were health campaigners able to move government decisively in the direction of compulsory pasteurisation.[14] This was attained in a limited form for the first time with the 1949 Milk (Special Designations) Act, introduced by the post-war Labour government, which allowed local authorities 'to render compulsory the use of special designations on sales of milk', including pasteurisation. Dr Edith Summerskill, Parliamentary Secretary at the Ministry of Food, described this final realisation of compulsory pasteurisation as 'a triumph over ignorance, prejudice and selfishness'.[15]

Summerskill's victorious observation alluded to the nutritional as well as the economic argument against pasteurisation. These aspects of the debate appear in the second half of this chronologically based chapter, which examines inter-war developments. The first half looks at the initial attempts to regulate production and sale, culminating in the 1914 Milk and Dairies Act, and the continuing resistance to regulation in rural communities in the years immediately following the war. Following the details in chapters 3 and 6 about voluntary and statutory fat and non-fat milk standards, this chapter concentrates on the specific debate about the perceived hazards of drinking cow's milk. It closes by reflecting on three related conflicts of interest – between rural and urban areas, the needs of agriculture and public health, and the Ministries of Agriculture and Health – which restricted the expansion of state regulation before 1939.

Cleanliness and Standards, 1885–1914

The first concerted attempt to introduce comprehensive legislation on the production and sale of milk did not come until the 1914 Milk and Dairies Acts (there were separate measures for England and Wales and Scotland). Before this, cleanliness of milk was regulated only to a limited extent, primarily via the 1885 Dairies, Cowsheds and Milkshops Orders and the 1901 Sale of Milk Regulations. The coverage of the 1885 Orders, issued by the Privy Council, was extremely uneven, largely because responsibility for making regulations had been delegated to local authorities. In 1907 the Local Government Board reported that in England and Wales, urban authorities were far more likely than rural authorities to have issued

---

[14] R. J. Hammond, *Food. Vol. II. Studies in administration and control* (London, 1956), pp. 253–7.
[15] Milk (Special Designations) Act, Public General Acts, 1949, chapter 34; Parliamentary Debates, Fifth Series, Vol. 21 February 1949, 1605.

regulations.[16] Outside London, where the City and Metropolitan authorities had made regulations, the figures were as shown in table 7.1.

Table 7.1 Rural and urban coverage of the 1885 Dairies, Cowsheds and Milkshops Orders in England and Wales (outside London), 1907

Councils	Issued	Not issued	% not issued
Borough	290	36	11
Other Urban	684	126	15
Rural Districts	493	165	25

Source: Local Government Board, Dairies, Cowsheds and Milkshops (Regulations), Parliamentary Papers, 152, 1907.

This trend, it should be emphasised, was of particular importance given the changes in the geographical profile of the dairy trade which had taken effect by 1907, with urban dairies giving way to rural dairies.[17] This development, combined with the comparative reluctance of rural councils to regulate the trade, had the effect of ensuring that a significant share of dairies, at least in England and Wales, were unregulated on the eve of the First World War. In 1919 an official inquiry concluded that the Dairies, Cowsheds and Milkshops Orders had been 'largely ineffective'.[18]

The impact of the 1901 Sale of Milk Regulations, stipulating that milk should comprise at least 3 per cent milk fat and 8.5 per cent of other solids, was also limited.[19] They were introduced in the wake of the 1894–6 House of Commons Select Committee hearings on Food Products Adulteration, which had devoted a significant amount of time to the question of milk, an item commonly topped up with water – 'the addition of the yield of the "cow with the iron tail"', as Alfred Hill, Medical Officer of Health for Birmingham, put it in 1893.[20] Representatives of the dairy industry referred the Select Committee to milk supply contracts that specified a minimum amount of fat content. The Aylesbury Dairy Company, for instance, required a minimum of 3.25 per cent milk-fat solids and 8.5 per cent of other, non-fatty solids, and ensured that this standard was being maintained through a system of regular sampling. From another supplier, John Thomas Horner of the Dairy Trade and Can Protection Society, the Select Committee actually drew the admission that a combined minimum solids standard of around 11 per cent was low rather than stringent.[21] Hence the 1901 regulations, demand-

---

[16] 'Dairies, Cowsheds and Milkshops (Regulations)', Parliamentary Papers, 152, 1907.
[17] Atkins, 'White Poison?', pp. 208–9.
[18] Final Report of the Committee on the Production and Distribution of Milk, 1919, Cmd. 483, p. 12.
[19] The regulations were issued under the 1899 SFDA by the Board of Agriculture.
[20] *Public Health*, 5, p. 355.
[21] Report, Food Products Adulteration, Parliamentary Papers, 1894, 253, pp. 28, 169, 211.

ing slightly lower minimum solids counts than Aylesbury and Horner, did not necessarily attempt to impose tougher standards than were already being observed by parts of the trade.

One objection to a minimum compulsory standard, voiced before the Select Committee by Richard Bannister of the Government Laboratory, was that it would merely formalise adulteration, with suppliers watering the milk so that it comprised no more than 11 per cent of solids.[22] Within a few years the Local Government Board began to suspect that Bannister had been right, suggesting that rural suppliers were 'robbing good milk of a large proportion of its cream so that it may just escape condemnation by the public analyst'. This increasingly widespread practice, known as 'toning', allowed suppliers to widen their profits margins considerably.[23] To the annoyance of many local authorities, moreover, traders whose produce failed to meet the prescribed standard often escaped conviction. In enforcing the regulations, local authorities were required to allow suspects to 'appeal to the cow', by admitting a second sample of milk from the original cow for analysis. If this appeal sample, taken directly from the beast, also fell below the standard, the charge of adulteration would not be upheld. In the 1920s the Ministries of Health and Agriculture received a steady stream of representations from English and Welsh Town and County Councils, pressing for the standard to be made absolute, and the 'appeal to the cow' abolished. For once the two Ministries were united on milk policy, rejecting these representations on the grounds that thousands of small farmer-producers would not have access to a chemical analyst, and that an absolute standard would further entrench the practice of toning milk down to the minimum fat and solid requirements.[24]

More important, however, than the loophole which allowed dairymen to sell poor-quality milk legally, was the absence of any minimum standard of cleanliness in the 1901 regulations. Nor had the 1885 Orders included any specific coverage of tuberculosis. Hence it was not actually an offence to supply milk that conveyed infectious diseases, whether of the bovine kind, such as tuberculosis contracted from a cow's udder, or of the human kind, such as scarlet fever or typhoid, passed through milk from a handler to a consumer. In the absence of central regulation a number of English urban authorities, including Birmingham and Manchester, sought to obtain local powers to control the quality of milk sold in their area of jurisdiction, including milk produced elsewhere and brought in. These initiatives were probably the original source of rural fears about the interventionist tendencies of urban 'outsiders'. Concerned about the trading complications arising from the potential proliferation of different local regulations, the Central Chamber of Agriculture (CCA) negotiated national 'model clauses' to combat tuberculosis with representatives of the Board of Agriculture, the Local Government Board and the urban corporations involved.[25] Given the involvement of the CCA these

[22] Report, Food Products Adulteration, Parliamentary Papers, 1894, 253, p. 363.
[23] Local Government Board, Annual Report, 1908–9, Cd. 4928, p. lxxxvii.
[24] Beckett to Cross, 18 June 1929, MH 56/79, Public Record Office (PRO).
[25] Matthews, *Fifty Years of Agricultural Politics*, pp. 42–4.

clauses, which formed the basis of several private Acts of Parliament introduced in 1900 and 1901, had only a limited impact on quality. According to Deborah Dwork the local measures were difficult to enforce and tended to result in milk being diverted from controlled areas to less-regulated markets.[26]

Effective central regulation began to emerge as a stronger possibility in the first decade of the twentieth century, as the work of the Royal Commission on Tuberculosis established conclusively between 1907 and 1914 that bovine tuberculosis could be transmitted to humans through cow's milk. The Royal Commission coincided with one of the few periods of concerted 'public interest' pressure for strengthened state regulation, driven by the Pure Food and Health Society of Great Britain. This brought together elite reformers, including by 1912 Waldorf Astor and Christopher Addison, who were to assume prominent roles in future debates about milk safety, and some agrarian MPs, notably Charles Bathurst, a Wiltshire Conservative and member of the Royal Agricultural Society and the Farmers' Club. The Pure Food and Health Society was particularly keen to emphasise the perceived link between potentially hazardous milk and infant mortality.[27] The Royal Commission and the Pure Food and Health Society both contributed to a developing general debate about milk safety, which resulted in the LGB making three attempts to introduce comprehensive legislation on Milk and Dairies: in 1909, 1912 and 1913. But despite the presence of farming representatives in the 'public interest' lobby, and just as they had helped to shape the local controls, dairy farmers, operating through the CCA, opposed these central regulations and sought to minimise their scope and impact.[28] This was implicitly acknowledged by one of the LGB's Medical Officers, Frederick Willis, who in 1913 informed the British Medical Association that the failure to secure legislation, for which there was an 'urgent need', reflected the 'great need for better education of the public on the question'. He also cited pressure on Parliamentary time, an entirely admissible explanation, given the upheavals arising from the 1909 'People's Budget' controversy and the Irish Home Rule Crisis in 1913.[29] The hesitant pace of intervention may also have reflected the Liberal government's unwillingness to court further rural opposition at a time when the Chancellor of the Exchequer, Lloyd George, was moving towards introducing a land tax which the land-owning community deeply resented.[30]

The nature of agricultural opposition to milk and dairies legislation was discussed at the Board of Agriculture when officials received from the LGB a draft of the 1913 Bill. Haygarth Brown, the Board's Superintending Inspector, welcomed the proposed system of inspection that was designed to counter 'toning', a practice

---

[26] Dwork, *War is Good for Babies*, pp. 60–1, 72–4.

[27] *British Food Journal*, March 1912, pp. 25–7, May 1912, p. 81, September 1913, p. 170, October 1913, p. 181, November 1913, pp. 205–7.

[28] Smith, *Retreat of Tuberculosis*, pp. 176–182.

[29] British Medical Council, Public Health Committee, 29 October 1913, SA/BMA Box No. 216, F105, Contemporary Medical Archives Centre, The Wellcome Institute for the History of Medicine (CMAC).

[30] Martin Pugh, *The Making of Modern British Politics, 1867–1939* (Oxford, 1982), pp. 118–20.

which threatened the livelihood of honest dairy farmers. But, in common with departmental colleagues, Haygarth Brown opposed the LGB's position on regulating for improved cleanliness and hygiene on dairy farms. The Board of Agriculture's view was summarised by Furnival Jones, its Legal Adviser, in a memorandum to Frederick Willis in January 1914. This maintained that 'the general application of stringent regulations might easily so restrict the production of milk as to more than counter-balance the advantage to be derived from the greater purity or better quality of the milk available for consumption'.[31]

Agricultural suspicion of regulation was given public expression when the 1914 Milk and Dairies Bill was debated in Parliament. Justifying its necessity, the LGB President, Herbert Samuel, cited the widespread prevalence of tuberculosis, particularly among children, adding that a far purer supply of milk was essential if the 'health of the people' was to be protected.[32] Samuel's Bill duly made it an offence to sell tuberculous milk, and gave local authorities numerous powers to combat the sale of dirty or contaminated milk, including registration and regular inspection of dairies, and the right to stop dairies from sending out supplies where contamination was suspected. A separate Scottish Bill, introduced simultaneously, was even more stringent, explicitly requiring local authorities to inspect all dairies and dairy cattle on an annual basis, obliging dairymen to notify local authorities of infectious diseases among cattle and staff and, in cases of contamination, to provide local authorities with a full list of customers.

Although both Bills were carried easily through Parliament, receiving Second and Third readings without a division, qualified opposition was voiced by agricultural MPs, including Charles Bathurst, the Wiltshire Tory who had been involved in the Pure Food and Health Society. He expressed distaste for 'restrictive legislation' which was 'imposed upon the agricultural industry', and warned that any further 'restrictions' would inevitably affect the supply of milk, reducing production and increasing prices. This opposition of dairy farmers to milk regulations represented an important contrast with their support for legislation, explored in chapter 3, which equally 'restricted' the behaviour of margarine producers. Yet Bathurst, along with the Central Chamber of Agriculture, the British Dairy Farmers' Association and the Central Land Association, supported the 1914 Bill, accepting it as a moderate response to a strong public health case for cleaner milk.[33]

This muted rural support reflected the LGB's attempt to balance the potentially conflicting public health and agricultural interests when framing the legislation. Samuel's role in 'reconciling the various interests' was particularly praised by his fellow Liberal MP Christopher Addison, who had played a significant role in framing the government's health insurance legislation in 1911.[34] An official at the

---

[31] Haygarth Brown minute, 8 July 1913; Jones to Willis, January (unspecified date) 1914, MAF 52/5, PRO.
[32] Parliamentary Debates, Fifth Series, Vol. 62, 945, 12 May 1914.
[33] Parliamentary Debates, Fifth Series, Vol. 63, 239–45, 9 June 1914.
[34] Christopher Addison, *Four and a Half Years* (London, 1934), p. 25.

Scottish LGB noted that the milk and dairies legislation would provide urban areas with cleaner milk, and hence help urban local authorities to secure much improved public health. But the memorandum concluded by emphasising the importance of not 'making these necessary safeguards unduly vexatious or burdensome to the rural communities engaged in providing milk'.[35] To this end, the Board of Agriculture and rural district councils, the competence of which farmers trusted above that of the LGB and county or burgh councils, were given a significant role in the administration of the legislation. Local authority guidelines on the registration and inspection of dairies would have to be agreed with the Board of Agriculture as well as the LGB, and in England and Wales local authority responsibility for ordering inspections and the cessation of contaminated supplies was given to the district as opposed to the county councils. In other words, inspections would be conducted by officers from the area where milk was produced, rather than by officers from the area – possibly some distance away – where the milk was sold and consumed. At a time when London, for example, was receiving much of its milk from as far north as Derbyshire and as far west as Devon, the requirement of such an assurance carried great resonance.[36] Bathurst observed that among the farmers' central objections to legislation was the fear of 'invasion' by 'ignorant and sometimes officious' urban authority officers, 'whose knowledge of farming matters, and particularly cattle, is probably non-existent'.[37] This fear, it should be emphasised, was based on the recent history of local control, in which the interventionist activism of urban authorities like Manchester and Birmingham had only been contained by the CCA's apparently determined efforts in the 1900–1 debate.

Paradoxically, perhaps, by giving extensive powers to rural local authorities and the Board of Agriculture, the legislation inadvertently fuelled rather than balanced the competing agricultural and public health interests. Addison, a London Liberal and committed public health reformer, insisted that effective administration could only be effected in the hands of larger authorities. Addressing Bathurst's main argument against county councils, Addison stated that their distance from the area of production actually put them in a stronger position to administer the law fairly than district councils. Perhaps with some justice, given the 1907 evidence from the Local Government Board that many rural districts had been reluctant to impose regulations on dairymen, Addison suggested that, 'human nature being what it is', an officer representing a rural council would find it hard to go 'against the interests of important producers in his own district'. A county council officer, on the other hand, would rarely face the same dilemma.[38] In a similar vein, while academic

---

[35] 'Milk and Dairies (Scotland) Bill, 1914', unsigned and undated, HH 64/47, Scottish Record Office (SRO).

[36] Edith H. Wetham, 'The London Milk Trade, 1900–1930', in Derek J. Oddy and Derek S. Miller (eds), *The Making of the Modern British Diet* (London, 1976), p. 70.

[37] Parliamentary Debates, Fifth Series, Vol. 63, 242, 9 June 1914.

[38] Parliamentary Debates, Fifth Series, Vol. 63, 249, 9 June 1914.

veterinarians favoured legislative intervention to counter the sale of tuberculous milk, including the compulsory slaughter of diseased beasts, practitioners in the field were opposed because their livelihood was dependent on the fellowship of farmer clients.[39]

The Milk and Dairies Bill attained the Royal Assent on 10 August 1914. This timing was highly unfortunate: like the Irish Home Rule Act and other recently adopted Parliamentary instruments, its operation was delayed by the outbreak of war. Under a postponement order issued in December 1914, the Milk and Dairies Act would have come into effect on 1 October 1915, but the regulatory framework in England and Wales was then adapted with the introduction of the 1915 Milk and Dairies (Consolidation) Act.[40] This added a number of minor details to the 1914 Act, and stipulated that the contents of the latter would not automatically come into effect until one year after international hostilities had ceased. This date was not officially judged to have arrived until 1 September 1921, when the final Peace Treaty was concluded, and hence the government resisted pressure from the BMA to introduce the legislation following the Armistice.[41]

For Christopher Addison, the first Minister of Health in Lloyd George's peacetime coalition government, this delay was unacceptable, and he attempted to force the pace early in 1920 by introducing a new Milk and Dairies Bill. This would have come into operation immediately, and proposed significantly tighter regulations than the postponed legislation. First, registration with local authorities by dairymen and dairy premises would have become obligatory, with the Minister allowed to prohibit trading by producers who acted outside the terms of their license. Second, all dairymen would have been required to maintain – for inspection by the Ministry of Health – records bearing particulars on production, purchasing, storage, cleansing methods and sales. Third, and perhaps most significant, given the concerns about rural district councils which Addison had expressed in 1914, the Bill would have entitled any sanitary authority within a county council area to enforce the provisions on stopping supplies and inspecting dairies and cattle. In other words, sanitary officers from a district of consumption could regulate dairies in a district of production, so long as both areas fell within the jurisdiction of the same county council.[42]

In May 1931, as Ministry of Health officials discussed a further initiative on clean milk, the papers showing Addison's Health Ministerial record on milk were recovered and studied. These confirmed the recollection of the First Secretary, Sir Arthur Robinson, that Addison's 1920 Bill had been dropped because of the combined opposition of farmers and Ministry of Agriculture officials. Robinson noted that he had been impressed 'by the vigour of his [Addison's] views as to the

---

[39] Smith, *Retreat of Tuberculosis*, p. 176.

[40] Milk and Dairies (Postponement of operation of Act) Order, 1914. The LGB circulated copies of the order to local authorities on 18 December 1914; MAF 52/5.

[41] British Medical Association Council, 22 January 1919, SA/BMA Box No. 216, F105, CMAC.

[42] Milk and Dairies Bill, 1920. Sections of the Milk and Dairies (Consolidation) Act, 1915, showing proposed amendments, Cmd. 696, 1920, Clauses 1–3.

obstructive attitude of the Ministry of Agriculture and the farmers in regard to a milk policy taking proper account of health considerations'.[43] The government's official explanation in 1920 for not proceeding with this Bill was thus not entirely correct, the Leader of the House, Andrew Bonar Law, telling Parliament that there was insufficient time for a 2nd Reading in the remainder of the Session, and the measure was withdrawn in December.[44]

The government had one other reason for dropping Addison's Bill. Following the sudden collapse of the post-war boom in the summer of 1920, Lloyd George's administration became preoccupied with the need to minimise public expenditure. On 9 December the government announced that any legislation involving expenditure, but not yet in force, was to remain in abeyance. This negated the prospect of further milk initiatives by Addison, but in the longer term it also had repercussions for the 1914 and 1915 Milk and Dairies Acts that were due to take effect in September 1922. It was in these terms, the need to avoid fresh public spending commitments, that the Scottish Board of Health explained in July 1921 to local authorities the decision to postpone once more the enforcement of the 1914 Act.[45]

The new governing emphasis on economy led to a crucial change of personnel at the Ministry of Health in April 1921. Addison, who had unapologetically spent significant sums of public money on projects – Housing most notably – that were geared to securing long-term public health improvements, was forced out by Lloyd George. In his diary George Newman, the Ministry's Chief Medical Officer, recorded his sadness at Addison's departure and, perhaps significantly, made no note of the arrival of the new Minister, the industrialist Sir Alfred Mond.[46] Unlike Addison, Mond was embarked on a political trajectory that took him out of the Liberal Party and into the Conservative rather than Labour ranks. And, as Minister of Health, Mond was responsible in 1922 for ending government grants for building houses, introduced by Addison in 1919.[47] Mond had connections with food reformers, being a founding patron of the People's League of Health in 1917.[48] This indicated the possible blurring of distinctions between business, social reformers and government, but his ministerial activities showed little sign of any progressive agenda. Under his guidance financial retrenchment became the cornerstone of the Ministry of Health's milk policy, and – in contrast to the LGB's delicate handling of the 1914 Act – there was little attempt to balance competing health and agricultural claims. Instead, responding to pressure from farmers who

[43] Memorandum by J. N. Beckett, 18 May 1931; note by Sir Arthur Robinson, 26 May 1931, MH 56/81, PRO.
[44] Parliamentary Debates, Fifth Series, Vols. 129, 42, 10 May 1920, 133, 400, 11 August 1920 and 135, 213, 1 December 1920.
[45] John Jeffrey, Scottish Board of Health, to J. L. Officer, Convention of Royal Burghs, 14 July 1921, HH 64/48, SRO.
[46] George Newman Diary, 14 April 1921, MH 139/4, PRO.
[47] A. J. P. Taylor, *English History, 1914–1945* (Oxford, 1965), pp. 197, 317.
[48] Jones, *Social Hygiene*, pp. 50–1, 71–6.

were complaining about the alleged cost of the 1915 Act, the Ministry initially sought to repeal it outright.⁴⁹ In February 1922, J. N. Beckett, the Health Ministry's regular monitor of food and drink matters, told Scottish Office and Board of Health representatives that as it would be impossible for some time to enforce the 1914 Act's 'expenditure provisions', there was 'no good hanging on to them'. Mond confirmed this departmental view later that month in a note to Robert Munro, the Scottish Secretary, seeking the latter's support for the removal of the 1914 and 1915 legislation from the Statute Book. Under pressure from local authorities, Scottish officials utterly rejected this but conceded instead their willingness to tolerate a period of further postponement.⁵⁰ The Ministry of Health modified its position accordingly. In a Cabinet Paper at the end of May Mond outlined the case for a three-year postponement on grounds of cost to farmers and rate-payers, estimating an annual burden on the latter of £750,000. Mond attempted to offset the impact of postponement on quality and safety by proposing an important practical step which would not involve 'throwing any material expenditure on the state, the local authorities or the trade'. This was simply to outlaw the deliberate sale of tuberculous milk. Without a system of registration and inspection Mond conceded that this would be a difficult offence to prove, but its effect 'would be most salutary'.⁵¹

Mond's Cabinet Paper formed the basis of the 1922 Milk and Dairies Amendment Act, which was rushed through Parliament in July in time to beat the date – 1 September – when the 1914 and 1915 Acts would otherwise have come into effect automatically. These Acts were postponed for a further three years, and the deliberate sale of tuberculous milk was outlawed. While the insertion of this latter clause was a response to the unease expressed by Scottish officials, it also reflected the growing influence on official thinking of medical opinion. Medical professionals had broadly accepted by the beginning of the twentieth century that milk was a vehicle for the transmission of bovine tuberculosis to humans. This view was endorsed by the Royal Commission on Tuberculosis in 1911, and advanced in the final report of the war-time Astor inquiry on milk production and distribution.⁵² Published in 1919, this offered no quantitative evaluation of the scale of the problem, but initiated public debate by concluding that the spread of tuberculosis and other infectious diseases could be reduced through increased attention to hygiene on dairy farms and the increased adoption of pasteurisation. The report recommended that an official definition of pasteurisation should be introduced.⁵³

The debate about the possibilities of pasteurisation was just beginning to take shape at the end of the First World War. Only at the start of the 1930s did the Min-

⁴⁹ Parliamentary Debates, Fifth Series, Vol. 151, 370, 1 March 1922.
⁵⁰ MacPherson (Scottish Office) note of conversation with Beckett, 8 February 1922; Mond to Munro, 27 February 1922; notes by Dr Leighton, 4 March 1922 and A. Stalker, 6 March 1922, HH 64/54, SRO.
⁵¹ 'Milk and Dairies Bill', CP 2004, 30 May 1922, copy in HH 64/48, SRO.
⁵² Atkins, 'White Poison', p. 225.
⁵³ Final Report of the Committee on the Production and Distribution of Milk, 1919, Cmd. 483, pp. 12–13.

istry of Health have a considered view on the subject, but when pressed to take immediate action against tuberculous milk Mond was drawn into commenting on the desirability of heat treatment in 1922. Sir William Watson Cheyne, Conservative MP for the Scottish Universities and a former President (1914–17) of the Royal College of Surgeons, observed in Parliament that unacceptably large numbers of infants were dying from tuberculosis caused by contaminated milk. The average tally of such deaths in the 1920s, it is worth re-emphasising, is considered to be around 2,000.[54] Watson Cheyne urged Mond that the 1915 Act was desirable on political as well as health grounds: designed to save the lives of children it would appeal to the new female electorate 'more than any topic you could take up'.[55] Persistent questioning throughout May from another Tory MP, Nicholas Gratton Doyle of Newcastle, about the condition of his city's milk, drew the admission from Mond that serious pollution of milk was not confined to the north-east and that it was advisable to boil all milk intended for consumption by children unless pasteurised. From James Sexton, one-time Liverpool dockers' leader and MP for St. Helens, this elicited the suggestion 'that it would expedite matters if a few of the distributors of impure milk were boiled as well as the milk'.[56]

In further postponing the 1914–15 regulations on registration and inspection, the 1922 Amendment Act was welcomed by dairy farmers. Percy Hurd, a Somerset Conservative MP, said he was glad that farmers were 'getting at least some consideration', and that measures which would have 'knocked out of production' two-thirds of London's suppliers had been deferred. In satisfying the farmers while introducing the first ever Milk Act, Mond was arguably balancing the interests of agriculture and public health, but – unlike the farmers – public health reformers were not impressed by his efforts. A particularly crushing verdict was expressed during the Bill's Second Reading by Mond's Ministerial predecessor, Christopher Addison, who emphasised – as Mond had privately admitted to Cabinet colleagues – that without a system of inspections the law against selling tuberculous milk would be difficult to enforce. Addison also lamented the absence in the Act of measures to stop contaminated supplies and counter the sale of dirty milk. Finally, attacking Mond's commitment to financial retrenchment, Addison argued that saving money by not appointing a small number of dairy inspectors was a false economy. As the Act would fail to clean up the milk supply, in the long term much larger sums would be spent treating patients with tuberculosis and other milk-borne infectious diseases.[57] In this respect Addison was undoubtedly correct. According to one recent estimate, each year in the 1920s local authorities and central government were spending about £9 million on the treatment, convalescence and after care treatment of patients suffering from milk-borne tuberculosis.[58] This was a signifi-

---

[54] Smith, *Retreat of Tuberculosis*, p. 186.
[55] Parliamentary Debates, Fifth Series, Vol. 151, 1916–17, 13 March 1922.
[56] Parliamentary Debates, Fifth Series, Vol. 153, 1134–5, 3 May 1922; Vol. 154, 345–6, 17 May 1922 and 1182–3, 24 May 1922.
[57] Parliamentary Debates, Fifth Series, Vol. 156, 2199–237, 12 July 1922.
[58] Smith, *Retreat of Tuberculosis*, p. 185.

cantly larger sum than the £750,000 annual 'burden' on the rate payer which Mond believed the 1915 legislation would involve. Despite this, and the various recent warnings about the dangers of the milk supply, too few in the House of Commons viewed the matter seriously enough to oppose farmers and the government.[59] Francis Acland, a Liberal who supported Addison on milk, speaking to a virtually empty chamber at 10pm during the 1922 Bill's Second Reading, noted that the vast body of MPs were 'more practically interested in other fluids than in milk'.

The postponement of the 1914 Act had at least one further important consequence. Its first clause allowed the government to issue regulations governing the conveyance and carriage of milk. Such guidelines were needed because railway stations, through which most of the urban supply passed, were dirty places. There was ample evidence that consumers would only be protected adequately if producers were legally required to secure the churns and other containers against contamination from steam, soot and the general elements. A Ministry of Food inspector, patrolling London's Paddington Station in 1919, reported that most of the milk-train wagons were filthy and that many of the churn lids contained water. This had obvious implications for the quality of the milk which wholesalers were buying at the station. In Dundee the Medical Officer of Health, inspecting the milk train at the city's West Station in 1921, noted that cans with badly fitting lids were filled with a mixture of milk and 'greasy dirty water'. There were, he added, numerous other 'opportunities for contamination', as wholesalers inspected and tested milk from different uncovered cans, standing at an open platform.[60]

The 1922 debate had been a reminder that in the sphere of milk policy commercial and public health interests could be mutually exclusive. This, arguably, was also a central theme of the operation of the National Milk Publicity Council (NMPC), established in 1920 with the support of dairy trade and farming and professional health bodies. These included the National Farmers' Union, the National Federation of Dairy Associations, the National Clean Milk Society, the Society of Medical Officers of Health and the Sanitary Inspectors' Association. A body of its kind had been recommended by the Astor inquiry, to promote milk sales by extolling its nutritional and health properties. The NMPC's formation clearly indicated a degree of willingness among producer and welfare groups to co-operate, and its existence recalled the alliance of farmer and health representatives which had come together in the pre-war Pure Food Society. The NMPC's development was duly encouraged by the Ministries of Health and Agriculture, although Sir Robert Morant, Permanent Secretary until his premature death in March 1920, was advised that any support which his department gave to the NMPC's development would have to fall well short of financial assistance. Providing money would lay the Ministry open to criticism 'for being allied too closely' with the trade organ-

---

[59] Addison, *Four and a Half Years*, p. 30.
[60] G. Sutherland Thompson to S. Montgomery, Milk Section, Ministry of Food, 19 March 1919, CC/MIL 80, National Museum of Labour History, Manchester; Scottish Board of Health, Third Annual Report, Cmd. 1697, 1921, pp. 67–8.

isations associated with the Council.[61] The impact of the NMPC is difficult to establish. But its operations were clearly hampered by the competing aims of its component groups, with Medical Officers of Health concerned about the potential difficulties of promoting increased sales without the introduction of new regulations – opposed by producers – that were needed to bolster public confidence. The strains became apparent in 1926 when the NFU advised its members to withdraw from the Council, amid arguments on the basis that welfare groups and other non-dairy organisations were over-represented. In addition, with the Council promoting milk provision for malnourished and impoverished children, too little was being achieved in increased cash sales.[62]

Voluntary grading versus compulsory pasteurisation, 1922–38

One aspect of the 1922 Amendment Act had been welcomed by Addison and some other health campaigners. Under temporary orders issued by the Ministries of Food and Health in 1919 and 1921, traders were entitled to sell their milk under a series of licensed designations. The 1922 Act placed this system on a permanent legislative footing, enabling producers to sell milk as 'Certified', 'Grade A (Tuberculin Tested)', 'Grade A' or 'Pasteurised'. Licenses for the first two grades were issued directly by the Minister of Health; the other two were obtained from local authorities. The conditions under which these licences were issued were initially published in the 1922 Milk (Special Designations) Orders, and finalised in a slightly revised form in the 1923 Milk (Special Designations) Orders, summarised in table 7.2.

Table 7.2 Grading definitions under the 1923 Milk (Special Designations) Orders

Designation	Permitted bacterial count (per cubic cm)	Special conditions
Certified	30,000	Cows inspected for TB quarterly; milk farm-bottled
Grade A (Tuberculin Tested)	200,000	Cows inspected for TB quarterly; milk delivered in sealed churns
Grade A	200,000	Cows inspected quarterly
Pasteurised	200,000	Retained for 30 minutes at 145–50°F, then cooled <55°F

Source: Milk (Special Designations) Orders, 1922 and 1923, copies in MH 56/88, PRO.

The Orders were prepared mainly by Dr J. M. Hamill of the Ministry of Health, along with Sir George Newman, the Chief Medical Officer. In July 1923 Newman advised Neville Chamberlain, Minister of Health, that the best form of milk was

[61] Cross to Sir Robert Morant, 20 January 1920, MH 56/74, PRO.
[62] Alan Jenkins, *Drinka Pinta* (London, 1970), pp. 80, 92–6.

that obtained from fully healthy cows in the cleanest conditions possible, cooled immediately and then distributed with the minimum of handling and delays. But the complexities of transport and distribution in 'a highly urbanised country such as England' ensured that safe and affordable milk for the general population could only really be provided by pasteurisation, which, if properly conducted, would render milk safe without injuring its nutritional properties.[63]

The final definition of pasteurisation was slightly different, it might be noted, from Newman's 1903 recommendation of holding milk at a minimum of 140°F for at least 20 minutes. When the 1922 Order appeared there was little opposition to the 30 minute and 145°F minimums, but trade objections were lodged against three other conditions initially attached to the pasteurisation definition in the 1922 Order. This had proposed, first, that a bacterial count of 30,000 per cubic centimetre should be fixed; second, that the pasteurised milk should contain no bacillus coli per one-tenth of a cubic centimetre; and, third, that the vessel bearing the milk should be labelled with the day of pasteurisation. Each of these conditions was revoked in response to pressure from the dairy trade, although the large increase in the permitted bacterial count was only temporary. The 1923 Order specified that from 1 January 1924 pasteurised milk could legally contain no more than 100,000 bacteria per cubic centimetre. Writing towards the end of his long career, some 20 years after the Order had been introduced, Arthur Enock, the veteran microbiologist and milk trader, described this as an undemanding standard.[64]

Voluntary grading had been originally advocated by Waldorf Astor in 1914, during the debate on Samuel's Milk and Dairies Act. Astor, who chaired the wartime inquiry on milk supply, was an unusual figure in holding direct agricultural and public health interests, being both a dairy farmer and a Governor of Guy's Hospital in London. In 1914 he had argued that the overall quality of supply would improve more rapidly if the government concentrated on rewarding the good producers rather than punishing the bad. Samuel had opposed grading, however, characterising it as a 'system under which the well-to-do classes can get the best milk by paying more for it, leaving the rest of the population to obtain whatever milk they can at the present price'.[65] Hence the 1914 Act had only volunteered a vague suggestion that the LGB might later define conditions under which 'certified milk' could be produced and sold.

Mond took a more positive view of grading, predicting that consumers would quickly learn the value of the special designations. As demand subsequently developed, the number of licensed producers and suppliers would increase and prices fall within reach of all social classes.[66] To some extent this faith in the voluntary approach was borne out by the development of the large dairy combines that were coming to dominate the larger urban markets. According to Gary D. Libecap, in

[63] Enock, *This Milk Business*, p. 113.
[64] *Ibid.*, pp. 113–15.
[65] Parliamentary Debates, Fifth Series, Vol. 63, 257, 290, 9 June 1914.
[66] Parliamentary Debates, Fifth Series, Vol. 156, 2200, 12 July 1922.

industries where competing products are not clearly distinguishable, the incentive to improve quality is greatest for large firms with large market shares.[67] The interwar milk trade is a good illustration of this model of general business behaviour. Firms like United Dairies, which provided much of London's pasteurised supply, were highly sensitive to the market advantages of pasteurisation, recognising that the process instilled greater public confidence in milk and duly increased demand. Ben Davis, United Dairies' Director of Laboratories, wrote a short pamphlet to this effect in 1933.[68] In 1934 about 90 per cent of supply in Greater London was pasteurised, as was around 60 per cent in Edinburgh and 66 per cent in Glasgow.[69] Yet the big distributors, for all their metropolitan and urban supremacy, did not quite supply the majority of consumers. In 1931, according to an inter-departmental committee of officials from the Ministries of Health and Agriculture, the 30 per cent of the national supply supplied by big distributors, including the Co-operative Wholesale Society, was definitely pasteurised. The committee was uncertain about whether another 20 per cent, distributed by small dairy firms, was pasteurised or not. Officials were aware, however, that the remaining 50 per cent, supplied by the thousands of small producer-retailers, was definitely not heat-treated.[70]

The inter-departmental committee had been established to consider whether any further changes to the law were necessary, the 1914 legislation having finally come into effect in 1925 despite the attempt by dairy MPs to hold it up again.[71] The Ministry of Agriculture wanted to change the law in 1931 in order to ease pressure on farmers by removing milk from the allegedly punitive Sale of Food and Drugs Acts, but the committee's findings persuaded the Ministry of Health that regulation needed to be tightened rather than relaxed.[72] Despite the introduction of wider inspections and the power to withhold contaminated supplies under the 1914 Act, the spread of milk-borne infectious diseases had continued to be a significant problem. In 1929 at least 65 people died in Brighton, having contracted a severe case of septic sore throat from contaminated milk.[73] Smaller tragedies, including milk-borne paratyphoid which killed seven people in Essex in 1931, provided further evidence of the limited impact of existing legislation, although fatalities were not always required to prompt official concern. In 1927 the Scottish Board of Health reported the case of a farmer whose milk had twice, within fourteen months, caused two major outbreaks of severe gastro-enteritis in Dundee. On the second occasion a veterinary inspector traced the epidemic to a cow stricken with mastitis, but the farmer continued to mix her produce with the rest of his herd's milk. The Scottish Board described the case as 'a signal demonstration' that

[67] Libecap, 'The Rise of the Chicago Packers', pp. 242–62.
[68] Ben Davies, *The Nation's Milk Supply*; copy in PP/JPH Box No. 14, A147, CMAC.
[69] *Food Manufacture*, July 1934, pp. 244–7.
[70] Inter-Departmental Committee, 'Interim Report', 24 February 1931, pp. 2–3, MH 56/88, PRO.
[71] Parliamentary Debates, Fifth Series, Vol 186, 1837–8, 20 July 1925.
[72] H. E. Dale (MAF) to Beckett, 17 October 1930, MH 56/88, PRO.
[73] *The Times*, 31 December 1929–18 January 1930.

the Milk and Dairies Act had still to prove itself as 'a practical means for avoiding outbreaks of infectious disease due to milk'.[74] The legislation had also made little impact on the supply of milk infected with bovine tuberculosis. According to the inter-departmental committee, 6.3 per cent of 14,235 samples analysed in 1930 by the Ministry of Health were tuberculous. This was alarming enough, but as distributors mixed produce from dozens of farms a small amount of infected milk could contaminate a much larger portion of overall supply.[75]

The extent of milk-borne infectious disease reflected the fact that pasteurisation remained confined largely to the urban supply. It was also due to the limited market progress of special designations, the other key element in the voluntary approach. While there were more than 200,000 ordinary producers in England, Wales and Scotland in 1930, there were just 216 certified producers, 264 Grade A (Tuberculosis tested) producers and 498 Grade A producers. For the bottling of Grade A (TT) and Grade A milk, in England and Wales a further 161 and 305 licenses were held.[76] The correspondingly high prices prompted occasional irate correspondence in the press. 'In my case', wrote Mrs A. H. Badger of West London to *The Times*, 'although I should like to have a pint of certified milk daily, I have to limit my consumption to half a pint, as the price for "certified" is 8d a pint instead of 3 and a half'.[77]

There were competing explanations for this absence of progress. Farmers and the Ministry of Agriculture (MAF) argued that quarterly inspections and the licence fees were prohibitively expensive. In 1923 MAF had actually pressed the Health Ministry to reduce the annual number of examinations for graded herds from four to two, describing itself as 'prepared to take the risk for the sake of increasing the supply [of graded milk]'.[78] There was, perhaps, some merit in this argument. The vast majority of farmers had less than 50 cows, and might well have been deterred by the flat rate annual fees of £5 for certified and £1.1.0 for the others, which would more obviously have served as an incentive for farmers with larger herds, capable of producing more significant quantities of premium milk.[79] At the same time the Ministry of Health maintained that the cost of quarterly inspections – the bare guarantee of safety – posed no special difficulty for 'careful farmers', and believed that the slow growth of demand was really the result of public uncertainty about the relative merits of the various grades.[80] Officials were themselves suspicious about Grade A, a term suggesting a premium of quality

---

[74] Scottish Board of Health, Annual Report, 1927, Cmd. 3122, pp. 206–7.

[75] Inter-Departmental Committee, 'Interim Report', 24 February 1931, p. 4, MH 56/88, PRO.

[76] Ministry of Health, Annual Report, 1930–1, Cmd. 3937, pp. 36–7; Department of Health for Scotland, Annual Report, 1931, Cmd. 4080, pp. 31–2.

[77] *The Times*, 25 January 1930.

[78] A. D. Hall (Chief Scientific Adviser, MAF) to Sir Arthur Robinson (MoH), 8 March 1923, MH 56/94, PRO.

[79] Smith, *Retreat of Tuberculosis*, p. 185.

[80] A. B. Maclachlan to Sir Arthur Robinson, 14 February 1923, MH 56/94, PRO; Francis McKee, 'The Popularisation of Milk as a Beverage During the 1930s', in David F. Smith (ed.), *Nutrition in Britain. Science, scientists and politics in the twentieth century* (London and New York, 1997), p. 129.

which they regarded as unmerited. There was also a widespread public belief, according to Arthur Enock, that 'certified' was certified as free from all disease-bearing organisms: it was actually only certified as having been produced and distributed under certain conditions.[81] But reform of the established voluntary system was virtually impossible, for Grade A producers would hardly agree to sell their milk as 'Grade B' or anything else which did not imply first class.[82]

The limited impact of the voluntary policy and the findings of the 1931 inter-departmental committee prompted Dr T. Carnwath, Senior Medical Officer at the Health Ministry, to conclude that compulsory pasteurisation was the only solution. 'I am confident', he wrote to George Newman, Chief Medical Officer, and Sir Arthur Robinson, First Secretary, 'that a clear pronouncement by this Department in favour of pasteurisation would do much to clear the air and encourage the reorganisation of the industry on modern lines.'[83] Although the Ministry eschewed any such immediate pronouncement, henceforth its unofficial private view was that only pasteurised milk could be regarded as truly safe. This qualified the Ministry's earlier endorsement of grading: while Certified and Grade A (TT) milk was free from tuberculosis, it could still convey infectious diseases like paratyphoid or scarlet fever.[84]

Support for compulsory pasteurisation was gathering strength in the 1930s. By 1934 the British Medical Association also believed that pasteurised was the only safe form of milk, and medical professionals did much to break down the main health or nutritional argument against pasteurisation.[85] This was the belief, once held by doctors as well as producers, that heat treatment destroyed milk's nutrients. Astor's 1919 inquiry had begun the process of reappraisal by showing that milk's most important qualities – vitamins A and B – were unharmed by heating.[86] After the 1930 Brighton epidemic, Public Health Professor Henry Kenwood emphasised that pasteurisation had no material affect on milk's 'wonderful nutritive properties', an observation confirmed by further research in the 1930s.[87] In 1934 the *British Medical Journal* carried the findings of a research project conducted two years previously in Lancashire. This involved 20,000 Lancashire school children, half of whom were given raw milk only and the other half pasteurised only during a four month period. Dr Ethel Elderton of University College London said the experiment provided no evidence that raw milk had an advantage over pasteurised in increasing the weight or height of the children. Elderton also reported identical results from a similar American project, in which those who drank raw milk actually grew less than those who drank pasteurised, and suffered more diphtheria, scarlet fever, intestinal disturbances and rickets.[88] New work in

---

[81] Enock, *This Milk Business*, p. 34.
[82] Memoranda by Cross, 16 July 1925 and MacFadden, 27 July 1925, MH 56/77, PRO.
[83] Carnwath to Newman and Robinson, 9 March 1931, MH 56/81, PRO.
[84] Maclachlan to Newman and Robinson, 18 March 1931, MH 56/81, PRO.
[85] British Medical Association Council, 7 November 1934, SA/BMA Box No. 216, F105, CMAC.
[86] Final Report of the Committee on the Production and Distribution of Milk, p. 7.
[87] *The Times*, 8 January 1930.
[88] Clipping from the *British Medical Journal*, 2 June 1934, PP/JRH, Box No. 14, A147, CMAC.

the 1930s buttressed Astor's earlier conclusions on the vitamin properties of pasteurised milk, revealing milk to be such a poor source of Vitamin C – 5 gallons of raw milk contained the equivalent of an ounce of fresh orange juice – that its loss through pasteurisation was irrelevant. Milk's essential goodness came from Vitamins A, B1, B2, D and E: A was completely unaffected by heat and the others only marginally altered.[89]

There was a secondary nutritional or health argument against pasteurisation, implying that it made old or diseased milk 'safe' for consumption, thus deflecting attention from the importance of obtaining pure milk from healthy cows and transporting it hygienically and promptly.[90] Until the later 1920s this was the position of many tuberculosis specialists, who also worried that pasteurisation would inhibit the transmission of immunising doses of TB in childhood.[91] An influential bacteriologist, R. Stenhouse Williams, who headed the small MAF-funded National Institute for Research in Dairying at Reading, opposed pasteurisation as a 'technical fix' which discouraged the production of clean milk. He was also sympathetic towards, if not entirely convinced by, the argument that milk's nutritional value was reduced by pasteurisation. It is believed that Williams' reluctance to endorse heat treatment deprived the research institute of much-needed funding from big pro-pasteurisation suppliers like United Dairies.[92] The view that heat treatment would retard the supply of clean milk was expressed with more prolonged vigour by producers of Certified and Grade A (TT) Milk, many of whom belonged to the National Clean Milk Society (NCMS), founded in 1915. In 1923 the NCMS hosted a national conference on pasteurisation at London's Guild Hall, where Lord Dawson, Physician to the Royal Family, stated, 'Pasteurisation may be necessary, it may even be good, but we can never insist too strongly or too often that pasteurisation can never make bad milk into good milk'.[93] This was a constant theme of statements issued by the Clean Milk movement's leading figure, Wilfred Buckley, who kept a certified herd at his own farm near Oxford, and who provided advice to various government departments and official inquiries throughout a lengthy public career. During the Brighton tragedy Buckley admitted that pasteurisation made milk safe, but insisted that the process did not 'convert bad milk into good milk'.[94] Indirectly, of course, this was an argument about the merits of graded milk in general and certified in particular: wider pasteurisation would have undermined the attraction, from the perspective of safety, of the milk supplied by Buckley and other graded producers.

[89] *Food Manufacture*, May 1936.
[90] Weltham, 'London Milk Trade', p. 69.
[91] Smith, *Retreat of Tuberculosis*, p. 190.
[92] Keith Vernon, 'Science for the Farmer? Agricultural Research in England 1909–36', *Twentieth Century British History*, 8 (3), 1997, pp. 329–31.
[93] Jenkins, *Drinka Pinta*, p. 46.
[94] *The Times*, 9 January 1930. For Buckley's career, see his obituary and an appreciation written by Edward Wise, a Labour MP and war-time colleague of Buckley's at the Ministry of Food; *The Times*, 28 October and 1 November 1933.

The weight of this latter argument against pasteurisation was gradually eroded, both by the strengthening medical evidence about the hazards of raw milk and, as indicated above, by commercial factors and the advance of the big dairy combines. The business argument for pasteurisation was simple: increased consumer confidence would promote increased sales. This was the position of United Dairies, the largest single milk retailer in the 1930s, although it did not attempt to consolidate its market advantage by pressing for compulsory pasteurisation. This perhaps reflected the company's sensitivity to concerns that it was already too large a combine; certainly its interests lay in remaining on good terms with farming suppliers. No such compunction governed the activities of the Glasgow Wholesale Milk Dealers' Association, which by 1936 was actively lobbying the government for the introduction of pasteurisation on a statutory basis.[95] The Ministry of Agriculture had indirectly recognised the link between improved safety and increased demand – assumed by the Ministry of Health in 1930 – in 1932, when it appointed the Milk Reorganisation Commission, under Sir Edward Grigg, a Tory MP from Cheshire. Grigg was asked to prepare a scheme under the 1931 Agricultural Marketing Act for regulating milk marketing in England and Wales, and to make recommendations for adoption in Northern Ireland and Scotland. While focusing chiefly on marketing mechanisms, Grigg's report, published on 6 February 1933, did not ignore quality and safety. It ruled out compulsory pasteurisation, saying this would have an 'adverse effect on the producer who has hitherto derived some advantage from close proximity to large consuming centres', but advocated reform of the confusing system of grades. He favoured abolishing these and introducing a scheme where the government paid premiums on milk sold by accredited producers, whose herds and production methods were inspected regularly and met prescribed bacteriological standards.[96]

Grigg's report was of great long-term significance, leading to the establishment of the Milk Marketing Board that governed milk retailing until its abolition in 1995. In the short term the system of premiums for designated producers was put into effect with the 1934 Milk Act. Unlike earlier Milk and Dairies legislation this was drafted entirely by the Ministry of Agriculture, and reflected MAF's assumption that the development of grading had been inhibited by cost. The new 'premiums' – or 'bribes', as they were called by Tom Williams, Labour's future Minister of Agriculture – could amount to 1d per gallon.[97] Grigg's other recommendation on grading, that the designations be simplified, was only partially realised. Following the recommendations of a report published by the Medical Research Council, primarily written by Professor G. S. Wilson of the London School of Hygiene and Tropical Medicine, the 1923 grades were abolished under the 1936 Milk (Special Designations) Order. Having gathered evidence from representatives of the

[95] Glasgow Wholesale Milk Dealers' Association (GWMDA), Minutes, 30 September 1936, UGD 352/6/1, Business Records' Centre, University of Glasgow (BRC).
[96] *The Times*, 30 January–13 February 1933.
[97] *Milk Act*, 1934, Clauses 9–10, *Public General Statutes*, 1934, chapter 51; Parliamentary Debates, Fifth Series, Vol. 290, 1209–15, 7 June 1934.

Ministries of Health and Agriculture and the Department of Health for Scotland, Wilson prescribed bacteriological standards for the five grades adopted under the new Order: 'Tuberculin Tested (Certified)', 'Tuberculin Tested', 'Accredited', 'Tuberculin Tested (Pasteurised)' and 'Pasteurised Milk'. Roughly speaking, Tuberculin Tested (Certified) and Tuberculin Tested replaced Certified and Grade A (TT) respectively, and Accredited was a substitute for Grade A. The Ministry of Health's attempt to re-designate this latter product as 'standard' was thwarted by officials at MAF.[98] The Order also introduced a new bacteriological test, the modified methylene blue reduction test, described by Arthur Enock as a simple and inexpensive process with only a very small experimental error. A given concentration of methylene blue, an aniline dye, was added to ten cubic centimetres of milk, incubating at body temperature, and the time for the dye to become decolourised then measured. Clean milk would decolourise the dye after seven or eight hours, moderately clean milk would take four and a half to six and a half hours, milk prepared without particular attention to cleanliness between one and four and a half hours and really dirty milk would take less than one hour.[99]

The 1934 Act was opposed by Labour leaders in Parliament as an inadequate weapon against impurity. Sir Stafford Cripps was particularly sceptical about the value of voluntary grading. 'Merely keeping a roll of tested herds', he said, 'is not good enough. It is the untested herds that are a danger.' These were the herds that would continue to infect the milk supply with tuberculosis and other serious diseases.[100] The number of licensed producers increased significantly following the introduction of the 1936 Special Designations Order. In England and Wales in 1938 there were 2,028 Tuberculin-Tested and 19,824 licence-holders; this compared with just 360 Certified and Grade A (TT) and 547 Grade A in 1931. In Scotland, where the old designations were retained, the number of Certified and Tuberculin-Tested licenses increased from 67 and 77 in 1931 to 134 and 1251 in 1938. Although this partially bore out the old Ministry of Agriculture argument that the pre-1934 growth of voluntary standards had been inhibited by the costs of registration and inspection, Cripps's warnings about the inadequacies of the system were not entirely unfounded. In England and Wales only 1808 of the 19,824 accredited licenses went to farmers who bottled their own milk.[101] Thus most graded produce was still exposed to the potentially contaminating journey from churn to bottle. In overall terms, moreover, the proportion of officially licensed producers remained small, with some 200,000 ordinary producers still operating in 1938.

The voluntary approach to improved safety and quality was confirmed by the government's failure to implement a White Paper, *Milk Policy*, issued in July 1937. This new initiative, which reflected the Ministry of Health's long-term aim by

---

[98] Ministry of Health, untitled memo, 30 May 1935, MH 56/95, PRO.
[99] Enock, *This Milk Business*, pp. 51–3.
[100] Parliamentary Debates, Fifth Series, Vol. 290, 1132, 1142, 7 June 1934.
[101] Ministry of Health, Annual Report, 1937–8, Cmd. 5801, p. 52; Department of Health for Scotland, Annual Report, 1938, Cmd. 5969, p. 59.

promising the future possibility of compulsory pasteurisation, had been prompted by renewed pressure from urban local authorities. Having attempted to introduce compulsory pasteurisation through local bye-laws, the Corporations of Glasgow and Poole were told by the government – on the advice of the House of Commons Ways and Means Committee – that such an important national issue could only be settled by national legislation. Undeterred, early in 1937 both Corporations arranged for a sympathetic peer to introduce such legislation in the House of Lords, and withdrew these measures only after the government had pledged its intention to publish the White Paper which appeared in July.[102]

The contents of this document were settled after lengthy negotiations between the Ministries of Health and Agriculture, with the latter adamant that compulsory pasteurisation should not 'inflict undue hardship on the milk producer'. MAF officials were particularly concerned about the tens of thousands of small producer-retailers, reminding the Minister, Walter Elliot, that the Conservative Research Department believed compulsion would put many of them out of business. MAF's general position on pasteurisation was changing, however, with officials finally recognising in March 1937 that, 'in the public interest and in the interests of the dairy interest itself', it could no longer be resisted in principle. In place of outright opposition, MAF's new strategy was to 'hold back' the Ministry of Health to a gradual extension of localised compulsion, subject to dairy farmers receiving 'adequate warning'.[103] Lengthy negotiations between the two Ministries ensued, with Ministers Elliot and Kingsley Wood involved, the former insisting that 'any policy of pasteurisation should include adequate safeguards for the producer-retailer'.[104]

These 'safeguards' were included in the White Paper. Aimed at promoting greater consumption by increasing public confidence in milk's purity and safety, this offered the prospect of local authorities applying to the Ministry of Health or Scottish Secretary of State for permission to order compulsory pasteurisation of milk supplied in their area. Orders would be granted 'subject to certain conditions' – the 'safeguards' sought by MAF. Local authorities intending to use the power would give two years' notice; tuberculosis-tested and sterilised milk were exempt; and small farmers – the producer-retailers – who produced milk from a single herd, would receive an additional three years' grace.[105] The next step, much delayed, was the introduction of the Milk Industry Bill in November 1938. Along with increased premiums for designated producers, this included the White Paper's provisions for compulsory pasteurisation. These were stoutly opposed by the National Farmers' Union and the National Federation of Milk Producers, representing the small dairy farmers, and consequently attacked in Parliament by the usual rural suspects on the Conservative backbenches. On 29 November the Prime Minister, Neville Chamberlain, was asked to withdraw the Bill by Sir Edward Ruggles-Brise and Sir Hugh

---

[102] Glasgow Wholesale Milk Dealers' Association, Directors' Annual Report, 27 April 1937 and Minutes, 29 June 1937, UGD 352/6/1, BRC.
[103] Memo by A. W. Street, Second Secretary, 1 March 1937, MAF 52/130, PRO.
[104] Note by Sir Donald Ferguson, Permanent Secretary, MAF, 6 April 1937, MAF 52/130, PRO.
[105] Milk Policy, Cmd. 5333, July 1937, p. 6.

O'Neill, the chairmen, respectively, of the Conservative Agricultural Committee and the 1922 Committee of Conservative Private Members. 'In view of the objections which have been raised in many quarters', Chamberlain postponed the Bill's Second Reading. His Minister of Agriculture, William Morrison, was then forced to resign, the clear victim of rural Conservatism's undying opposition to tighter milk regulation. When compulsory pasteurisation was eventually introduced by the post-war Labour government, the Minister responsible, Edith Summerskill, praised the 1938 Bill and Morrison's pioneering efforts, attributing his demise to the same forces of 'ignorance' and 'selfishness' which had opposed compulsory pasteurisation.[106] Morrison's immediate successor in December 1938 was reassuringly rural, Colonel Sir Reginald Hugh Dorman-Smith, a recent past President (1936–7) of the NFU, and the Bill was quietly dropped in January 1939.[107] Milk distributors in Glasgow regretfully – and correctly – surmised that with the appointment of Dorman-Smith there was no prospect of future legislation which included compulsory pasteurisation.[108] Separate failed attempts to have the Bill re-introduced by the People's League of Health, and by the BMA, the Royal College of Surgeons, the Society of Medical Officers of Health and the Joint Tuberculosis Council were all reported in *Food Manufacture*. The journal itself declared pure milk to be an urgent priority and criticised the postponement of the legislation.[109] Viscount Astor, who had been prominent in earlier inter-war debates about milk, observed that in undermining the Bill the farming lobby had once again inhibited improvements in quality and safety.[110]

Conclusion: conflicts of interest

The absence of compulsory pasteurisation before the Second World War supports P. J. Atkins' view that milk remained a potentially dangerous, even lethal, substance until the 1920s. Indeed, with some justice it should be said that milk was still a hazardous drink in 1939. Compulsory pasteurisation was seen by the Ministry of Health and the medical profession as the only guarantee of milk's safety and therefore essential in the interests of public health, but in 1938 its introduction had been resisted by the Ministry of Agriculture and dairy farmers on the grounds that it would damage the commercial interests of producers. Its continuing absence hence brings into focus three, over-lapping conflicts of interest which have featured in this chapter on milk's pre-1939 regulatory framework: between rural and urban areas, between agriculture and public health, and between the Ministries of Agriculture and Health.

---

[106] Parliamentary Debates, Fifth Series, Vol. 461, 21 February 1949, 1606.

[107] *The Times*, 19–30 November and 12 December 1938; Parliamentary Debates, Fifth Series, Vol. 341, 885, Vol. 342, 606 and Vol. 343, 18.

[108] Glasgow Wholesale Milk Dealers' Association, Directors' Annual Report, 25 April 1939, UGD 352/6/1, BRC.

[109] *Food Manufacture*, January 1939, p. 1, May 1939, pp. 148–50.

[110] Viscount Astor and Seebohm Rowntree *British Agriculture: The principles of future policy* (London, 1939), pp. 192–3, 200–5, 208.

Throughout the period political and trade representatives of farming areas frequently complained about the manner in which milk regulations were shaped by urbanites who did not understand the imperatives of country life. To obviate the danger of meddling county council officials descending on farms from distant urban centres, in 1914 farming MPs successfully insisted that local authority responsibilities under the Milk and Dairies Act be invested in rural district councils. During the passage of the 1934 Milk Act these MPs maintained that talk of contaminated supplies was greatly over-exaggerated by 'those who live in towns': the product, essentially, of fevered and ignorant urban imagination.[111] Rural opposition to regulation was bolstered by the vital political relationship between farmers and the Conservative Party. It is highly significant that Tories only advocated tighter regulation if they had a direct personal involvement in medicine or public health. Sir Francis Fremantle, who in 1920 unsuccessfully pressed Lloyd George's Coalition to proceed with Addison's Milk and Dairies Bill, was a governor of both St Guy's and St Bartholomew's Hospitals and President of the Incorporated Society of Medical Officers of Health.[112] In articulating the hazards of milk from the Conservative benches Fremantle was joined by Sir William Watson Cheyne, President of the Royal College of Surgeons from 1914 to 1917, and Sir Ernest Graham-Little, a dermatologist in a London children's hospital. In the main, however, Tories seldom failed to support the farmers, their traditional rural allies.

Conservative-based rural opposition to urban interference intersected with the second conflict which prevented a tighter regulatory framework from emerging, the competing interests of agriculture and public health. Supporters and opponents of regulation alike argued that their aims were synonymous with those of the public in general, but each offered an entirely different interpretation of this 'public interest', and how it was served by regulation. Both sides accepted that an abundant supply of clean and fresh milk was a pre-requirement of improved public health. Public health reformers viewed tighter regulation as the best way of securing such a supply, and argued that improved public confidence in the product's safety would greatly increase demand for milk. Yet the public health lobby was divided over the means to this end, with many medical professionals and social reformers opposing compulsory pasteurisation until the 1930s. Fragmented opposition undoubtedly made things easier for the dairy farmers who resisted heat treatment by statute, insisting that quality or safety improvements would be outweighed by rising costs and a diminution in the quantity of supply. With the perceived high costs of regulation – inspections, licenses and most importantly the possibility of being ordered to cease operations where infection was suspected – many farmers, particularly in the 1920s, threatened to withdraw from milk production altogether. Dairy farmers who issued these threats were manipulating the 'public interest' argument which linked milk consumption with public health,

---

[111] See the remarks of R. J. Russell, MP for Eddisbury in Cheshire; Parliamentary Debates, Fifth Series, Vol. 290, 1173, 7 June 1934.

[112] Parliamentary Debates, Fifth Series, Vol. 135, 1245, 1 December 1920.

effectively saying that regulation would damage public health by reducing the volume of milk available.

In attempting to balance the competing agricultural and public health interests, the state rarely challenged this notion that the commercial interests of farmers coincided with those of the wider public. This partly reflected the parsimonious nature of the Ministry of Health in the early 1920s. Mond delayed the introduction of the 1914–15 legislation because it was opposed by farmers, but also because he believed it would be too expensive for local authorities and ratepayers. But the real explanation for the timidity of state regulation was the difference of view between the Ministries of Health and Agriculture. Lobbying vigorously and effectively on behalf of the largest body of dairy farmers, the small producer-retailers, the Ministry of Agriculture blocked pasteurisation and countered criticism of the 1922 system of grading by modifying it in 1934 to include 'premiums' (what the Labour Party called 'bribes') to farmers who produced designated milk.

The compromise which emerged from these three, intersecting conflicts was the ineffective policy of voluntary standards. The system of Special Designations, adopted permanently under the 1922 Act, was an acknowledgement that overall quality was unacceptable. But by simply leaving the task of securing much-need improvements to farmers the state absolved itself of real responsibility in an area of major public importance. In any event grading was a failure – no wholesale improvement in quality resulted. Dairymen were hardly united in admiration for the system, with the majority of farmers citing the expense of veterinary inspections and licences as an excuse for refusing to participate. But even when the objection on grounds of cost was removed under the 1934 Act, and replaced with the financial incentive of premiums for licensed producers, the overwhelming majority of producers chose to remain unlicensed. Public health critics of grading, meanwhile, saw it as a distraction. The BMA was reluctant to regard graded milk as safe unless it had also been pasteurised, and concerned that the public were confused by the number of graded products available. Ministry of Health officials took the same view, but also believed that any attempt to introduce a less-confusing system of voluntary grading would be futile. Where the different qualities of the competing grades were transparent, how many producers would choose to advertise the fact that their milk was only the second or third best available? The 1936 designations certainly did little to dispel any potential public confusion. Professor Wilson, it emerged, had been a reluctant architect of the 1936 Order. His report for the Medical Research Council, while providing definitions for several new grades, included the frank recommendation that from a strict public health perspective there should only really be two categories: milk suitable for human consumption, and milk not suitable for human consumption.[113] With this Professor Wilson articulated sentiments which had been expressed by numerous medical professionals and politicians – including a handful of Conservatives as well as

---

[113] Enock, *This Milk Business*, p. 53; Professor Wilson repeated this distinction in an article published in *Food Manufacture*, March 1936.

Labour and Liberal members – since 1914. Market competition led to the adoption of pasteurisation by leading dairy combines, but these corporations did not seek to consolidate their advantage with regulation. The defective system of voluntary grading, designed to mask the irreconcilable conflict of interest between the needs of public health and the commercial aims of the mass of dairy farmers, was not bolstered by the local option of compulsory pasteurisation until the Labour government introduced what Edith Summerskill described as 'the Milk (Save the Children) Bill' in 1949.[114]

---

[114] Parliamentary Debates, Fifth Series, Vol. 461, 1605, 21 February 1949.

8

Conclusion

This study has shown that the evolution of Britain's food laws can usefully be analysed using regulatory perspectives that have been applied to the development of American legislation. Elements of 'public interest', capture and bureaucratic discretion all contributed to the timing, character and limitations of the regulatory process, at times resembling and sometimes diverging from equivalent developments across the Atlantic. The British food regulation debate reveals the existence of a broad policy community of food reformers, commercial interests and government officials. The precise mix of groups and individuals varied slightly, depending on the issue or commodity involved. Thus analysts were omnipresent, but doctors featured more in discussions of milk, preservatives and health issues. Agrarian pressure groups were very prominent between 1880 and 1914 when butter, margarine and milk received particular attention and their successful lobbying passed responsibility for milk and butter standards to the Board of Agriculture. By the 1920s farmers' organisations were largely absent from the discussions of general food laws, featuring instead in the important but narrower controversy over milk and other new marketing schemes. This focus represented a further stage in the evolution of policy-making communities at the level of the individual commodity which became a fundamental feature of British agriculture from the 1940s.

Despite the problematic nature of the concept, there was a distinct 'public interest' reform movement which campaigned for regulation to control the quality and safety of food production and distribution. Its fundamental character was evident in the anti-adulteration campaign of the 1850s which was inspired by Wakley and Hassell, using the medical press and the professional research of analytical chemists to highlight fraudulent and dangerous adulteration. Analysts and doctors remained the most consistent presence before the various official inquiries and investigations of food quality and standards to 1938. This was a consequence of the reformers' key achievement, the provision in the 1860 Act which allowed local authorities to appoint Public Analysts. Although many authorities preferred not to implement the policy or restricted their analyst's duties, the slow expansion in the number of analysts provided an institutional base from which the profession could pursue its campaign for further and stricter regulation. The same trend occurred for Medical Officers of Health who occupied a similar role in the local enforcement of the adulteration acts. Both professions strengthened their capabilities as pressure groups through the formation of their own organisations, the Society of Public Analysts and the Incorporated Society of Medical Officers of Health. Their advocacy of consumer interests co-existed with efforts to promote their own professional status, including determining the qualifications and remuneration for their posts. Indeed the SPA's campaign for a national system of uniform standards was clearly an attempt to strengthen the authority of its members. This was in some ways a paradoxical goal, given that a central system of minimal standards could reduce the analysts' local discretion and influence, but their long campaign was predicated on the hope of achieving a more secure professional position and steadily expanding the scope of regulation. The reform campaign also included specialist pressure groups, such as the Bread and Food Reform League or later the People's League of Health, both dominated by middle-class social reformers and philanthropists. And concern about adulteration was shared too by working-class organisations, most notably the burgeoning Co-operative movement which emphasised the sale of pure food in Co-op stores as a central component of its fair trade ideology. The various strands of the reform movement qualify Olson's emphasis on the disincentives to organising the mass of consumers. While most consumers remained outside the reform campaign, numerous associations and societies were formed to lobby in their name.

Business attitudes toward regulation were diverse, reflecting differences of interest between firms and sectors, changing circumstances and their experience of the regulatory system itself. Although such diversity undermines straightforward notions of capture or business privilege, both elements provide certain insights. If capture is used in Stigler's sense of business initiating demands for regulations to provide competitive advantages, the picture is mixed. In the 1850s and 1860s manufacturers and retailers were on the defensive in the face of the anti-adulteration campaign inspired by Wakley, Hassall and other reformers. As Burnett and Horrocks have noted, some firms adjusted their operations in response to these criticisms. By the 1860s and 1870s, however, a new phase was evident with manufacturers and London commodity brokers determined to shape new legislation that legitimised their products. This pressure combined direct personal influence, such as Jeremiah Colman's place on the 1874 Select Committee, with organised lobbying by London tea dealers and coffee producers and importers. A further element appeared during the 1880s in the form of landowners from dairying areas and butter producers and traders who were anxious to obtain new laws that would handicap the emergent margarine industry. These agrarian pressure groups were also the prime movers in the campaign for butter regulations in the early 1900s, culminating in the Butter and Margarine Act of 1907. Landed interests from grain-growing districts were responsible for the series of unsuccessful Pure Beer Bills during the late nineteenth and early twentieth centuries.

The rural lobbying was a protectionist response to the agricultural depression. The same basic motivation was evident in the successful campaign by British-based manufacturers of condensed milk for regulations to impede US imports in the early 1920s. In addition the debates about mixtures, or compound foods, in the 1870s and the protracted conflicts about butter and margarine involved producers of a premium product attempting to undermine the reputation and marketing strategies of cheaper substitute commodities. Similar strategies were apparent in relation to vinegar before and after the First World War, and cheese and ice-cream in the 1920s and 1930s. All of these business-led initiatives are consistent with Stigler's assumption that regulation is primarily a product of producer interests intent on erecting barriers to entry. It also lends support to Olson's argument that smaller groups who are directly affected by a measure are easier to organise. But the examples of business initiating regulation also highlight the problematic nature of capture theories since a successful campaign required the defeat of rival and equally committed and self-interested producers. If this aspect increases the significance of the lobbying by business, it also means that not all interests can be satisfied. Margarine producers and traders opposed the Margarine Act of 1887 and there were divided views about the later butter regulations, the use of preservatives, and standards for milk, vinegar and other commodities. Sometimes, as with vinegar, the competing interests ensured a stalemate, precluding any legislation. But there is an important qualification, namely that business advocacy of regulation was most pronounced when targeted on specific measures designed to impede a competitor. When the proposed regulation was of a general character, such as the various SFDAs between 1872 and 1938 or the preservatives regulations, the food industry was more often on the defensive, opposing or seeking to limit any intervention rather than sponsoring new measures. Only in 1874 were business representatives advocating changes to general laws in order to legitimise mixed or processed articles.

Bureaucratic discretion featured at several stages of the regulatory process. The legislative framework was partly shaped by local government which influenced the timing and extent of enforcement. In some areas the SFDA was largely inoperable before 1899. The most active authorities, notably Kensington vestry or Bermondsey, directly lobbied the LGB and later the Ministry of Health about food issues. Further pressure was exerted at times through peak organisations such as the County Councils' Association. Public analysts and Medical Officers of Health were responsible for the operation of the food and drugs laws at the local level. The analyst's scientific expertise was involved in determining the composition of a sampled food and, in addition, the certificate of analysis required a judgement about whether the commodity was legitimate. Usually the local Medical Officer of Health then advised on whether the evidence warranted prosecution, though the final decision often lay with the council's health committee. These local officials were also able to take the initiative in sampling particular foods, thereby focusing attention on a particular additive, product or supplier. Their opinions were, of course, subject to the scrutiny of the courts where the analyst's certificates could be challenged as factually inaccurate or an alleged adulteration could be declared a legitimate trade practice. The analysts' professional standing remained precarious to the

1890s, largely due to their uneasy relationship with the Government Laboratory and the conservatism of officials at the LGB. But analysts were consulted regularly about the food laws and throughout the period from 1875 to 1938 active and campaigning analysts exercised considerable influence when supported by their local council. Charles Cassal and Alfred Hill typified this aspect of bureaucratic initiative, the latter having the added advantage of being the local Medical Officer of Health in Birmingham, and Otto Hehner's lengthy career spanned the establishment of the SFDA in the 1870s, the arsenic debate in the 1900s, and the preservatives inquiry in the 1920s. In their appearances before official inquiries and through the SPA's lobbying, such analysts and doctors linked local and national politics. By the 1920s the presence of analysts on the Preservatives Committee signalled a significant advance into the policy-making process. Yet no individual Public Analyst or the SPA possessed the status or decisive influence achieved by Harvey Wiley in the United States. This reflected the stronger state-level powers and institutional base of American food reformers: active states were clearly far more influential than, say, a London vestry. Wiley's political acumen and his pivotal role as lobbyist, bureaucrat and associate of manufacturers contrasted with the narrower remit and more technical role of George Buchanan of the LGB's Foods Section. Wiley's position, head of the Bureau of Chemistry in the Department of Agriculture, also combined agrarian and health concerns in a way that became more fragmented in the British case where both the LGB and the Board of Agriculture had responsibilities for standards by 1899.

The medical profession established an earlier, greater and more integrated presence in national government with the appointment of doctors as officials with responsibility for food matters in the LGB and Ministry of Health. This reflected the doctors' expertise across a wide range of public health issues compared to the analysts' concentration on food quality. The national involvement of doctors in food policy received its main impetus from Buchanan's initiatives in response to the turn of the century food scares over arsenic in beer and the quality of imported meats. Buchanan investigated the arsenic poisonings directly and was secretary to Kelvin's Royal Commission which, along with other contemporary inquiries, recommended the creation of an external advisory body on foods or an LGB research unit. When the latter option was selected, Buchanan established and directed the new Foods Section. Although small, this provided a central research capability and the reports by Buchanan and other food inspectors made public policy recommendations. Experts in the LGB are usually seen as subordinate to civil servants and Ministers and detached from the policy-making process, but Buchanan used the Foods Section's reports and the panic over imported meat to convince John Burns, the President of the LGB, to extend considerably his department's powers to regulate foods by introducing the 1907 Public Health Act. It signalled that safeguarding health rather than eliminating fraud was the priority for central government. Buchanan's influence was greatest in the context of food scares which lends support to Skocpol's view that crisis conditions created the best opportunities for bureaucratic initiative. Yet food developments do not bear out Skocpol's logic

Conclusion

entirely. According to this, the First World War, in producing a general state of crisis, should have increased the autonomy of the state and its capacity to intervene. In the event, there were mixed effects, reflecting the priority given to the demands of mobilisation. Proposed legislation was abandoned in the case of food standards and suspended in the case of milk, effectively disrupting the unsteady course of pre-war policy making. During the war central government assumed greater control of food supplies, particularly after 1916, and introduced its own food standards as part of the rationing schemes. But these initiatives and the wartime Ministry of Food were only temporary.

From 1920 central oversight of food regulation passed to the new Ministry of Health and the Ministry of Agriculture. Politicians and civil servants in the Ministry of Health were anxious to maintain their influence over food policy, establishing the Preservatives inquiry and later the Willis committee on food standards in order to avoid any prospect of responsibility passing to other Departments or agencies. At the same time the new Ministry firmly identified health protection as its central priority. Bureaucratic initiative remained influential in the principal legislation of the 1920s: the preservatives regulations were proposed by a committee dominated by officials and scientists from various departments. When the committee proclaimed preservatives to be an unambiguous health risk, the Ministry firmly supported legislation while seeking compromise with manufacturers and retailers over the detail and timing of the new regulations. Subsequently, however, Ministers, civil servants and officials accepted the food industry's claims that further controls were unnecessary and would indeed constitute harassment. This attitude explains the slow progress and cautious outcome of the inquiry on food standards in the 1930s. In the absence of new health concerns, bureaucratic initiatives were confined to the new marketing schemes and subsidies provided by the Ministry of Agriculture. The Ministry of Health's evident caution recalled the conservatism of the LGB, although in a very different economic and political context from the 1880s and 1890s when Preston-Thomas had summarised his department's preference for local rather than central direction. Much had changed, but the comparison emphasises that there was not a continuous or direct progression towards greater or stricter regulation: the process was contested, fitful and uncertain. This resembles the evolution of the US Pure Food and Drug laws which were a product of lengthy debate and, apart from a phase of activism around 1906–7, were applied cautiously until being revised in the 1930s.

'Public interest' reformers, commercial interests and government officials all contributed to the debates about food quality and standards. Both reformers and business groups were increasingly organised, developing national associations to present their views to Parliament and government departments. Their relative influence is not always easy to disentangle. Paulus argued that the 1899 SFDA embodied a key compromise, defining the parameters of legitimate trade for manufacturers and retailers and ensuring the position of analysts and local authorities in implementing the law. Although compromise was important, regulation evolved not through repeated agreement between all sides, but rather through a series of shifting alliances. Analysts and doctors consistently advocated further intervention. Their primary contribution was in initiating debate and maintaining pressure on the food industry and government. Their agitation prompted a defensive response by business, seeking minimal regulations within which to operate. But the reformers' constant presence makes it difficult to see them as a decisive influence because, as in the United States, legislation occurred only intermittently following protracted pressure and debate. The SPA greeted most new food legislation as a welcome, but limited and belated, advance. The preservatives regulations of 1925, arguably the reformers' greatest achievement, were the result of over three decades of lobbying by which time many producers and retailers had turned to new methods of keeping foods, notably refrigeration, which did not involve chemical preservatives. Similarly doctors and analysts sustained their critique of milk quality for more than four decades. By the 1930s their arguments had convinced the Ministry of Health of the need for compulsory pasteurisation, but even then the measure was not finally adopted until 1949. In this case the milk trade's defence of its established operations delayed change, emphasising the limitations of the food reformers' influence in the face of commercial resistance.

Commercial interests were, by contrast, more influential. The introduction of the Margarine Act, the Condensed Milk regulations and standards for milk and butter were a product of organised lobbying by producers and traders with, except in the case of condensed milk, support from farmers. The prospects of regulation were increased where the intention was to disadvantage overseas competitors. Analysts and doctors provided valuable support to the case for intervention, but the actual focus of these specific regulations indicates that business influence was decisive. Business interests might have been expected to resolve their problems without regulation. Certainly some manufacturers pursued their own strategies of branding and quality control. In some districts farmers and shopkeepers had scope to use their local political influence over the operation of the food laws. Business looked to the state for support primarily in search of protection from imported produce at times of overproduction. Unable to obtain tariffs, agrarian interests and butter trades looked to the food laws as a form of social regulation that might stymie their competitors. This interpretation explains the interwar developments when farming interests gained more direct support through marketing schemes and then subsidies and were no longer so interested in obtaining new food laws.

The emphasis on specific or target regulations leaves the question of general legislation, such as the SFDA and preservatives regulations. Such broad measures lacked a specific pro-regulation lobby among producers or retailers and the various hearings and debates usually revealed diverse views. The industry's heterogeneous character could have given the initiative to the reformers. This was the result in the case of the preservatives regulations in the 1920s where bureaucratic initiative, namely the Ministry of Health's concern about health risks, was an added influence. Yet, although the food manufacturers considered themselves on the defensive at this stage, they then acted to influence the fine detail of the regulations and promoted the 1928 SFDA, which guaranteed uniform administration of the regulations. Manufacturers then dissuaded the government from introducing a general system of food standards. This opposition to general standards and regulations reflected three broad developments. First, as Paulus argued, the compromises in the SFDA of 1899 were regarded as broadly acceptable by manufacturers and retailers as a legal framework consistent with their established practices. Second, the food manufacturers, through the Manufacturing Confectioners' Alliance and the Food Manufacturers' Federation, preferred to maintain their own control over food quality. Manufacturers were particularly anxious to resist inspection of their factories and warehouses. The leading manufacturers' strategy was to rely on gaining the maximum share of an expanding market, free of restrictions, rather than seeking to use regulations to exclude or disadvantage their smaller rivals. With Paul Cadbury and others articulating this view, the major manufacturers made no attempt to promote general food laws. Third, and similarly, there was no pressure for regulation from smaller firms who might have looked to the state to control the activities of larger producers. This suggests that the small firms accepted the leadership of Cadbury and others and were perfectly content with the basic framework of the 1899 SFDA. Only when these arrangements were disrupted by new developments, as when courts applied various different standards for preservatives, did the industry support regulation in order to obtain greater uniformity. This offers a contrast to the American case where the imposition of food laws by the individual states has been portrayed as a factor leading manufacturers to seek uniformity through national regulations. In Britain manufacturers were apparently less concerned by local laws, partly because the burden fell on retailers and partly because the 1899 SFDA had created acceptable definitions of legitimate trading.

The debates about food regulation cast some light on whether business was a privileged group due to its fundamental economic role. According to Kolko, US food regulations were conservative since they did not threaten the place of business in society and this was generally the case in Britain. Only the Co-operative movement offered a challenging vision and philosophy, but this aspect did not surface consistently in the area of food quality and standards. Elements of privilege were evident too in that officials and Ministers were always concerned not to interfere unduly with commercial activities. Those regulations that were adopted generally aimed to establish a broad framework within which producers and distributors could operate rather than directly controlling their affairs. At a lower level, however, the notion of business privilege is less distinct due to the rivalry among different business interests. In their various efforts to capture the regulatory process, one group's success could be at the expense of a rival. In addition the representatives of business did not regard themselves as privileged, or sufficiently so, but often considered themselves on the defensive, notably over the preservatives regulations, and requiring to re-assert their position in the face of what they saw as the domineering views of social reformers.

As McCraw suggested, many different pressure groups used their own notions of the 'public interest' as convenient rhetoric in the debates about food regulation. Their different definitions of the term illuminate the different assumptions and tensions in the debates about Britain's food laws. The reforming analysts and doctors based their definitions of 'public interest' on the original anti-adulteration issues: food should be safe to eat and not include unnecessary or fraudulent ingredients. The 1875 SFDA enshrined these two elements as the fundamental definitions of adulteration, ensuring that the concepts remained central to the operation of the food laws. Between 1875 and 1938 the health aspect became increasingly important, even though government and industry emphasised the decline of dangerous adulterations, with regulators regarding food safety as their main priority. This reflected the broad scope of the health issue since new developments presented additional potential hazards. The food safety aspect centred initially on particularly dangerous additives such as red lead or mercury, but also came to encompass the longer-term effects of exposure to small quantities of new additives, such as the food preservative chemicals. At times health concerns extended to questions of nutrition and diet, as with the fat content of milk or the quality of machine-skimmed condensed milks. Generally 'public interest' arguments for regulation were made in terms of the potential hazards to particularly vulnerable groups, especially infants and invalids. This partly reflected the considerable attention paid to milk products, but also served to counter the assumption that adult consumers were either not at risk or, as legally responsible consumers, required no special protection. The importance attached to health hazards was heightened periodically by food scares which gave new impetus to the debates about food. Analysts and the SPA remained concerned with emphasising fraudulent adulteration, while medical opinion placed more stress on health risks. For the analysts, the potential for fraud required not simply compulsory labelling, but precise specification standards so that consumers knew what they were purchasing. A commodity should have certain defined characteristics, preferably an established chemical composition, that were reproduced in each item. This definition of adulteration as fraud was present in the 1875 Act and remained part of the debate, but the analysts' desire for precise descriptions attracted far less support from other reformers or the public than did concerns with health.

Business definitions of 'public interest' varied according to whether the individual was supporting or opposing a particular regulation. When advocating a regulation, commercial pressure groups adopted versions of the reformers' 'public interest' case, usually claiming that a rival product was a fraudulent adulteration in its composition, description or advertising. This emphasis was most apparent in the campaigns against margarine where the butter trade made far less effort to raise health or nutritional objections. Opposition to regulation was generally based on three broad views. First, manufacturers argued that particular foods were nutritious, sometimes linked to an emphasis on the availability of cheap food as particularly important. In this respect food producers and distributors offered their own definition of 'public interest' rooted in the availability of inexpensive foods as the priority for public health and the welfare of consumers. This approach was used effectively by margarine interests to counter their critics' depiction of the product as fraudulent. The importance of cheap food was influential in the thinking of

Conclusion

government officials and it limited, for example, the LGB's support for protectionist measures that would have prohibited margarine, and was still important for politicians and officials in the Ministry of Health between the wars. Hence there was a persistent tension between those commercial interests which made essentially protectionist demands for regulation and the business opposition to regulation which emphasised the importance of cheap imported foods. Second, and related to cheap food, manufacturers and traders claimed that their products were designed to satisfy consumers' tastes. This addressed claims of fraudulent adulteration by placing consumer choice in a central position and essentially offered a model of the food industry as one where perfect competition operated sufficiently to make regulation unnecessary. Consumers were pictured as knowledgeable about the composition of different products. Thus they were able to exercise freedom of choice and required no special protection. A third, and also related, defence was that manufacturers had their own commercial motives for supplying safe and unadulterated foods. This point was emphasised by the suppliers of branded and packaged goods like Colman and Cadbury. It was an important defence, partly because it had substance, reflecting emerging trade practice, and partly because it buttressed the argument that market forces operated effectively, with the industry trusted to act responsibly to protect its own reputation and sales. The state accepted a good deal of this logic and as a result paid less attention to the operations of smaller manufacturers and retailers on the assumption that the behaviour of the leading firms was representative of the industry generally.

Bibliography

Government papers

Public Records Office, Kew

Current Guide (1999).
DSIR 16 Department of Scientific and Industrial Research.
DSIR 26 Government Laboratory.
MAF 36 Board of Agriculture and Ministry of Agriculture and Fisheries, food policy.
MAF 52 Ministry of Agriculture and Fisheries, milk policy.
MAF 101 Ministry of Agriculture and Fisheries, Public Analysts, Empire Marketing Board.
MH 56 Ministry of Health, food policy, including milk, preservatives and food standards; Local Government Board, food contamination.
MH 58 Ministry of Health, People's League of Health resolutions.
MH 107 Local Government Board, Personal Files.
MH 113 Local Government Board, food policy.
MH 139 Ministry of Health, Diaries of Sir George Newman.

National Archives of Scotland (Scottish Records Office), Edinburgh

HH 62 County Medical Officers of Health, Annual Reports.
HH 64 Scottish Office, food and milk policy.

Records of business and other organisations

Bakery and Allied Traders' Association Minutes, Food and Drink Federation Library and Archives, London.
British Food Manufacturers' Federation, Food and Drink Federation Library and Archives, London.
British Medical Association, Contemporary Medical Archives Centre, The Wellcome Institute for the History of Medicine, London.
Consumers' Council, National Museum of Labour History, Manchester.
Glasgow Wholesale Milk Dealers' Association, Business Records' Centre, University of Glasgow.
James Keiller and Son Ltd., Dundee City Archives.
Rowntree Mackintosh, Borthwick Institute, York.

Bibliography

Private papers

John Burns, Diary, British Library Manuscript Collection.
J. R. Hutchison, Contemporary Medical Archives Centre, The Wellcome Institute for the History of Medicine, London.
Sir Thomas Edward Thorpe, Royal Society Library, London.

Official publications

Board of Agriculture (Intelligence Division), Annual Report (1900).
Board of Agriculture and Fisheries (Intelligence Division), Annual Report of Proceedings under the SFDA for 1903, 1904, Cd. 2187.
Board of Agriculture and Fisheries, Annual Report of Proceedings under the Sale of Food and Drugs Acts for 1904, 1905, Cd. 2637.
Departmental Committee to inquire into the desirability of regulation under the Sale of Food and Drugs Act, 1899, for Milk and Cream, Minutes of Evidence, 1901, Cd. 484.
Departmental Committee to inquire into the desirability of regulation under the Sale of Food and Drugs Act, 1899, for Milk and Cream, Report, 1901, Cd. 491.
Report of the Departmental Committee on the Composition and Description of Food, 1933–4, Cmd. 4564.
Final Report of the Committee on the Production and Distribution of Milk, 1919, Cmd. 483.
Final Report of the Departmental Committee Appointed by the Board of Agriculture to Inquire and Report upon the Desirability of Regulations for Butter, Minutes of Evidence, 1904, Cd. 1750.
First Report of the Royal Commission to Inquire into Arsenical Poisoning from the Consumption of Beer and Other Articles of Food and Drink, July 1901, Cd. 692.
Final Report of the Royal Commission to Inquire into Arsenical Poisoning from the Consumption of Beer and other Articles of Food and Drink, 1903, Cd. 1848.
Royal Commission to Inquire into Arsenical Poisoning from the Consumption of Beer and other Articles of Food and Drink, Minutes of Evidence and Appendices, Vol. 1, 1901, Cd. 1845.
Royal Commission to Inquire into Arsenical Poisoning from the Consumption of Beer and other Articles of Food and Drink, Minutes of Evidence and Appendices, Vol. 2, 1902–1903, Cd. 1869.
HMSO, Census of Production, Vols. 1–5 (1907–34).
House of Commons, Sub-Committee of the Standing Committee on Trusts, Report on Vinegar, 1921, Cd. 1355.
Inter-Departmental Committee, Sale of Bread by Weight (1921), Cmd. 1400.
Interim Report of the Departmental Committee appointed by the Board of Agriculture to Inquire and Report upon the Desirability of Regulations for Butter, 1902, Cd. 944.
Local Government Board in England and Wales, Annual Reports (1899–1918).
Local Government Board in Scotland, Annual Reports (1899–1913).
Local Government and Public Health Consolidation Committee, Third Interim Report, December 1937, Cmd. 5628.
LGB (Medical Department), Reports of Inspectors of Foods, Nos. 1–14, (London: HMSO, 1906–1916).
LGB, Annual Report. Supplement Containing the Report of the Medical Officer of Health,

1905–6, Cd. 3656.
Ministry of Agriculture, Food and Fisheries, Departmental Committee on Distribution and Prices of Agricultural Produce, Interim Report on Milk and Milk Products, 1923, Cmd. 1854; Final Report, 1924, Cmd. 2008.
Ministry of Agriculture, Food and Fisheries, Food Quality and Safety: A century of progress (London, 1975).
Ministry of Health, Annual Reports (1920–38).
Ministry of Health, On the State of the Public Health. Annual Report of the Chief Medical Officer (1932).
Parliamentary Debates, Third, Fourth and Fifth Series.
Public General Acts: passed in various years from 1875.
Report by the Food Council on the Question of Short Weight and Measure in the Sale of Foodstuffs, Evidence (1925), Vols. 1–4.
Report by the Food Council on the Question of Short Weight and Measure in the Sale of Foodstuffs, 1926, Cmd 2591.
Report from the Select Committee on Adulteration of Food Act (1872). Proceedings and Minutes of Evidence, Parliamentary Papers, 1874 (262), VI, 243.
Report from the Select Committee on the Butter Substitutes Bill, Parliamentary Papers (208), 1887.
Report from the Select Committee on Marking of Foreign Meat, 25 August 1893, Parliamentary Papers, 1893–4, 214.
Report of the Select Committee on the Butter Trade, 1906 (245).
Report from the Select Committee on the Sale of Food and Drugs Act (1875) Amendment Bill, Parliamentary Papers, 1878–9 (155), X.1.
Report of the Departmental Committee Appointed to Inquire into the Use of Preservatives and Colouring of Food, 1902, Cd. 833.
Report of the Departmental Committee on Beer Materials Conducted by the Board of the Inland Revenue, 1899, C. 9171.
Report of the Departmental Committee on the Working in Great Britain of the Fertilisers and Feedingstuffs Act, 1893, 1905, Cd. 2372.
Report to the LGB by Dr JM Hamill on the presence of calcium sulphate in Baking Powder and Self-raising flour, 1911, Cd. 5614.
Report to the Local Government Board on Recent Epidemic. Arsenical Poisoning Attributed to Beer, January 1901, Cd. 459.
Report on Food Products Adulteration, Parliamentary Papers, 1894 (253).
Report on Food Products Adulteration, Parliamentary Papers, 1895 (363).
Report on Food Products Adulteration, Parliamentary Papers, 1896 (288).
Sale of Milk Regulations, 1901, Statutory Rules and Orders, No. 657 (London, 1901); No. 355 (London, 1902).
The Scottish Board of Health and Scottish Department of Health, Annual Reports (1920–38).

Periodicals and newspapers

The Analyst
The Brewers' Almanack
British Food Journal and Analytical Review
British Medical Journal

Bibliography

Co-operative News
The Economist
Food Manufacturers' Federation Bulletin
Food Manufacture
The Grocer
Ice Cream Industry
Public Health
Lancet
The Times

Books and articles

Addison, Christopher, *Four and a Half Years* (London, 1934).
Addison, Paul, *Churchill on the Home Front, 1900–1955* (London, 1992).
Akerloff, Gary, 'The Market for "Lemons": quality uncertainty and the market mechanism', *Quarterly Journal of Economics*, August 1970, pp. 488–500.
Anderson, Oscar E., *The Health of a Nation: Harvey J. Wiley and the fight for pure food* (Chicago, 1958).
Astor, Viscount and Rowntree, Seebohm, *British Agriculture: The principles of future policy* (London, 1939).
Atkins, P. J., 'Sophistication Detected: Or the adulteration of the milk supply, 1850–1914', *Social History*, 16(3), 1991, pp. 317–39.
Atkins, P. J. 'White Poison? the social consequences of milk consumption, 1850–1930', *Social History of Medicine*, 5, 1992, pp. 207–27.
Barnett, L. Margaret, *British Food Policy in the First World War* (London, 1985).
Bartrip, P. W.J. 'How Green Was My Valance? Environmental arsenic poisoning and the Victorian domestic ideal', *English Historical Review*, 109, September 1994, pp. 891–913.
Bellamy, Christine, *Administering Central–Local Relations, 1871–1919: The Local Government Board in its fiscal and cultural context* (Manchester, 1985).
Blank, Stephen, *Industry and Government in Britain: The Federation of British Industries in politics* (Farnborough: Saxon House, 1973).
Bolger, Patrick, *The Irish Co-operative Movement: Its history and development* (Dublin, 1977).
Brown, Kenneth D., 'John Burns at the Local Government Board: A reassessment', *Journal of Social Policy*, 6(2), 1977, pp. 157–70.
Brown, Kenneth, *John Burns* (London, 1977).
Burnett, John, 'The Baking Industry in the Nineteenth Century', *Business History*, 5 (1/2), 1962–3, pp. 98–108.
Burnett, John, *Plenty and Want* (third edition, London, 1989).
Campbell, John L. et al. (eds), *Governance of the American Economy* (Cambridge, 1991).
Casson, Mark, 'Brands: Economic ideology and consumer society', in Geoffrey Jones and Nicholas J. Morgan, (eds), *Adding Value: Brands and marketing in food and drink* (London, 1994), pp. 41–58.
Casson, Mark, *The Economics of Business Culture: Game theory, transaction costs, and economic performance* (Oxford, 1991).
Chalmin, Philippe, *The Making of a Sugar Giant. Tate and Lyle, 1859–1989* (New York, 1990).
Chandler, Alfred D., *Scale and Scope: The dynamics of industrial capitalism* (Cambridge,

MA., 1990).

Coller, Frank H., *A State Trading Adventure* (Oxford, 1925).

Collins, E. J. T., 'The "Consumer Revolution" and the Growth of Factory Foods: Changing patterns of bread and cereal-eating in Britain in the twentieth century', Derek J. Oddy and Derek S. Miller (eds), *The Making of the Modern British Diet* (London, 1976).

Collins, E. J. T., 'Brands and Breakfast Cereals in Britain', Geoffrey Jones and Nicholas J. Morgan (eds), *Adding Value: Brands and marketing in food and drink* (London, 1994), pp. 237–58.

Coppin, Clayton A. and High, Jack, 'Umpires at Bat: Setting food standards by government regulation', *Business and Economic History*, 21, 1992, pp. 109–19.

Corley, T. A. B., 'Nutrition, Technology and the Growth of the British Biscuit Industry, 1820–1900', Derek J. Oddy and Derek S. Miller (eds), *The Making of the Modern British Diet* (London, 1976), pp. 13–25.

Corley, T. A. B., 'Consumer Marketing in Britain, 1914–60', *Business History*, 29(4), October 1987, pp. 65–83.

Cox, Graham, Lowe, Philip and Winter, Michael, 'The origins and Early Development of the National Farmers' Union', *Agricultural History Review*, 39, 1991, pp. 30–47.

Crossick, Geoffrey and Haupt, Heinz-Gerhard, *Shopkeepers and Master Artisans in Nineteenth Century Europe* (London, 1984).

Crossick, Geoffrey and Haupt, Heinz-Gerhard, *The Petite Bourgeoisie in Europe, 1780–1914: Enterprise, family and independence* (London, 1995).

Davidson, R. and Lowe, R., 'Bureaucracy and Innovation in British Welfare Policy, 1870–1945', in W. J. Mommsen (ed.), *The Emergence of the Welfare State in Britain and Germany, 1850–1945* (London, 1981), pp. 107–130.

Davies, Ben, *The Nation's Milk Supply: Its hygienic production and control* (London, 1933).

Dictionary of National Biography, 1922–1930 (Oxford, 1937).

Dingle, A. E., 'Drink and Working-Class Living Standards in Britain, 1870–1914', *Economic History Review*, 35(4), November 1972, pp. 608–22.

Drummond, J. C. and Wilbraham, A., *The Englishman's Food: A history of five centuries of English diet* (London, 1939).

Dwork, Deborah, *War is Good for Babies and Other Young Children: A history of the infant and child welfare movement in England, 1898–1918* (London, 1987).

Dyer, Bernard and Ainsworth, Mitchell, *The Society of Public Analysts: Some reminiscences of its first fifty years and a review of its activities* (Cambridge, 1932).

Edgerton, D. E. H. and Horrocks, S. M., 'British Industrial Research and Development before 1945', *Economic History Review*, 67(2), 1994, pp. 213–38.

Enock, Arthur Guy, *This Milk Business: A study from 1895 to 1943* (London, 1943).

Eyler, John M., *Sir Arthur Newsholme and State Medicine* (Cambridge, 1997).

Fenton, James, 'Preservatives and Colouring Matter in Food', *Public Health*, August 1924, pp. 284–6.

Finlay, Mark R., 'Early Marketing of the Theory of Nutrition: The science and culture of Leibig's extract of meat', in Harmke Kamminga and Andrew Cunningham (eds), *The Science and Culture of Nutrition* (Amsterdam, 1995).

Fitzgerald, Robert, *Rowntree and the Marketing Revolution, 1862–1969* (Cambridge, 1995).

Fraser, W. Hamish, *The Coming of the Mass Market, 1850–1914* (London, 1981).

Gaffin, Jean and Thoms, David, *Caring and Sharing: The centenary history of the Co-operative Women's Guild* (Manchester, 1983).

Gardiner, A. G., *Life of George Cadbury* (London, 1925).

Bibliography

Glucksman, Miriam, *Women Assemble: Women workers and the new industries in interwar Britain* (London, 1990).
Gourvish, T. R. and Wilson, R. G. *The British Brewing Industry, 1830–1980* (Cambridge, 1994).
Grant, Wyn, *Business and Politics in Britain* (Basingstoke, first edition, 1987, second edition, 1993).
Gurney, Peter, *Co-operative Culture and the Politics of Consumption in England, 1870–1930* (Manchester, 1996).
Hall, P., *Governing the Economy: The politics of state intervention in Britain and France* (Cambridge, 1986).
Hamlin, Christopher, *A Science of Impurity: Water analysis in nineteenth Century Britain* (Bristol, 1990).
Hammond, R. J., *Food. Vol. II. Studies in administration and control* (London, 1956).
Harris, Jose, *Private Lives, Public Spirit: Britain, 1870–1914* (London, 1993).
Heer, Jean, *World Events, 1866–1966: The first hundred years of Nestlé* (Rivaz, Switzerland, 1966).
Hehner, Otto, 'Chemicals in Food: Increasing Use of Preservatives: An analyst's view', *The Times*, 30 October 1923.
Hennessy, Peter, *Whitehall* (London, 1990).
High, Jack (ed.), *Regulation: Economic theory and history* (Ann Arbor, 1991).
Hobsbawm, E. J., *Industry and Empire* (London, 1968).
Horrocks, S. M., 'Nutrition Science and the Food Industry in Britain, 1920–1990' in Adel den Hartog, *Food, Technology, Science and Marketing: European diet in the twentieth century* (East Linton, 1995), pp. 7–18.
Horrocks, Sally M. 'Quality control and research: the role of scientists in the British food industry, 1870–1939', in John Burnett and Derek J. Oddy (eds), *The Origins and Development of Food Policies in Europe* (Leicester, 1994), pp. 130–45.
Horrocks, Sally M., 'The business of vitamins: nutrition science and the food industry in inter-war Britain', in Harmke Kamminga and Andrew Cunningham (eds), *The Science and Culture of Nutrition* (Amsterdam, 1995), pp. 235–8.
Hosgood, Christopher, 'The "Pigmies of Commerce" and the Working-Class Community: Small shopkeepers in England, 1870–1914', *Journal of Social History*, 22, 1988–9, pp. 439–60.
Hosgood, C. P., 'A "Brave and Daring Folk"? Shopkeepers and trade associational life in Victorian and Edwardian England', *Journal of Social History*, 36, 1992, pp. 285–308.
Howe, Anthony, *Free Trade and Liberal England, 1846–1946* (Oxford, 1997).
Hunt, E. H. and Pam, S. J., 'Prices and Structural Response in English Agriculture, 1873–1896', *Economic History Review*, 50(3) Autumn 1997, pp. 477–505.
Hunter, Lynette, 'Nineteenth and Twentieth Century Trends in Food Preserving: Frugality, nutrition or luxury', in C. Anne Wilson, *Waste Not, Want Not: Food preservation from early times to the present day* (Edinburgh, 1991), pp. 142–8.
Ilersic, A. R., *Parliament of Commerce: The story of the Association of British Chambers of Commerce, 1860–1960* (London, 1960).
Jeffreys, James B., *Retail Trading in Britain, 1850–1950* (Cambridge, 1954).
Jenkins, Alan, *Drinka Pinta* (London; 1970).
Jeremy, David J. (ed.), *Dictionary of Business Biography*, Vol. I (London, 1984).
Johnston, J. P., 'The Development of the Food Canning Industry in Britain during Inter-war Period', in Derek J. Oddy and Derek S. Miller, *The Making of the Modern British Diet*

(London: 1976).
Jones, Greta, *Social Hygiene in Twentieth Century Britain* (London, 1986).
Jones, Geoffrey and Morgan, Nicholas J. (eds), *Adding Value: Brands and marketing in food and drink* (London, 1994).
Kamminga, Harmke and Cunningham, Andrew (eds), *The Science and Culture of Nutrition* (Amsterdam, 1995).
Kent, William, *John Burns: Labour's lost leader* (London, 1950).
Kindleberger, C. P., 'Standards as Public, Collective and Private Goods', *Kyklos*, 36(3), 1983, pp. 377–96.
Kindleberger, C. P., 'Group Behaviour', *Journal of Political Economy*, 59(1), 1951, pp. 30–47.
Kitson Clark, George, *Portrait of an Age: Victorian England* (London, 1953, reprinted 1977).
Kitson Clark, George, *The making of Victorian England* (Oxford, 1962).
Klein, B. and Leffler, K., 'The Role of Market Forces in Assuring Contractual Performance', *Journal of Political Economy*, August 1981, pp. 615–42.
Kolko, Gabriel, *The Triumph of Conservatism: A reinterpretation of American history, 1900–1916* (Chicago, 1967).
Konig, N., *The Failure of Agrarian Capitalism: Agrarian politics in the UK, the Netherlands and the USA, 1846–1919* (London, 1994).
Langlois, Richard N. and Robertson, Paul L., *Firms, Markets and Economic Change: A dynamic theory of business institutions* (London, 1995).
Libecap, Gary D., 'The Rise of the Chicago Packers and the Origins of Meat Inspection and Antitrust', *Economic Inquiry*, 30, April 1992, pp. 242–62.
Lindblom, Charles, *Politics and Markets: The world's political economic systems* (New York, 1977).
Liverseege, J. F., *Adulteration and Analysis of Food and Drugs* (London, 1932).
Macdonagh, Oliver, *Early Victorian Government, 1830–1870* (London, 1977).
Macleod, Roy (ed.), *Government and Expertise: Specialists, administrators and professionals* (Cambridge, 1988).
MacLeod, Roy M., *Treasury Control and Social Administration: A study of establishment growth at the Local Government Board, 1871–1905* (London, 1968).
Marrison, A. J., 'The Tariff Commission, Agricultural Protection and Food Taxes, 1903–1913', *Agricultural History Review*, 34, 1986, pp. 171–87.
Marsh, David and Rhodes, R. A. W. (eds), *Policy Networks in British Government*, (Oxford, 1992).
Marx, Karl, *The Eighteenth Brumaire of Louis Bonaparte* (Moscow, 1934).
Mathias, Peter, *The First Industrial Nation: An economic history of Britain, 1700–1914* (Second edition, Oxford: Methuen, 1983).
Matthews, A. H. H., *Fifty Years of Agricultural Politics: Being the history of the Central Chamber of Agriculture, 1865–1915* (London: P. S. King & Son, 1915).
McCraw, Thomas K., 'Regulation in America: A review article', *Business History Review*, 49, 1975, pp. 159–83.
McIvor, Arthur J., *Organised Capital: Employers' associations and industrial relations in northern England, 1880–1939* (Cambridge, 1996).
McKee, Francis, 'The Popularisation of Milk as a Beverage during the 1930s' in Smith, David F. (ed.), *Nutrition in Britain: Science, scientists and politics in the twentieth century* (Amsterdam, 1997), pp. 123–41.
Middlemas, Keith, *Politics in Industrial Society: the experience of the British system since 1911* (London, 1979).

Bibliography

Miliband, Ralph, *The State in Capitalist Society* (London, 1969).
Mowat, Charles Loch, *Britain between the Wars, 1918–40* (Oxford, 1955).
Murray, Keith A. H., *Agriculture* (London, 1955).
Oddy, Derek J. and Miller, Derek S. (eds), *The Making of the Modern British Diet* (London, 1976).
Oddy, Derek, J. and Miller Derek S. (eds), *Diet and Health in Modern Britain* (London, 1985).
O'Grada, Cormac, 'The Beginnings of the Irish Creamery System, 1880–1914', *Economic History Review*, 30(2), May 1977, pp. 284–305.
O'Rourke, Kevin, 'The European Grain Invasion, 1870–1914', *Journal of Economic History*, 57(4), December 1997, pp. 775–801.
Offer, Avner, *Property and Politics, 1870–1914: Landownership, law, ideology and urban development* (Cambridge, 1981).
Ogus, Anthony I., *Regulation: Legal form and economic theory* (Oxford, 1994).
Olson, Mancur, *The Logic of Collective Action: Public goods and the theory of groups* (Cambridge, MA, 1965).
Orwell, George, *The Road to Wigan Pier* (London, Penguin reprint, 1962).
Ovendon, Richard, *John Thomson (1837–1921): Photographer* (Edinburgh, 1997).
Paulus, Ingeborg, *The Search for Pure Food: A sociology of legislation in Britain* (London, 1974).
Peltzmann, Sam, 'Toward a More General Theory of Regulation', reprinted in George J. Stigler (ed.), *Chicago Studies in Political Economy* (Chicago, 1988), pp. 234–66.
Perren, Richard, *Agriculture in Depression, 1870–1940* (Cambridge, 1995).
Perren, Richard, 'The Retail and Wholesale Meat Trade, 1880–1939', in Derek J. Oddy and Derek S. Miller, (eds), *Diet and Health in Modern Britain* (London, 1985), pp. 46–65.
Perry, P. J., (ed.), *British Agriculture, 1875–1914* (Oxford 1973).
Phillips, Jim and French, Michael, 'The Pure Beer Campaign and Arsenic Poisoning, 1896–1903', *Rural History*, 9 (2), 1998, pp. 195–209.
Phillips, Jim and French, Michael, 'Adulteration and the Food Law, 1899–1939', *Twentieth Century British History*, 9 (3), 1998, pp. 350–69.
Plimmer, R. H. A. and Plimmer, V. G., *Food and Health* (London, 1925).
Plummer, Alfred, *New British Industries in the Twentieth Century* (London, 1937).
Pollard, Sidney, *The Development of the British Economy, 1914–1980* (London, 1983).
Pugh, Martin, *The Making of Modern British Politics, 1867–1939* (Oxford 1982).
Pugh, Martin, *Women and the Women's Movement in Britain, 1914–59* (London, 1992).
Reader, W. J., *Metal Box: A history* (London, 1976).
Rhodes, R. A. W., *Understanding Governance: Policy networks, governance, reflexivity and accountability* (Buckingham, 1997).
Richards, Thomas, *The Commodity Culture of Victorian England: Advertising and spectacle, 1851–1914* (Stanford, 1990).
Rio Tinto Zinc, *The Borax Story* (1953).
Ritschel, Daniel, *The Politics of Planning: The debate on economic planning in Britain in the 1930s* (Oxford, 1997).
Rubinstein, W. D., *Men of Property: The very wealthy in Britain since the industrial revolution* (London, 1981).
Russell, Colin A., *Chemists by Profession* (Milton Keynes, 1977).
Scott, Gillian, *Feminism and the Politics of Working Women: The Women's Co-operative Guild, 1880s to the Second World War* (London, 1998).

Searle, G. R., *Morality and the Market in Victorian Britain* (Oxford, 1998).
Self, Peter and Storing, Herbert J., *The State and the Farmer* (London, 1962).
Shaw, Gareth, 'The European Scene: Britain and Germany', John Benson and Gareth Shaw, (eds), *The Evolution of Retail Systems, c. 1800–1914* (Leicester, 1992), pp. 17–34.
Sinclair, Upton, *The Autobiography of Upton Sinclair* (London, 1963).
Skocpol, Theda, 'Political Responses to Capitalist Crisis: Neo-Marxist theories of the state and the case of the New Deal', *Politics and Society,* 10 (2), 1980, pp. 155–202.
Smith, David F. and Nicolson, Malcolm, 'Nutrition, Education, Ignorance and Income: A twentieth century debate', in Harmke Kamminga and Andrew Cunningham (eds), *The Science and Culture of Nutrition* (Amsterdam, 1995), pp. 288–318.
Smith, David F., 'Nutrition Science and the Two World Wars', in David F. Smith (ed.), *Nutrition in Britain: Science, scientists and politics in the twentieth century* (Amsterdam, 1997), pp. 142–65.
Smith, F.B. *The Retreat of Tuberculosis, 1850–1951* (London, 1988).
Stenton, M. and Lees, S. (eds.), *Who's Who of British Members of Parliament. Vol. I: 1832–1885* (Brighton, 1981).
Stevenson, John, *British Society 1914–1945* (London, 1984).
Stigler, G. J., 'Can Regulatory Agencies Protect the Consumer?', in G.J. Stigler (ed.), *The Citizen and the State: Essays on regulation,* (Chicago, 1975).
Sullivan, Mark, *Our Times: The United States 1900–1925. Vol. II. America finding herself* (New York and London, 1927).
Supple, B. E., 'Income and Demand, 1860–1914', in Roderick Floud and Donald McCloskey (eds), *The Economic History of Britain since 1700, Vol. II* (Cambridge, 1981), pp. 121–43.
Taylor, A. J. P., *English history, 1914–1945* (Oxford, 1965).
The Retail Meat Trade: A practical treatise by specialists in the meat trade, Vol. I (London, 1928).
Tomlinson, Jim, *Public Policy and the Economy since 1900* (Oxford, 1990).
Trentmann, Frank, 'The Transformation of Fiscal Reform: Reciprocity, modernisation and the fiscal debate within the business community in early twentieth century Britain', *Historical Journal,* 39, 1996, pp. 1005–48.
Turner, John (ed.), *Businessmen and Politics: Studies of business activity in British politics, 1900–1945* (London, 1984).
Vernon, Keith, 'Science for the Farmer? Agricultural research in England, 1909–36', *Twentieth Century British History,* 8(3), 1997, pp. 310–24.
Wagner, Gillian, *The Chocolate Conscience* (London, 1987).
Walton, J. K., *Fish and Chips and the British Working-Class, 1870–1940* (Leicester, 1992).
Walvin, James, *The Quakers: Money and morals* (London, 1977).
Ward, A. G., 'Advising on Food Standards in the United Kingdom', in MAFF, *Food Quality and Safety: A century of progress* (1975), pp. 26–8, 38.
Weatherall, Mark, 'Bread and Newspapers: The making of "A Revolution in the Science of Food" in Harmke Kamminga and Andrew Cunningham (eds), *The Science and Culture of Nutrition, 1840–1940* (Amsterdam, 1995).
Webb, Catherine, *The Woman with the Basket – The History of the Women's Co-operative Guild, 1883–1927* (Manchester, 1983).
Weir, Ronald, *The History of the Distillers Company, 1877–1939* (Oxford, 1995).
Weltham, Edith H. 'The London Milk Trade, 1900–1930', in Derek J. Oddy and Derek S. Miller (eds), *The Making of the Modern British Diet* (London, 1976).
Wilkins, Mira, 'When and Why Brand Names in Food and Drink?', in Geoffrey Jones and

Nicholas J. Morgan (eds), *Adding Value: Brands and marketing in food and drink* (London, 1994), pp. 15–40.

Williams, Iolo A., *The Firm of Cadbury, 1831–1931* (London, 1931).

Williamson, O. E., *Markets and Hierarchies: Analysis and anti-trust implications* (New York and London, 1975).

Wilson, C. Anne, *Waste Not, Want Not: Food preservation from early times to the present day* (Edinburgh, 1991).

Wilson, Charles, *The History of Unilever*, Vol. I (London, 1954).

Winstanley, Michael J., *The Shopkeeper's World, 1830–1914* (Manchester, 1983).

Wohl, Anthony S., *Endangered Lives: Public health in Victorian Britain* (London, 1983).

Wood, Donna J., *Strategic Uses of Public Policy: Business and government in the Progressive era* (Pittsburgh, 1986).

Wood, Donna J., 'The Strategic Use of Public Policy: business support for the 1906 Food and Drug Act', *Business History Review*, 59, Autumn 1985, pp. 403–32.

Wright, Louise, *The Road from Aston Cross: An industrial history, 1875–1975* (Leamington Spa, 1975).

Young, James Harvey, 'The Science and Morals of Metabolism: Catsup and benzoate of soda', *Journal of the History of Medicine and Allied Sciences*, 23, 1968, pp. 86–104.

Young, James Harvey, *Pure food: Securing the Federal food and drugs act of 1906* (Princeton, 1989).

Index

Acland, F. (MP) 171
Addington, Lord 153–4
Addison, C. (MP) 137, 164–6, 170–2
   Minister of Agriculture 76–7
   Minister of Health 110, 167–8, 182
Addison, P. 81
Adulteration Act, 1872 16, 33–6
adulteration of food 1, 4–5, 124, 127, 158–9
   coffee 48–9
   legal definitions 34, 36–7, 52, 144, 192
   'sophistication' 30–1, 54–5, 60, 157
   statistics 53
   see also Sale of Food and Drugs Acts
Adulteration of Seeds Act, 1901 46
advertising 16–17, 36, 38, 47, 125–6, 192
agricultural interest groups 22–3, 46, 57, 185–6, 190
Agricultural Marketing Acts, 1931–3 136, 178, 189
Agricultural Produce (Grading and Marking) Act, 1928 136
agriculture 9–10, 22–3, 35, 50–1, 62–3, 135–6
   impact of imports 13, 22–3, 68
   research 28–9
   see also dairy producers
Agriculture and Fisheries, Board of 22, 26, 46, 72, 79
   condensed milk standards 132
   Departmental Committee on Butter (1902) 58–9, 107–8, 128
   Departmental Committee on Milk (1900–1) 56–8, 107–8
   milk policy 164–6
   powers under SFDA (1899) 51–2, 54–6, 63–4, 128–9, 133, 160
Agriculture and Fisheries, Ministry of
   food standards 136, 150
   milk pasteurisation and policy 159, 161, 163, 167–8, 171, 174–5, 177–81
   Preservatives Inquiry, 1923 115, 120
Akerloff, G. 3–4
alcoholic spirits 40–1, 64
Allen, A. H. (Public Analyst)
   1874 Select Committee 36
   1887 Select Committee 42
Allied Bakers 18
American Milk Products 132
Analyst, The 31, 39, 126
Anglo-Swiss Condensed Milk 129
Appleton, T. H. (Rowntree's) 28, 126
Armour 132
arsenic poisoning
   Halifax, 1902 75
   in beer (1900–1) 10, *passim* 66–78, 83
   in manufactured goods 67
   see also Royal Commission on Arsenic Poisoning
Association of Biscuit Manufacturers 18
Association of British Chambers of Commerce 23
Association of British Chemical Manufacturers 114
Asquith, H. H. (MP) 81
Astor, W. (MP) 137, 164, 173, 181
   chair of war-time committee on milk production 169, 171, 177
Atkins, P. J. 15, 158–60, 181

Index

Attfield, J. 103–4
Aylesbury Dairy Company 101, 162–3

Badger, A. H. (West London milk consumer) 175
Bakery and Allied Traders' Association 111, 117, 119, 123
Balfour, A. J. (MP) 70
Bannister, R. (Somerset House) 48, 163
Barclay, G. (Manchester wholesaler) 41
Barnett, L. M. 138
Bartrip, P. W. J. 67
Bathurst, C. (MP) 164–6
Beckett, J. N. (Ministry of Health) 110–11, 115, 120–1, 132, 141, 145–6, 150–1, 157, 169
beer 13, 102
beer materials *passim* 67–78
  see also 'pure beer'
Bell, J. (Principal, Somerset House) 41–5
Bellamy, C. 80
Bennion, E. (National Bakery School) 17
Benson, J. 13, 21
Biggart, J. (Association of Public Analysts in Scotland) 26
Blackwells 16, 101
Blank, S. 24
Borax Consolidated Ltd. 100
Borden 130
Boseley, L. K. 126
Bostock & Co. 67–8, 70–2, 74–5
bovine tuberculosis 158, 160, 164, 169–70, 175, 177
Bovril 17, 55
bread 17–18, 127, 129, 138, 143
Bread and Food Reform League 38, 129, 186
brewers *passim* 16, 68–78, 114, 117, 126
  chemists 69–70, 75–6
Brewers' Almanack, The 71
Bright, J. (MP) 42
Brighton, deaths from contaminated milk in 158, 174, 176–7
British Analytical Control 30, 91, 124, 126, 135
British Dairy Farmers' Association 57, 98
British Food Journal 30, 55, 135
British Ice Cream Association 29

British Medical Association 102, 110, 113, 164, 167, 176, 181, 183
British Medical Journal 68, 70, 73, 75, 91, 115–16, 118, 151, 176
British Pharmacopoeia 125
Brock, L. G. (Ministry of Health) 141–2
Buchanan, G. S. (LGB Foods Section) 68, 70–2, 79, 82–3, 92–4, 106–7, 122, 188
Buckley, W. (National Clean Milk Society) 177
Burnett, J. 4–5, 13, 15–16, 21, 27, 33–4, 37–8, 39, 52, 54, 124, 186
Burns, J. (MP, President, LGB) 78, 80–1, 83, 88, 91–2, 107–9, 136–8, 188
butter 10–12, 20, 38, 50, 97, 100, 102, 119, 149, 185
Butter and Margarine Act, 1907 62–4, 107, 128, 140, 186
Butter Association 59–60
butter producers
  1894–6 Select Committee 45, 50
  1906 Select Committee 59, 61
  Irish 41–2, 59, 61, 64
  Margarine Act, 1887 41–2
butter standards 10, 56, 58–64, 149, 185, 190

Cadbury, G. 36–8
Cadbury, P. S. 25, 149, 156, 191
Cadburys 18, 25, 126, 193
  advertising 16, 36, 38, 47
  employment of chemists 28
Campbell, J. 6, 60
Campbell-Bannerman, H. (MP) 66, 81, 92
Campden Research Station 28–9
canning 16–18, 29, 84, 94, 96–7, 130
Carnwath, T. (Ministry of Health) 176
Cassal, C. (Public Analyst) 188
  British Analytical Control 30, 39, 55
  status of Public Analysts 39
  views on preservatives 97–8, 101–2, 105, 108–9
Casson, M. 4
Central Chamber of Agriculture 22, 57, 60, 63, 68, 70, 101, 163–4, 166
Chalmin, P. 12

Chamberlain, A. N. (MP)
  Minister of Health 112, 116–17, 121–2, 145, 172
  Prime Minister 180–1
Chambers of Commerce 23
Chandler, A. D. 16
Chaplin, H. 72, 76
Chapman, A. C. (Public Analyst) 76
chemical analysts 1, 26, 31, 75
  see also scientists in food processing
Cheshire cheese 133, 147–8, 160, 187
Cheyne, W. W. (MP) 170, 182
Chicago stockyards and packing plants 66, 83–95
Chivers 28–9, 137
Churchill, W. S. (MP)
  considers position at LGB 81
  reviews *The Jungle* 87
Clynes, J. R. (MP) 139
cocoa 14, 16, 35–8, 47–9, 81, 85, 113
coffee 12, 48–9
Coffee Association of London 48
Collins, E. J. T. 17–18
Collins, G. (MP, Scottish Secretary of State) 151
Colman, J. (MP)
  1874 Select Committee 35–8, 85, 186
  1894–6 Select Committee 48
  Margarine Act, 1887 42
Colman's 16–17, 27, 126, 137, 193
  1894–6 Select Committee 47
  advertising 47
  employment of scientists 27
Committee of Civil Research 145–6, 155
Conan Doyle, A. 137
Condensed Milk Defence Association 25, 56–7,
condensed milk standards 129–132, 156, 160, 187, 190, 192
Confectionery & Preserved Food Manufacturers' Association 25
Conservative Party, The 160, 180–2
Consumers' Council 138–40, 142–3
Coppin, C. A. 9
Co-operative movement 139, 143, 191
  anti-adulteration 39, 186
  beer materials 77
  in retailing 20–1, 26

  Preservatives Inquiry, 1923 116
  views on standards 127–8, 147
Co-operative News 77, 127–8
Co–operative Wholesale Society 27–8, 41, 61–2, 174
Corley, T. A. B. 14, 17
Country Brewers' Society 70–1, 73–4, 76
County Councils' Association 63, 147, 187
Court of Reference 46, 79, 81, 92, 98, 105, 127, 129, 137–8
Cox, G. 23
Cranbrook, Lord 42
cream 160
Cream Trade Protection Society 107–9
Creed, E. (Kings College Hospital, London) 113
Cripps, R. S. (MP) 179
Crosse & Blackwell 16, 18, 137, 152
  employment of scientists 28
Crossick, G. 26–7
Cunningham, A. 28

Daily Express 113, 137
Daily Mail 129
Dairies, Cowsheds and Milkshops Orders, 1885 161–3
dairy producers 13–15, 22, 38, 56, 159–61, 168–9, 174–5, 177, 179–82, 190
Dairy Trade and Can Protection Society 56–7, 100, 162–3
Dalziel, J. (MP) 62
Davies, B. (United Dairies), 15, 174
den Hartog, A. P. 27
Department of Scientific and Industrial Research 121
Dingle, A. E. 13
Dorman-Smith, R. H. (MP, Minister of Agriculture) 181
Doyle, N. G. 170
Droop Richmond, H. (Aylesbury Dairy Company) 57, 58
Drummond, J. C. (People's League of Health) 147
Dundee 18, 127, 171, 174
Dwork, D. 159, 164
Dyer, B. (Public Analyst) 55, 60, 62

Edgerton, D. E. H. 28

Index

Elderton, E. 176
Elliot, T. (MP, Board of Agriculture) 59–62
Elliot, W. (MP, Minister of Agriculture) 147, 180
Ellis-Richard, P. A. (Public Analyst) 112
Empire Marketing Board 120–1
employment
   agricultural 13, 84
   food manufacturing and distribution 14–15, 152–3
Enock, A. 160, 173, 176, 179
Epps, H.
   1894–6 Select Committee 48
Evans, J. (Public Analyst) 151
Eyler, J. M. 80

Faber, H. 49
Federation of British Industry 24–5, 139
Fertilisers and Feedstuffs Act, 1893 46
Finlay, M. R. 27
First World War
   impact on food policy 138, 141, 167, 189
   stimulus to agriculture 76
Fitzgerald, R. 17
food consumption 12–14
Food and Drugs Act, 1938 124, 153–5, 157
Food and Drugs Bill, 1913 136–7
Food and Drugs Bill, 1914 138
Food Council, The 143
food imports 12–13, 106–7
   impact of Chicago scare 87–9
Food Manufacture 17, 28–9, 31, 121, 135, 151, 153, 181
food manufacturers 1, 9, 11–12, 15–19, 23, 31–2, 51, 55
   evidence of unhygienic conditions 125, 140–2, 152, 157
   industrial concentration 152–3
   interest groups 23–5, 190–1
   views on standards 124, 126–7, 147–51, 156
Food Manufacturers' Federation 25, 112, 117–19, 121–3, 135–6, 139, 142–4, 148–50, 152, 156, 191
   Research Association 28, 118, 152–3
Food, Ministry of 124, 138–40, 143, 171, 188

food retailers 9, 11–12, 19–21, 25–7, 31, 34, 45–7, 49, 51, 55, 64, 110, 141–3, 190–1
   impact of Chicago scare 88–9
   interest groups 25–7
   regulation 26
   views on standards 127, 150
food standards and definitions 10, 31, *passim* 124–57
   Ministry of Health Departmental Inquiry, 1929–34 124, *passim* 145–53
Foreign Meat Regulations, 1909 107
Foster, Sir W. (MP)
   chairs 1894–6 Select Committee 45–6
   criticism of margarine regulation 51–2, 63
Fraser, W. H. 14, 17
Fremantle, F. E. (MP) 182
Fry, J. S.
   1874 Select Committee 35–8
Fry's 16, 18, 28, 38
   1894–6 Select Committee 47–8, 51
   advertising 47

Gardiner, A. G. 36
Gladstone, W. E. (MP, Prime Minister) 68, 74
Glasgow Corporation 98, 180
Glasgow Wholesale Milk Dealers' Association 178, 180–1
Glaxo 137
Glucksman, M. 15
Government Laboratory 40, 44–5, 82, 97, 99, 104, 126, 128, 188
   milk standards 56, 163
   see also Inland Revenue Laboratory, Somerset House
Graham-Little, E. G. (MP) 182
Grant, W. 7, 23–4
Greenwood, A. (MP, Minister of Health) 153, 158
Grey. E. (MP, Foreign Secretary) 88
Grigg, E. (Milk Reorganisation Commission) 178
Grocer, The 25–6, 139
   1894–6 Select Committee 45–7
   advertising copy 47
   butter standards 61, 63
   impact of Chicago scare 88–9

Preservatives Inquiry, 1923 114, 118
  views on Public Analysts 43–4
Guinness, W. (MP) 76
Gurney, P. 21, 26, 139

Hall, P. 8
Hamill, J. M. (LGB Foods Section, Ministry of Health) 108–9, 112, 134, 172
Hamlin, C. 33
Harcourt, W. (MP) 74
Harris, J. 2–3, 7–9, 12, 79
Hassall, A. H. (Royal Free Hospital, London) 33, 185–6
Haupt, H. G. 26–7
Health, Department of (Scotland) 146, 151, 155, 168–9, 179
Health, Ministry of 10, 25, 30–1, 66, 96, 138
  approach to food regulation 124–5, 132–4, 136, 139–42, 157, 159, 189–90, 193
  condensed milk standards 131–2
  Departmental Inquiry on Food Standards, 1929–34 124, *passim* 145–53, 156
  general character 110
  milk pasteurisation and policy 163, *passim* 167–84, 190
  Preservatives Inquiry, 1923 110, 112–15, 117–19, 121, 123
Health, Scottish Board of 112
Hehner, O. (Public Analyst) 40
  1887 Select Committee 42
  background and career 30–1, 188
  beer materials 70, 75–7
  condensed milk standards 131
  letter to *The Times*, 1923 30, 112
  views on preservatives 96–8, 101–2, 112
Heinz 28, 117
Hicks-Beach, M. (MP, Chancellor of the Exchequer) 69, 74
High, J. 9
Hill, A. (Medical Officer of Health and Public Analyst) 99, 101, 162, 188
Hilton Young, E. (MP, Minister of Health) 146, 153
Hobsbawm, E. J. 18, 21
Holmes, C. J. 29

Hopkins, G. F. 112, 116, 129
Horlicks 28
Horrocks, S. M. 27–8, 30, 126, 148, 152, 186
Hosgood, C. P. 21
Hovis 17
Howe, A. 81
HP Foods 17
Hume-Williams, E. W. (MP) 109
Huntley & Palmers 16, 18, 28, 137
Hurd, P. A. (MP) 170

ice cream 29, 148, 187
Ice Cream Association 29, 133
Ice Cream Industry 29, 133
ICI 29
Idris, T. (MP) 94
Idris and Co. 114–15
Ilseric, A. R. 23
industrial concentration 18–19, 32, 152–3
information costs, 3–4, 60–2
Inland Revenue Act, 1880 68–70, 74
Inland Revenue Departmental Committee on Beer Materials (1896–99) 69–70, 75, 77
Inland Revenue Laboratory 98
Innes Rogers, J. (London Chamber of Commerce) 30
Institute of Chemistry 30, 39
International Tea Company 26

Jackson, G. (Manchester and Salford Milk Dealers' Association) 42–3
jam 14, 18, 74, 101, 103, 114, 121, 135, 138–40, 143–4, 148, 150, 156
Jeffreys, J. B. 13, 21
Jeremy, D. J. 16–17, 27, 36, 38
Jones, Geoffrey 4
Jones, Greta 150

Kamminga, H. 28
Kearley, H. (MP, Lord Devenport) 26, 45, 58, 79
Keiller's 18, 25, 126–7
  employment of chemists 28, 126, 152
Kelvin, Lord 71–2, 74–6, 78–9, 81
Kensington 98–9, 105, 108–11, 115, 117, 122

Index 209

Kenwood, H. 176
Kindleberger, C. P. 125
Kitson Clark, G. 1, 7–8, 81, 83
Kolko, G. 7, 9, 84–5, 90, 93, 191

Labour Party, The 143
Lamb, J. (NFU) 76
Lampitt, L. H. (Lyons) 148
Lancet 33, 55, 67, 70–1, 72–3, 83, 85–86, 88, 90–1, 94, 97–9, 111, 115–16, 126, 151
Lane, W. (MP, Cork butter merchant) 41
Langlois, R. N. 3
Law, A. B. (MP) 168
Lees, S. 35
Lever Brothers 18, 28
Libby 132
Libecap, G. D. 4, 173–4
Liberal governments (1905–1914) 62–3, 66, 78, 81, 164
Liebig's Extract of Meat 27, 82 93–4
Lindblom, C. 7
Linlithgow Report on food prices, 1924 135–6
Lipton's 20, 26
Lloyd, F. J. (British Dairy Farmers' Association) 57, 58, 98
Lloyd-George, D. (MP, Prime Minister) 63, 167–8, 182
local authorities
    1894–6 Select Committee, 46
Local Government Board (England and Wales) 1, 5, 10, 156
    enforcement of SFDA 47–8, 52, 80, 138
    Foods Section 66, 78–9, 82, 92–4, 106, 109, 111, 122, 129–30, 134, 140–1, 188
    general character 66, 79, 81, 189, 193
    milk policy 158–9, 161–6
    views on food regulation 41, 46
    views on preservatives 97–8, 105, 107–10
Local Government Board (Scotland) 5, 52–4, 166
London and County Vinegar Brewers' Association 133
London Butter Association 49

London Chamber of Commerce 23, 30, 139
    1894–6 Select Committee 46, 48–9, 127
    1906 Select Committee 61
    Preservatives Inquiry 114, 117
Long, W. (MP)
    President, Board of Agriculture 11, 51
    President, LGB 70–1, 73–4
Lowe, P. 23
Low, J. S. (LGB) 141

McAlley, R. (Public Analyst) 42–3
Macara, T. (Food Manufacturers' Research Association) 119
McCraw, T. K. 2, 191
MacDonagh, O. 1, 81, 83
MacFadden, A. (LGB Foods Section, Ministry of Health) 82, 106–7, 111–12, 120, 123, 132, 140–2
Machin, S. (FMF) 121, 145
McIvor, A. 25
Maclachlan, A. B. (Ministry of Health) 146, 151
MacLeod, R. 1, 33, 39, 80–1
McVitie & Price 16
Malt Vinegar Brewers' Association 134, 148, 155
    see also vinegar standards
Manchester and Salford Milk Dealers' Association 42
Manchester Brewers' Central Association 70–1
Manufacturing Confectioners' Alliance 25, 113, 122, 148–9, 152, 156, 191
margarine 18, 97
    regulation under SFDA 50–2, 63–4
    sold as butter 10–11, 26, 41
Margarine Act, 1887 11, 41–2, 45, 49, 64, 187, 190
margarine producers 25, 192–3
    1894–6 Select Committee 50
Marrison, A. J. 23
Marsh, D. 8
Marx, K. 5
Matthias, P. 13
Maxwell, H (chairman, LGB Departmental Inquiry, 1899–1900) 99, 120
Maypole Dairy Company 20, 50, 54

meat inspection and slaughtering
  in Britain 87
  see also Chicago stockyards and packing plants
Medical Officers of Health 37, 39–40, 54, 57, 67, 71, 75, 92, 99, 101, 103, 111, 126, 147, 158, 171–2, 181, 186–7
medical profession 185, 188, 192
  milk pasteurisation and policy 160–1, 181, 190
  views on preservatives 99–104, 116–7
Medical Research Council 178, 183
Merchandise Marks Act 49, 63
merger activity 18, 20
Metal Box Company 18
Metropolitan Grocers' and Provision Dealers' Association 49–50
Middlemas, K. 24
Miliband, R. 7
milk
  adulteration 37, 40, 44–5, 128, 137, 159
  grading 172–3, 175–6, 178–9, 183–4
  infectious properties 158, 160, 164, 169–71, 174, 176–7
  pasteurisation 160–1, 169–70, 173–4, 176–81, 183–4, 190
  preservatives 97–101
  standards 42–3, 56–8, 148, 185, 190
  vitamin properties 176–7
  see also bovine tuberculosis; dairy producers
Milk Act, 1934 178–9, 182–3
Milk and Dairies Act, 1914 138, 161, 165, 167–71, 173–4, 182–3
Milk and Dairies Amendment Act, 1922 169–72, 193
Milk and Dairies Bill, 1920 167, 182
Milk and Dairies (Consolidation) Act, 1915 167–70, 183
Milk Industry Bill, 1938 180–1
Milk Marketing Board 133, 178
milk producers
  changes to SFDA, 1875 42
Milk (Special Designations Act), 1949 161, 184
Miller, D. S. 12, 14, 17, 29
Moir & Son 16

Mond, Sir A. (Lord Melchett) 29, 134
  Minister of Health 168–71, 173, 183
Morant, R. (Permanent Secretary, Ministry of Health) 171
Morrison, W. (Minister of Agriculture) 181
Munro, H (MP, LGB) 81, 112
Munro, R. (MP, Scottish Secretary) 169
Murray, K. A. H. 13
mustard 35, 48, 155

National Association of Creamery Proprietors and Wholesale Dairymen 119–20
National Clean Milk Society 171, 177
National Confederation of Employers' Organisations 24
National Council of Women of Great Britain and Ireland 143
National Farmers' Union 22, 133, 147, 180
National Federation of Dairy Associations 171
National Federation of Grocers' Associations 26–7, 45, 59, 63, 89–90, 92, 94–5, 114, 117–18, 127, 134, 139, 143, 150
National Federation of Meat Traders 87, 149
National Food Canning Council 29
National Milk Publicity Council 171–2
National Pure Food Association 137
Neill, C. (US Presidential Inquiry, 1906) 83, 87, 90, 92
Nestlé 117, 129–31
Newman, Sir G. (Chief Medical Officer) 142, 145–6, 168
  milk pasteurisation and policy 160–1, 172–3, 176
  views on adulteration 31, 157
  views on preservatives 110, 115
New Statesman 135

Oddy, D. 12, 14, 17, 28, 29
Offner, A. 22
Ogus, A. 2, 4, 125
Olson, M. 5, 21, 39, 186–7
O'Neill, H 181
O'Rourke, K. 13

Orwell, G. 14
Oxo 17

Paddington Station, London 171
Parliamentary Select Committees
  Adulteration (1856) 33
  Adulteration Act, 1872 (1874) 1, 34, 36, 69, 152
  Butter Substitutes Bill (1887) 41–2
  Butter Trade (1906) 59–62
  Food Products Adulteration (1894–6) 38, 45–51, 79, 98, 129, 162
  Marking of Foreign Meat (1893) 91
  Sale of Food and Drugs Act, 1875, Amendment Bill (1878–9) 41
Paulus, I. 5, 33–4, 39–41, 51, 55–6, 159, 189, 191
Peek, Frean 16–18, 25
Peek, Sir H. (MP)
  1874 Select Committee 35, 37, 44, 85
  supports 1875 SFDA 37
Peltzman, S. 8
People's League of Health 113, 146–7, 151, 168, 181, 186
perfect competition 2–4, 50
Perren, R. 12
Pharmacy Act, 1869 34
Plummer, A. 16
Plunkett, H. (MP) 58–9
policy networks 8, 22–3, 56
Pollard, S. 18
Pope, W. 116
Portland, Duchess of 137
preservatives 29, 84, *passim* 96–123, 130, 132, 149, 185
  cream 107–110
  dairy products 107
  Government Laboratory report on extent of in 1900 97
  legal position under SFDA 97
  LGB Departmental Inquiry, 1899–1900 79, 81, 85, *passim* 99–109
  Ministry of Health Departmental Committee,1923 30–1, 112–15
Preservatives Regulations, 1925 10, 96, 124, 144, 156, 187–91
  business response 117–20, 145
Preston-Thomas, H. (LGB) 48, 80, 189

product quality 4
Public Analysts 30, 36–7, 46, 77, 79, 82, 96, 99, 122, 136, 138, 149, 185, 187, 192
  advocacy of standards 124–6, 133, 144
  status 39–40, 42–4, 188
  see also Society of Public Analysts
Public Health Act, 1890 5
Public Health (Condensed Milk) Regulations, 1923 132
Public Health (Milk and Cream) Regulations, 1912 108–9, 119
Public Health (Regulations as to Food) Act, 1907 66–7, 83, 92–4, 107, 111–12, 131, 188
  Parliamentary opposition 93
'pure beer' 69, 74
Pure Beer Bills 69, 73, 76–8, 186
Pure Beer Campaign 70, 72–4, 77
Pure Food Act (USA), 1906 84–5, 189
Pure Food and Health Society of Great Britain 137–8, 164–5, 171

Quilter, C. (MP) 69–70, 72, 76, 77

Reader, W. J. 14
Reckitts 18
Rees Jones, E. 29
regulation
  bureaucratic discretion 7–8, 39, 82–3, 122, 185, 187–8, 190
  capture 6–7, 37–9, 40–1, 64, 83, 85, 109, 125, 132, 185–6
  public interest 2–5, 7, 10, 34, 37–8, 40–2, 54, 62, 64–5, 83, 85, 91, 101, 110, 120, 122, 124–6, 130, 133, 136, 138, 159–60, 164, 182–3, 185, 189, 191–2
Reynolds, E. S. (Manchester Royal Infirmary) 67–8
Reynolds, J. (US Presidential Inquiry, 1906) 83, 87, 90, 92
Rhodes, R. A. W. 8
Rhondda, Lord (Food Controller) 109
Richards, T. 17
Ritschel, D. 24
Robertson, P. L. 3
Robinson, A. (Permanent Secretary, Ministry of Health) 110, 145–6, 167, 176

Roosevelt, T. (US President) 83, 85, 88–90, 95
Rowntree 16–17, 25, 38
   employment of scientists 27–8, 31, 126, 152
Royal College of Surgeons 102, 181
Royal Commission on Arsenic Poisoning, 1901 71–8, 81, 129, 140, 188
Royal Commission on Food Prices, 1925 118, 143
Royal Commission on Tuberculosis, 1907 164, 169
Rubinstein, W. D. 16
Ruggles-Brise, E. A. (MP) 76, 180
Russell, C. A. 34

St. John Barne, F. (MP) 69
Salamon, A. (Manchester brewers' chemist) 75–6
Sale of Butter Regulations, 1901 56, 128
Sale of Food and Drugs Acts, 1875 and 1899 1, 4–5, 10, 27, 34, 51, 63–4, 69, 85, 124–6, 138, 145, 160, 174, 189–91
   appeal system 40, 44
   compulsory measure (1899) 52
   definitions of adulteration 36–7, 192
   establishes Public Analysts 30, 37
   focus on retailers 19, 27, 31, 36–7, 51, 64, 157
   impact on adulteration 52–4
   impact on manufacturers 27, 37–8
   'informal sampling' 53–4
   local operation 26, 37, 39–40, 52–4, 187
   manufacturer's invoice as warranty 46–7, 51
   private sampling and prosecutions 49–50, 60
Sale of Food and Drugs Act, 1928 119, 136, 154
Sale of Food and Drugs Act Amendment Act, 1879 40
Sale of Food Bill, 1920 140–1
Sale of Food Order, 1921 143
Sale of Milk Regulations, 1901 56, 58, 128, 161–3
Samuel, H. L. (MP, President, LGB) 109, 165, 173
Sanderson, J. (Coffee Association of London) 48
Sassoon, P. A. D. G. (MP) 138
scientists in food processing 27–31, 126
Sclater-Booth, G. (MP) 1, 34, 42, 44
Scottish Wholesale Co–operative Society 120
Second Industrial Revolution 15
Sewell Read, C. (MP)
   beer materials 70, 72, 75
   chairs 1874 Select Committee 34–5, 37
Sexton, J. (MP) 170
Shaw, G. 13, 21
Shippam, G. 114, 149
Simon, J. 34
Sinclair, U. 91
   The Jungle 66, 83–8, 94
Skocpol, T. 8, 188–9
Smith, A. (*Lancet* sanitary correspondent)
   articles on Chicago 85–8, 90, 94
   meets Sinclair 86
Smith-Carington, N. W. (MP) 76
Society of the Chemical Industry
   Food Group 28, 147–8
Society of Public Analysts
   1894–6 Select Committee 45–6, 51
   agreements with manufacturers 121, 124, 133–5
   beer materials 70
   government recognition of 30, 40
   milk standards 56–7
   organisation and activities 39
   Preservatives Inquiry, 1923 115
   relations with Somerset House 43–5
   views on food regulation 31, 41, 52, 157
   views on standards and definitions 31, 46, 129, 131, 136–8, 144–8, 150–1, 155–6, 186, 190
   see also Public Analysts
Somerset House (Inland Revenue Laboratory) 40–1, 44
   milk standards 42–3
   see also Government Laboratory
Spencer Low, J. (LGB) 141
Stenhouse Williams, R. 177
Stenton, M. 35
Stevenson, J. 16
Stigler, G. J. 4, 6, 114, 186

Index

St Ivel 137
sugar 13, 68–9
Sullivan, M. 84
Summerskill, E. C. (MP) 161, 181, 184
Supple, B. 14

Tate & Lyle 18, 28
Tattersall, C. (Medical Officer of Health, Salford) 67
tea 12–14, 20, 34–5, 54, 81, 127, 138, 140, 143, 148, 186
Tea Dealers' and Grocers' Association 34, 186
technological innovation
 in food processing 16–17, 27–31
temperance movement 77–8
Thorpe, T. E.
 butter standards 58
 head of Government Laboratory 45
 LGB Departmental Inquiry, 1899–1900 99
 relations with SPA 45
Times, The 89–90, 112, 116, 137, 175
Tomlinson, J. 24
Trade, Board of 25, 44, 132, 134, 144
Trentmann, F. 23
Troyte, G. J. A. (MP)76
tuberculosis 99
 see also bovine tuberculosis
Turner, J. 23–4

Unilever 18
Union Cold Storage 20
United Dairies, 28, 61, 117, 120, 131, 174, 177–8
United Kingdom Alliance for the Suppression of the Liquor Trade 77
United States Department of Agriculture 83, 90, 188

Vallance, J. (Scottish Department of Health) 151

Van Den Bergh, H. 50
Van Houten's 47
Veale. D. N. (Ministry of Health) 117–18, 120
vinegar standards 133–5, 155–6, 187
vitamins 28, 176–7

Wagner, G. 36, 38
Wakley, T. (*Lancet*) 33, 185–6
Walton, J. K. 25
Walvin, J. 36
Watson Cheyne, W. (MP, Scottish Universities) 170, 182
Weatherall, M. 129
Webb, B. 81
weights and measures 143–5
whisky 78
Wiley, H. (US Department of Agriculture) 84–5, 94, 105–6, 137, 188
Wilkins, M. 4, 60
Williams, I. A 36
Williams, T. (MP) 178
Williamson, O. E. 3
Willis, F. (LGB) 164–5
 chair of food standards inquiry 144, 146–8, 150–2, 156, 189
Wilson, C. 18
Wilson, G. S. (London School of Hygiene and Tropical Medicine) 178–9, 183
Winstanley, M. J. 21, 25
Winter, M. 23
Wood, D. J. 6, 9
Wood, H. K. (MP, Minister of Health) 153–4, 180
Women's Co-operative Guild 127–8, 143
Wright, L. 17
Wyndham West, H. (Manchester Sessions Court Recorder) 44

Young, E. H. (MP) 153
Young, J. H. 9, 84–5

EU authorised representative for GPSR:
Easy Access System Europe, Mustamäe tee 50,
10621 Tallinn, Estonia
gpsr.requests@easproject.com

www.ingramcontent.com/pod-product-compliance
Ingram Content Group UK Ltd.
Pitfield, Milton Keynes, MK11 3LW, UK
UKHW021835140426
5217IPUK00021B/1460